Care and Social Change in the Irish Welfare Economy

edited by
Bryan Fanning
Michael Rush

University College Dublin Press
Preas Choláiste Ollscoile
Bhaile Átha Cliath

First published 2006
by University College Dublin Press
Newman House
86 St Stephen's Green
Dublin 2
Ireland
www.ucdpress.ie

ISBN 978-1-904558-82-8

Cataloguing in Publication data
available from the British Library

Typeset in France in
Adobe Garamond and Trade Gothic
by Elaine Burberry
Index by Jane Rogers
Text design by Lyn Davies
Printed in England on acid-free paper
by Antony Rowe Ltd

For
Matt and Mary Fanning
Mick and Peggy Rush

Contents

Contributors to this volume

SIOBHAN BRADLEY is Research Development Officer in the Centre for Social and Educational Research, Dublin Institute of Technology. She has conducted extensive research on the impact of societal changes on early childhood care and education policies in Ireland and most recently conducted research into the design of an accessible childcare model for all households in Ireland on behalf of the National Women's Council of Ireland.

BRYAN FANNING is a senior lecturer in the UCD School of Applied Social Science. He obtained his doctorate from the University of London. He is the author of *Racism and Social Change in the Republic of Ireland* (Manchester University Press, 2002), *Evil, God, the Greater Good and Rights* (Edwin Mellon, 2007), co-editor of *Ireland Develops: Administration and Social Policy 1953–2003* (IPA) and *Theorising Irish Social Policy* (UCD Press, 2004). He is the editor of *Immigration and Social Change in the Republic of Ireland* (Manchester University Press, 2006).

ALICE FELDMAN is a lecturer in the UCD School of Sociology. Her research interests include: race/ethnicity, migration and the politics of identity/difference; and socio-legal studies, social movements and social change. She is currently working on a number of research projects, including: the development of immigrant-led organisations and participation of 'new' communities in civil society in the North and South of Ireland; anti-racism practice and activism in Ireland; changing identities in contemporary Ireland, and the development of codes of practice for research with minority ethnic communities.

MARTIN GEOGHEGAN is a lecturer in the School of Applied Social Studies at University College Cork. He has undertaken research and published in the areas of community development, social work, civil society and social movements. He is the co-author of *The Politics of Community Development* (A & A Farmer, 2004).

NÓIRÍN HAYES is a senior lecturer and researcher at the Dublin Institute of Technology where she lectures in child development and early childhood education and is the director of the Centre for Social and Educational Research (CSER). She is currently Chair of the management board for the Centre for Early Childhood Development and Education (CECDE) and of the Ballymun Development Group for Children and Young People. She is a founder member and vice-chair of the Children's Rights Alliance. Dr Hayes was a member of the recent NESF Project Team on Early Childhood Care and Education. She has published widely and her publications include the textbook *Early*

Childhood: An Introductory Text, 3rd edn (Gill & Macmillan, 2005) and a report on children and policy in Irish, *Children's Right – Whose Right? A Review of Child Policy Development in Ireland* (Policy Institute, TCD: 2002).

GABRIEL KIELY is Professor of Social Policy and Social Work at UCD. He is the Irish member of the European Observatory on the Social Situation, Demography and the Family. His books include *Finding Love: Counselling for Couples in Crisis* (1989). He is co-editor of *Family Policy: European Perspectives* (1991), *Irish Social Policy in Context* (UCD Press, 1999) and *Contemporary Irish Social Policy* (UCD Press, 1999/2005,) and *Theorising Irish Social Policy* (UCD Press, 2004)

MARY ELLEN MCCANN has extensive experience in community drugs work in Dublin. For 17 years, she worked in Ballymun, and was one of the first to attempt to draw attention to the rise in heroin use in the early 1980s. Under her direction, the Youth Action Project (YAP) came to be recognised as a leader in the field, accessing funding from a variety of sources, national and European, to develop its work. She has been to the fore in promoting community approaches to drugs issues, and has been active at local level and at policy level. She is vice chairperson of the National Advisory Committee on Drugs. She was awarded her PhD by Dublin City University and moved to the UCD School of Applied Social Science, in 2001.

TINA MACVEIGH is a teaching and research fellow in the UCD School of Applied Social Science, where she teaches social policy theory and welfare economics. Her doctoral research work consists of an analysis of Irish primary education policies within a rights-based perspective. In addition to teaching and research, she continues to be involved with community-based projects seeking to raise awareness and develop a rights-based approach to issues of poverty and disadvantage.

KEVIN MURPHY is a teaching fellow in the UCD School of Applied Science. His doctoral research involves examining the principles and practice of sustainable development and how these impact upon social policy. His work focuses on how the social pillar of sustainable development has been conceptualised, paying particular attention to the development of education for sustainable development in Ireland.

FRED POWELL is Professor of Social Policy at University College Cork. He has written extensively in the areas of social policy and social work. His books include *The Politics of Irish Social Policy 1600–1990* and *The Politics of Social Work*. He is the co-author of *Social Policy: Voluntarism in Ireland* and *The Politics of Community Development*. His publications have appeared in journals including: *Social Policy and Administration, British Journal of Social Work, European*

Journal of Social Work and *Administration*. He has been a member of the National and Social and Economic Committee, Royal Irish Academy since 1999.

MARIA PIERCE is a PhD student affiliated to the Social Policy and Ageing Research Centre, School of Social Work and Social Policy, Trinity College, Dublin. Previously, she lectured in the UCD School of Applied Social Science. She has extensive experience as a researcher in the areas of gender equality, lone parents and the delivery of social and information services. Her latest publications include *Minority Ethnic People with Disabilities in Ireland: Situation, Identity and Experience* (Equality Authority, 2003).

SUZANNE QUIN is an Associate Professor in the UCD School of Applied Social Science. She is the author of *Uncertain Lives, Untimely Deaths* (Avebury, 1996). She is a co-editor of *Theorising Irish Social Policy* (UCD Press, 2004), *Contemporary Irish Social Policy* (UCD Press, 1999), *Disability and Social Policy in Ireland* (UCD Press, 2003) and *Mental Health and Social Policy in Ireland* (UCD Press, 2005). She is the co-editor of *Understanding Children* vols 1 and 2 (Oak Tree Press, 2001)

VALERIE RICHARDSON is a senior lecturer in the UCD School of Applied Social Science. She is the Irish representative on the European Observatory on the Social Situation, Demography and the Family. Her research is mainly in the area of Irish and European family policy, child care policy and practice, lone parents and adoption. Her most recent research was a study on traditional adoption in Ireland for the Crisis Pregnancy Agency

MICHAEL RUSH is a lecturer in the UCD School of Applied Social Science and co-ordinator of the Housing and Community Studies undergraduate programme. His published work includes articles on comparative family policy, reproductive work and sports policy. He has been a contributing author to *Irish Social Policy in Context* (UCD Press, 1999) and *Theorising Irish Social Policy* (UCD Press, 2004). His research publications include *Including Children: Disability, Diversity and Additional Needs* (Waterford Childcare Committee) and *Causes and Consequences of Joy-riding in Priorswood*. His PhD research is a comparative investigation into fatherhood and the cultural politics of social policy and reproduction.

NESSA WINSTON is a lecturer in the UCD School of Applied Social Science. She is the author of *Between Two Places: Emigrant Integration and Identity* (European Cultural Foundation, 2002) and the co-author of *Housing Policy Review 1990-2002* (Stationery Office, 2004). Her research and teaching interests include: migration, race, ethnicity and social policy; housing policy; social policy evaluation. Recent research projects include a study of returning older Irish migrants; a study of the Irish in Britain and a review of Irish housing policy.

Abbreviations

ABP	area-based partnerships
ADM	Area Development Management Ltd
AFDC	Aid to Families with Dependent Children
BTC	Breaking the Cycle
CDB	City/Country Development Board
CDP	Community Development Programme
CE	community employment
CECDE	Centre for Early Childhood Development and Education (St Patrick's College, Dumcondra)
CHW	Community Health Worker
CORI	Conference of Religious in Ireland
COSAC	An Chomhairle Sport agus Caiteamh Aimsire (National Council for Sport)
CPA	Combat Poverty Agency
CSO	Central Statistics Office
CSPE	Civil Social and Political Education (in the Secondary School curriculum)
CWC	Community Workers Co-op
CWO	Community Welfare Officer
DCU	Dublin City University
DIT	Dublin Institute of Technology
EOCP	Equal Opportunities Childcare Programme
ERC	Educational Research Centre
ESC	European Social Charter
ESRI	Economic and Social Research Institute
EU	European Union
FDI	Foreign Direct Investment
FRM	Fathers Responsibility Movement
G8	Group of 8 (leading industrial nations)
GAA	Gaelic Athletic Association
GDP	Gross Domestic Product
GNP	Gross National Product
HDR	Human Development Report (of the United Nations)
HEA	Higher Education Authority
HFEA	Human Fertilisation and Embryology Authority
HIV	Human Immunodeficiency Virus
HRB	Health Research Board
HSCL	Home/School/Community Liaison

HSE	Health Service Executive
IBC	Irish Bishops Council
ICE	Interdepartmental Committee on Emigration
ICPO	Irish Commission for Prisoners Overseas
IDA	Industrial Development Agency
IEA	Irish Economic Association
IBEC	Irish Business and Employers Federation
ICESR	International Covenant on Economic and Social Rights
IECE	Irish Episcopal Commission for Emigrants
IPA	Institute of Public Administration
IPH	Institute of Public Health in Ireland
ISC	Irish Sports Council
ISSP	International Social Survey Project
LDTF	Local Drugs Task Forces
LGFA	Ladies Gaelic Football Association
MU	Mothers' Union
NAPS	National Anti-Poverty Strategy
NCCA	National Council for Curriculum and Assessment
NCO	National Children's Office
NDA	National Disability Authority
NDP/CSF	National Development Plan – Community Support Framework
NDST	National Drug Strategy Team
NESC	National Economic and Social Council
NESF	National Economic and Social Forum
NGB	National Governing Bodies (of sports)
NGO	Non-government organisation
NILDD	National Intellectual Learning Disability Database
NPSD	National Physical and Sensory Database
NQHS	National Quarterly Household Survey
NSWQB	National Social Work Qualification Board
NWCI	National Women's Council of Ireland
OECD	Organisation for Economic Co-operation and Development
OHCHR	Office of the High Commissioner for Human Rights (UN)
OPFP	One Parent Family Payment
PPF	Programme for Prosperity and Fairness
PWDI	People With Disabilities Ireland
RCPCH	Royal College of Paediatrics and Child Health
RDTF	Regional Drugs Task Force
SIRP	Southern Integrated Research Partnership
SMI	Strategic Management Initiative
SPC	Strategic Policy Committee

SPC	Strategic Policy Committee
SSPA	Survey of Sports and Physical Activity
SWA	Supplementary Welfare Allowance
TANF	Temporary Aid to Needy Families
TCD	Trinity College, Dublin
UCD	University College Dublin
UCL	University College, London
UN	United Nations
UNESCO	United Nations Educational, Scientific and Cultural Organisation
UNHCHR	United Nations Office of the High Commissioner for Human Rights
USFI	The Unmarried and Separated Fathers of Ireland
USI	Union of Students in Ireland
WCED	World Commission on Environment and Development
WHO	World Health Organisation
WITH	Women in the Home
YAP	Youth Action Project

Introduction

Context, change, challenges and care

Bryan Fanning
Michael Rush

Care and Social Change in the Irish Welfare Economy is part of the UCD Press Irish social policy series. It is a companion volume to *Contemporary Irish Social Policy* (2005) which examines different functional areas of Irish social policy such as education, housing and health, and to *Theorising Irish Social Policy* (2004) which locates it in terms of conceptual debates including globalisation, communitarianism, individualism, rights and difference. *Care and Change in the Irish Welfare Economy* is to some extent a sequel volume to *Irish Social Policy in Context* (1999). Like that earlier volume it is principally focused on key prevalent issues facing Irish social policy makers. These include the need to respond to changes resulting from immigration and shifts within the Irish welfare economy that have created new needs for social care.

    Care and Social Change in the Irish Welfare Economy differs in structure and emphasis from its 1999 predecessor to reflect recent considerable changes in Irish society. For example, immigration presents new challenges to Irish policy makers and students of Irish social policy. Economic prosperity has not resolved the problem of social exclusion. A care deficit has resulted from increased female participation in paid employment and the decline of informal care labour. Recent social, demographic and economic changes have presented Ireland with major new challenges in responding to the care needs of children, older people and people with disabilities. Dramatic changes in the social and economic profile of Irish society are changing the shape of the environmental and physical landscape. Distinctions between urban and rural life have become blurred. Rural Ireland, no longer synonymous with agriculture, is increasingly being reshaped into a suburban commuter hinterland. For growing numbers life in twenty-first-century Ireland is characterised by long commutes between the workplace and the dormitory town and by a trade off between high housing costs and time poverty. Within this context questions of social and environmental sustainability need to be addressed.

Context

The first section addresses several aspects of the institutional context of twenty-first-century Irish social policy. This institutional context is considered in chapter 1 as a *mixed economy of welfare* within which the state acts as a provider of welfare goods and services and regulator of welfare effort by private and voluntary sectors and, to a lesser extent, of informal care. Chapter 2 focuses on the role of *governance*, as distinct from government, in the ongoing shaping of Irish social policy. Here the governance mechanisms of social partnership that mediate between different interests in Irish society are examined as regulators of conflict within Irish society. Chapter 3 focuses on the *politics of care* and the nature of social-interdependence within the new welfare economy.

In chapter 1, Fanning examines structural shifts in welfare interdependencies over time. The reference in the chapter title to a new welfare economy draws attention to shifting balances between public, private, voluntary and informal provision as a consequence of increased participation by women in paid employment. The chapter also considers the consequences of immigration on the welfare economy of twenty-first-century Ireland. Immigrants are examined as providers as well as users of welfare goods and services. For services, stratifications resulting from differential rights for immigrants and non-citizens living in Ireland are seen to impact upon interdependencies within the mixed economy of welfare. In chapter 2, Geoghegan and Powell address the evolving relationship between governance and social policy in Ireland. It begins by locating Ireland within the international spectrum of welfare models. The forces that have shaped Irish social policy reveal conflicts between the modernising agendas of the secular state and the more traditionalist agenda associated with the Catholic Church. The corporate model of social partnership governance that emerged from these conflicts is examined as the bearer of conflicts between different social policy aspirations. The central lens through which these conflicts and structures are examined is the bottom up one of civil society. If the focus of chapter 2 is upon power relations, that of chapter 3 (Rush) is upon *the politics of care* that influences and is affected by the economic and power relationships which regulate Irish social policy. The concept of care as introduced in chapter 3 is identified as central to any consideration of present and future welfare choices. The politics of care, that is the business of shaping care relationships and paying for social care, has emerged as a central preoccupation of Irish social policy debates.

All three contextual chapters challenge presumptions that social policy is never limited to what states do in terms of welfare effort. Chapter 1 emphasises a functional model of welfare interdependency and examines how this is affected in the case of immigrants by stratified entitlements to state-provided welfare goods and services. The governance of social policy is never value free. As chapter 2 emphasises, it cannot be divorced from power relationships within and between different sectors represented in decision-making processes. The focus in chapter 3 on care interdependencies draws attention to a further range of power relationships. In the Irish case much responsibility for care still rests within the informal sector. Historically this sector has been portrayed in terms of the privatised household headed by a male breadwinner supporting unpaid care work by women either as a manifestation of subsidiarity (by Catholic conservatives) or patriarchy (by feminists). Many of the domains of care considered in subsequent chapters begin within informal relationships where care is provided unpaid, often by women frequently with inadequate outside support. As noted in chapter 3, and in a number of subsequent chapters, the demography of social care in Ireland is complex, shifting and increasingly politicised.

Social change and welfare futures

A number of chapters in this book are preoccupied with the future both in terms of the need to develop social policy responses to new challenges arising from immigration and the environment, and with regard to social repro-duction. Some chapters in the second section of *Care and Social Change in the Irish Welfare Economy* are concerned with questions of social reproduction and the need for a social policy focus on addressing social exclusion and disadvantage so as to minimise the reproduction of inequalities from present to future generations. In particular, attention is drawn to the consequences of educational disadvantage (chapter 4) and potential inequalities resulting from racism (chapter 5).

   Shifts within the Irish mixed economy of welfare and in the politics of care can be understood as responses to demographic change. The context within which these changes have occurred is one of unprecedented economic prosperity. Yet relative inequalities in areas such as health and education have persisted with potentially damaging consequences for the future of Irish society. In particular, high levels of educational disadvantage on the basis of socio-economic status have persisted. The focus in a number of chapters is upon relevant concepts to address the consequences of social and environ-mental change such as sustainability (chapter 7) and social capital (chapter 8). Prosperity and changing lifestyles also have implications for social policy. For example, chapter 8 examines the relationship between education, sport and health at a time when the physical fitness of children and young people has become a major social concern. The role of sport and sporting organisations in Ireland is related to debates about individual and collective social capital.

Collectively the chapters in this section emphasise the need for long-term approaches to social policy in relation to the environment, education, public health and social diversity. These by necessity require an emphasis on social research, whether the focus is upon the experiences of immigrants (chapter 6) or some other element of Irish society.

The concerns identified within the different chapters have a number of thematic commonalities. Major themes addressed in the context of social change and welfare futures are directly linked to policy development – for example the requirement for *evidence-based social policy* addressed in chapter 6 and the recognition of the usefulness of National Governing Bodies of Sports (NGBs) user data to public health debates in chapter 8. Similarly the limitations of available data on the economic and social well-being of ethnic minorities are considered in chapter 5. A central theme within this section on social change and welfare futures is the requirement to underpin theoretical debates in relation to social inclusion, social integration, social disadvantage and social capital with empirical data to capture the realities of housing, health, education and the impact of racism, social exclusion and poverty on individual and collective well-being. These chapters provide a framework for the practical application of social science to the development of a new welfare economy.

Care

Questions about care provision, responsibility for care and about the economic value placed on care work have moved to the forefront of the Irish social policy agenda. These are complex questions that have an impact – as chapters in this section emphasise – on a wide range of groups in Irish society. Chapter 9, on reproductive work, locates family change and changing attitudes to the organisation of family life in Ireland in an international comparative context. Changing attitudes to marriage, cohabitation and one-parent families and demographic changes are examined in the context of a new welfare economy where an increasing number of married mothers, cohabiting mothers and lone mothers are in paid employment. The childcare question as addressed in chapter 10 is related to changing family structures and change in the gender composition of the Irish labour market. Chapter 11 examines relationships between the different but complementary social and health care needs of children with disability. The underdevelopment of provision in the Irish case is emphasised, and the implications of an uneven geographical services of children with disabilities and their families are examined.

The social care infrastructure deficit is again highlighted in chapter 12 which examines social care provision for older people. Here the very modest role of public provision contrasts with an ongoing and controversial encroachment of the private sector into the residential care of older people. Chapter 12 highlights the dilemmas facing Irish society as demand for social care among people outgrows the family and the voluntary and community sector and the private 'for profit' sector emerges as the primary beneficiary of statutory policy and public funding. Chapter 13 highlights the transnational consequences of twentieth-century emigration for Irish social policy. During the twentieth century emigration functioned as dead hand on social policy insofar as it removed the political requirement to deal with many social problems. Now, to a limited extent, acknowledgements of Irish responsibility to the welfare needs of older emigrants have emerged. Finally in chapter 14, the ongoing role of the voluntary and community sector in the provision of health and social care is discussed. This chapter makes clear that the new welfare economy has retained a strong dependence upon community and voluntary participation in the delivery of primary health and social care, particularly in relation to addictive behaviour and social exclusion. Overall the third section of the book highlights the shifting demography of social care in the context of the mixed economy of Irish welfare.

Local history, comparative analysis

Since its initiation in 1999 the UCD Press series has developed into a significant body of academic work on Irish social policy. Each volume to date has been produced by an editorial team located in the Department of Social Policy and Social Work at UCD Dublin; the Department was renamed as the UCD School of Applied Social Science in 2005. The series began under the direction of Professor Gabriel Kiely, who since 1971 has made immense leadership contributions in the field of Irish social policy. In 1978 he received the first PhD in social work to be awarded by an Irish university. He became one of the first academics in Ireland to promote family policy as a distinct field in the wider domain of social policy analysis. In 1984 he became a founder member of the Family Studies Centre in UCD and went on to become one of the two Irish representatives on the EU Observatory of European Family Policies that subsequently became the EU Observatory on the Social Situation, Demography and the Family, serving there until 2002. In 1998 he was appointed Jean Monnet Professor of European Family Policies. This book along with others in the series owes much to his stewardship.

His is an influence that has helped to shape the series into a body of work that offers a distinct critique of Irish social policy: one similar in scope and focus but quite distinct from the British social policy series produced by the Open University. One aim of the UCD series is to locate Irish social policy within the broader international literature and to provide a critical mass of points of reference for comparative analysis. This aim cannot be achieved without a focus on what is distinctive about Irish institutions and welfare interdependencies, ideological perspectives and social problems. The local matters very much but cannot be understood without some wider perspective. Without such a focus there can be no escape from parochial Irish exceptionalism, from international academic indifference or misunderstanding and there can be no theoretical innovation. The UCD Press series that now includes *Care and Social Change in the Irish Welfare Economy* provides academics and students within Ireland with a resource that aims to foster such understandings.

Part 1   Context

Chapter 1

The new welfare economy

Bryan Fanning

Introduction

Irish society has changed significantly in recent years. A period of economic expansion over the last decade, often referred to as the Celtic Tiger, has depended upon an increase in paid female employment. Immigration, again driven by economic expansion, has changed Irish society into a visibly multicultural one. The consequences of these changes have impacted upon Ireland's welfare economy in a number of respects. For example, the increased participation of women in paid employment has increased the need for paid childcare provision outside the home. Immigrants, like other members of Irish society, are not merely economic actors. Some, such as those working in the health sector, are providers of welfare. They have social insurance, health, education and training needs like other members of society and as parents they seek to provide for the welfare of their children. This chapter examines the development of the Irish mixed economy of welfare. The welfare economy or 'the mixed economy of welfare' are terms that refer to the balance between the respective roles of the state, the market, the voluntary sector and individuals (and their families) as providers and recipients of welfare goods and services. This chapter considers how the balance between state, voluntary and market provision of welfare goods and services has become altered by immigration and recent social change. It examines how existing welfare stratifications and those resulting from differential rights for immigrants and non-citizens living in Ireland have impacted upon interdependencies within the mixed economy of welfare.

A mixed welfare economy

The role of the state in Ireland, as elsewhere, in securing the welfare of its citizens is one that has developed over time but it is not the case that all welfare, *in this sense*, is provided through the actions of the state. A mixed economy of welfare has persisted within contemporary society even if the balance of welfare provided by individuals for themselves and reciprocally for others has shifted towards a formal role for the state whose role and responsibilities in the provision of welfare are determined by law. The role of the state as a provider of welfare is one that has developed over time. As well as directly providing welfare goods and services funded through taxation, the state has come to regulate those purchased by individuals and families or provided by charitable groups and organisations within society.

The emergence of the state as a provider and regulator of welfare has given it a central role in shaping the mixed economy of welfare. The provision of welfare by a balance of public, private, voluntary and informal sector activity is referred to as welfare pluralism. This pluralism in the provision of welfare occurs with a mixed economy characterised by private purchase of services whether from public, private or voluntary sectors, provision or redistribution of services by the state, which can purchase services on behalf of its citizens or provide grant aid, subsidy or tax relief to other sectors which provide welfare services (Fanning, 1999: 52). Four sectors engaged in the provision of welfare can be identified:

- *A public sector* that includes welfare provision, financed, managed or regulated by the state.
- *A private sector* that provides welfare goods and services for profit to those who can pay. The largest single purchaser of these is often the state, which may, for example, purchase places for public patients in private nursing homes. Individuals might also purchase welfare goods and services from the private sector.
- *A voluntary sector* which includes welfare provision on a charitable basis and self-help and mutual-aid groups. Some parts of the voluntary sector may be dependent upon state funding whilst others may provide welfare goods and services to groups whose needs are not addressed or funded by the state.
- *An informal sector* consisting of the informal provision of welfare through friends, families and within communities. Examples include the care of children, the aged and people with disabilities by members of the same household.

The precise role of the state – as provider and regulator – is one that has changed over time so that we can identify an ongoing restructuring of the welfare economy with particular shifts when societies agree to extend or change the balance of provision, for example through constitutional change or legislation. The role of the market within the welfare economy can be influenced by legislation and government regulation. Some forms of welfare provision, such as education and health, were initially developed by the religious voluntary sector and subsequently became subject to regulation by the state. Other forms, such as social security, were initially developed by the state. Present-day welfare institutions are often built on the foundations of the past.

Historical context

(i) State provision and regulation

The role of the state in Ireland, as elsewhere, is that of provider and regulator of welfare provision. Article 45.1 of *Bunracht na h'Éireann* the 1937 Constitution states: 'The State shall strive to promote the welfare of the whole people by securing or protecting as effectively as it may as social order in which justice and charity inform all the institutions of the national life'. In practice this role is circumscribed by legislation. For example, rights and entitlements to public services and benefits are determined by law. It is also the case that the specific role of the state as provider and regulator differs for different areas of social policy.

Before independence in 1922, Irish social policy was shaped by British legislation. The first comprehensive scheme for the establishment of government welfare services in Ireland occurred under the Poor Relief Act, 1838 that established workhouses with a parish or union of parishes as an administrative unit. From 1851 a system of means-tested free medical attendance on the sick poor in their houses or in dispensaries build by each union area was developed. This means-tested dispensary system persisted within the post 1922 Irish state providing the foundations of the current mixed economy of health care.

The Health Act, 1953 introduced means tested statutory (medical card) entitlement to some 'free at point of access' health care services such as those provided by general practitioners. Under this system some users – those entitled to a medical card – could access public health services without charge. Those not so entitled had to pay for health care at points of access (doctors, surgeries and hospitals). State regulated health insurance schemes were primarily designed to allow those who could afford it to insure themselves voluntarily against the costs of hospital care (Nolan, 1991: 131). In 1933 some 65 government-approved societies administering health insurance for about half a million people were amalgamated into one body, the National Health Insurance Society (Coughlin, 1984: 211). The responsibilities of the Society were transferred to the Minister of Social Welfare under the Voluntary Health Insurance Act, 1951. A 'two-tiered' health care system developed which distinguished between a level of publicly available health care, available free at point of access for those with medical cards (though with some charges for others), and additional public and private services where entitlement was based upon ability to pay (Tormey, 2003: 193–4). In the Republic, health care expenditure became financed to a greater extent than in the UK by charges and private insurance, with these totalling 25 per cent compared with seven per cent in the UK by 1975 (Nolan, 1991: 175). The Irish health system, as such, has developed as a mixture of public, voluntary and private provision funded by taxation and charges. By contrast, the British NHS is primarily funded by taxation rather than by fees and charges to patients.

Irish social insurance provision originated in British legislation prior to 1922. Non-contributory Old Age pensions – financed by central government taxation and administered by the Department of Local Government and Public Health – were introduced in 1908. Unemployment insurance – financed by employee, employer and state contributions – was introduced in some areas of employment in 1911. After 1922 the Irish social welfare system expanded gradually with the introduction of contributory and non-contri- butory Widows and Orphans Pensions in 1935 (ten years after similar pensions were introduced in Britain) and children's allowances in 1944 (a year before these were introduced in Britain). The Social Welfare Act (1952) set up a new department to take responsibility for social security functions that until then had been held by several departments. The Act also extended coverage of unemployment insurance and benefits for widows and orphans. In Britain by contrast comprehensive welfare reforms had been simultaneously introduced in 1948 resulting in a more extensive system of state welfare provision.

(ii) Denominational welfare

After independence the new state acquired a predominantly Catholic ethos. The institutionalisation of Catholicism was reflected in, for example, legislation on divorce, contraception, adoption and censorship. The Catholic Church possessed a 'non-decisional' form of power. It had the capacity to mobilise politically in defence of its interests but rarely had to because these could be anticipated and addressed in a 'non-political' and non-contentious manner. As good Catholics, legislators and voters were deeply committed to expressing their faith in the laws and institutions of the country (Kennedy, 2001: 249). This was particularly evident in the area of health care where the principle of Catholic denominational control over health services for Catholics coincided with a Catholic ideological control over health care provision as a whole.

During the nineteenth century, separate Protestant and Catholic education and health systems had developed in Ireland. The development of some Protestant evangelical schools from the eighteenth century was followed, after the repeal of the Penal Laws, by a fast growing Catholic school system. Schools were owned and controlled by the religious voluntary sector. Efforts by the British government, from 1811, to promote a non-denomi- national education system in Ireland through a system of grant aid to schools failed. After some initial engagement within the state funded system, the most prominent Catholic provider of 'free schools', the Christian Brothers, opted to remain self financing (fee-paying schools for the Catholic middle classes were established to fund 'free' education for others).

The major hospitals in Ireland had been established under voluntary (i.e. Catholic and Protestant religious) control prior to the foundation of the new state. The system of Protestant voluntary hospitals expanded in the nineteenth century with the establishment of an eye and ear hospital in 1814, a children's hospital in 1821 and a maternity hospital in 1826. These were joined by Catholic voluntary hospitals following the establishment of St Vincent's by the Irish Sisters of Charity in 1815 and the Mater Hospital by the Sisters of Mercy some thirty years later (Robins, 2003: 154). Religiously separate welfare institutions persisted within the new state after independence.

In health, as in education, the impetus for maintaining a dual system was a sectarian concern with imposing a Catholic ethos on all provision for Catholics. For example, from 1944 the Archbishop of Dublin, Dr McQuaid, included an edict in diocesan regulations that 'the Church forbids parents and guardians to send a child to any non-Catholic school, whether primary, secondary or continuation or university' (Whyte, 1980: 306). Similar separatism ensured the persistence of a separate Protestant school and hospital system after independence even as the state became explicitly identifiable with Catholicism (Fanning, 2002: 39). The Catholic hierarchy successfully opposed, for example, the participation of Catholics in the proposed National Anti-Tuberculosis League in 1942 because of alarm at the Protestant flavour of its leadership. It proposed instead that the League be subsumed within the predominantly Catholic Irish Red Cross (Barrington, 1987: 162). Yet religious tolerance was constitutionally enshrined. In practice the state went out of its way to protect the minority's religious rights through special measures aimed at keeping small Protestant schools open and by insisting that no child could be required to take religious instruction without parental agreement (Fanning, 2002: 40). The difficulties of sustaining a separate health system for Protestants exceeded those in education, with the result that the Protestant minority was dependent upon a system governed by Catholic ethics and operational control. A growth in state involvement in health funding was accompanied by the supremacy of a Catholic ethos in the system as a whole (Barrington, 1987: 126).

(iii) Persistent welfare pluralism

The Irish welfare economy continues to reflect the emergence during the nineteenth century of two demarcated state and religious voluntary spheres of provision. The role of the state developed as a provider of benefits and social insurance and as regulator of the welfare economy as a whole. In this it could be seen to adhere to the ideological liberal ethos of the nineteenth-century

Poor Law and of the early twentieth-century expansion of employment related social insurance. This emphasised a minimal role for the state, the principle of individual (voluntary rather than compulsory) responsibility for social insurance and, where possible, a minimal role for the state. The second religious voluntary sphere was dominated by Catholicism. Insofar as the Church preceded the state as a provider of welfare goods and services, particularly in the areas of education and health, it resisted any encroachment by the state. This principle of autonomy from the state was referred to as the principle of subsidiarity in Catholic social doctrine. In theory subsidiarity meant the devolution of responsibility for welfare to the family. In practice, it was used to defend the Church's position as moral guardian from state interference. For the most part these two spheres co-existed without conflict. The political conflict in 1951 about what became known as 'The Mother and Child Scheme' was the most notable exception. In this case the Church criticised what it interpreted as efforts by the state to undermine the near-monopoly of the religious orders in hospital care and the Church's opposition to socialised, or state-controlled medicine (Foster, 1989: 572).

From the 1960s an ideological shift occurred within the Church whereby the state was likely to be criticised from doing too little rather than for encroaching upon existing voluntary provision (Whyte, 1980). The with-drawal of religious personnel from the provision of health and social services, as a result in the decline in religious vocations, created gaps which were increasingly filled by the statutory sector and other non-religious voluntary agencies. An increased preoccupation with the co-ordination of voluntary and statutory provision within a statutory framework that identifies roles and responsibilities of these different providers is evident within recent legislation and policy proposals. For example, the Child Care Act, 1991 emphasised co-ordination between health services run by the Department of Health and the voluntary sector. Policy documents such as *Shaping a Healthier Future: A Strategy for Effective Health in the 1990s* (Department of Health, 1994) pro-posed service agreements between the larger voluntary agencies and the health boards. The *Supporting Voluntary Activity* Green Paper, on the community and voluntary sector and its relationship with the state, advocated an enabling role for the state in the development of the voluntary sector (Department of Social Welfare, 1997: 22). The mixed economy of health care in Ireland can be seen to have changed over time. The role of the state has increased. The nature of the voluntary sector and interrelationships between the state and the voluntary sector have also changed over time. These have been shaped by the legacy of subsidiarity, new approaches to partnership in the provision of welfare and the increased financial dependence of the voluntary sector upon the state.

A gendered welfare economy

The relationship between the family as a site of welfare and the state as provider and regulator of welfare is again one that has changed over time. In the Irish context, dominant Catholic ideological perspectives about social policy have historically emphasised limiting state encroachment upon families. For example under Article 41.1.2 of the 1937 Constitution; 'The State . . . guarantees to protect the Family in its constitution and authority, as the necessary basis of social order and as indispensable to the welfare of the Nation and the State'. In effect, the 1937 Constitution prescribed a specific role for women within the welfare economy. As it was put in Article 41.2.1: 'In particular the State recognises that by her life within the home, woman gives to the State a support without which the common good cannot be achieved'. The Constitution went on to specify how this support to the common good would be achieved. 'The State shall, therefore, endeavour to ensure that mothers shall not be obliged by economic necessity to engage in labour to the neglect of their duties in the home.' (Article 41.2.2) What this meant in practice changed to some extent over time. Until the 1970s discrimination in employment and a ban on married women remaining in the civil service were arguably understood as means of regulating gender roles in accordance with the Constitution. The emphasis on the unpaid role of women as carers within the Irish welfare economy was sustained in part by discrimination.

Unpaid care work, mostly by women, constitutes a significant element of the Irish welfare economy, yet, since the introduction of social insurance in 1911, entitlements to state benefits have been explicitly linked to paid work. The National Insurance Act, 1911 established a social insurance system designed to ensure that the male breadwinner could provide for his family. Women were conceptualised as dependants, entitled to benefits only through their relationships with men as wives or daughters. Even when women engaged in socially insured paid employment they were legally entitled to lesser rates of benefit. These distinctions persisted after the Unemployment Assistance Act, 1933. Efforts to address female poverty, such as the Widows and Orphans Pension Act, 1935, took the form of developing separate categories of benefit for women rather than addressing such inequalities. The result was a gendered two-tiered system based on a distinction between benefits linked to previous paid employment (Unemployment Assistance, predominantly accessed by men) and means tested Home Assistance (formally called Poor Relief and accessed by women (McCashin 2004: 32). Under the Widow and Orphans Pension Act, 1935 the entitlements of widows to pensions depended on their dead husbands' contributions. If their husbands had sufficient contributions their widows got a widows pension. If not, they were eligible for Home Assistance.

Although rates of Unemployment Assistance for single men and single women were equalised under the Social Welfare Act, 1952 discriminatory practices such as the marriage bar (lifted in 1973), the marriage grant, small stamps (lower contributions and lower rates of benefit for shorter periods of time) for married women and the payment of adult dependant's allowances in respect of them were maintained. Unemployment Assistance was extended to male employees engaged in private domestic service and agriculture in 1953. It was not extended to women in similar occupations until 1966. The First Commission on the Status on Women, established in 1970, produced many recommendations on equal pay for women. The Employment of Married Women Act, 1973 revoked discrimination against married women in the civil service and the Employment Equality Act, 1977 addressed pay inequalities. A number of other acts addressed the benefit entitlements of women. However, insofar as separate benefit categories for women were retained, such as Deserted Wife's Allowance (introduced in 1970), Unmarried Mothers Allowance, 1973 and Single Woman's Allowance, 1974 the system remained a male-breadwinner one. Many of the benefits introduced during the 1970s envisaged women remaining in the home. Further reforms during the 1980s and 1990s were driven by the European Union. For example, the EU Equal Treatment Directive, 1979 emphasised removing discrimination against married women from social welfare schemes in respect of sickness, accident and unemployment. It envisaged women as ordinarily engaged in paid employment. It emphasised social policies aimed at supporting female as well as male breadwinners. In 1990 the various categories of lone mothers' benefits were reformed as lone parent benefits. The basis of entitlement to these was reconstituted from the relationship female claimants had/or did not have with men to one based on individual and equal entitlement to benefits as citizens.

Social and demographic change

(i) Gender

The overall participation of women in paid employment remained fairly constant between 1961 (29 per cent) to 1993 (34 per cent). What changed most was the participation of married women. Just 7.1 per cent of these were engaged in paid employment in 1971. This had risen to 30.9 per cent by 1989 and 47.8 per cent by 2003 (Richardson, 2003). From 1990 to 2000 the percentage of married women with young children in paid employment rose from 42.2 percent to 55.2 per cent. (McCashin, 2004: 72). By 2003 it was estimated that the overall female participation rate in the workforce stood at 48.8 per cent. These statistics indicate that married women with children were more likely to be engaged in paid employment than women as a whole.

In the 2002 Census the highest participation rates of married women in the workforce (75.5 per cent) were found to be for women between the ages of 25 and 34 years, that is ages when women are most likely to have young children. Women are more likely not to be engaged in paid employment than men. Of the 555,600 persons who described themselves in 2003 as engaged on home duties, 98.9 per cent were women (Quarterly National Household Survey: First Quarter, 2003). Women continue to participate in paid employment to a lesser extent than men and spend more time as carers in the home. This affects their income levels detrimentally. A 1997 study indicated that about three quarters of the gap between men's and women's hourly wages can be attributed to the fact that women, under current social and economic structures, typically spend less time in the labour market than men and more time as carers in the home. (Richardson and Rush, 2006). Research has consistently found that women's salaries are lower than men. Women also accrue lesser entitlements to employment related benefits and pensions because these are related to time spent and earnings obtained from paid employment.

The assumptions set out within the 1937 Constitution about the role of women in Irish society (dependants) and the welfare economy (unpaid carers) have been severely tested by social and economic change. The proposition set out in Article 41.1.2 that 'by her life within the home, woman gives to the State a support without which the common good cannot be achieved' has been challenged in the era of the 'Celtic Tiger' by economic and social policy norms that presume that women will ordinarily be engaged in paid employment. Similarly, the assumption under Article 41.2.2 that mothers shall not be obliged by economic necessity to engage in labour to the neglect of their duties in the home has been undermined by the growing participation of women in the economy and upon the economic necessity of dual-income households. The rapid expansion of the economy during the 1990s, measured in terms of increased Gross National Product (GNP), has been partially the result of the increasing participation of women in paid employment, and the further expansion of the economy is seen to necessitate further increases in female paid employment. As summarised by the Forum on the Workplace of the Future in 2003; 'A more diverse workforce, comprising an increasing proportion of women, older workers, non-Irish workers and people with disabilities, poses significant challenges for work places in areas such as work-life balance, equal opportunities, flexible employment arrangements and changes in the organisation of work (Forum on the Workplace of the Future, 2003: 22) The Forum's National Workplace Strategy (2004) identified a need for approximately 420,000 additional workers by 2010, with 150,000 of these required from outside the state. In 2004 the Forum made two key recommendations:

- Workplace policies are now needed to encourage more female participation, at present 20% below that of men, and to encourage older workers
  to remain at work, as well as a coherent immigration policy
- Barriers to women's participation in the workforce should be removed
  and practical solutions for the provision of childcare supports and arrangements put in place (Forum on the Future of the Workplace: 2004).

During the 1990s, at the cusp of the Celtic Tiger era, Irish social policy
debates remained preoccupied with the Catholic social values articulated in
Article 41 of the Constitution. For example, the Report of the Commission
on the Family (1998) expressed concerns that women should not be forced to
take up paid employment. Furthermore, the Commission depicted childcare
provision outside the home as a minority need (Commission on the Family,
1998: 62).

However, the Commission's emphasis on preserving the 'right' of mothers
not to engage in paid employment was sidelined by an increased emphasis on
economic individualism (Kiely, 2004: 64). Within this debate a Catholic
emphasis on the primacy of the family became to some extent subordinated
by a neo-liberal emphasis on the primacy of the market (Fanning, 2004a: 14)
This could be seen in the replacement of unpaid maternal childcare for the
most part by private sector provision rather than public provision or state-
funded provision. Inadequate childcare provision has been consistently identified over the last number of years as the major inhibitor to women's
participation in the labour market. Ireland has traditionally subscribed to the
'maximum private responsibility' model of childcare as described in the
OECD review of childcare policies (1991) where the state intervenes only to
provide a safety net of minimal childcare support for the poor or children at
risk (Richardson, 2003).

(ii) Immigration
In 1961 just over one million people were employed in the Republic of
Ireland. By 2004 this had risen by 783,000 to 1,836,000. By 2004 the total
population had exceeded four million (O'Hagan and Newman, 2005).
Between 1995 and 2000 almost one quarter of a million people (248,100)
emigrated to Ireland. This amounted to an aggregate figure of seven per cent
of the total population as recorded in the 1996 census. About half were
returned Irish emigrants. Some 18 per cent (45,600) were immigrants from
the United Kingdom. Thirteen per cent (33,400) came from other EU countries and seven per cent (16,600) came from the United States. Twelve per
cent (29,400) came from the rest of the world (Mac Éinrí, 2001: 53). Since this
initial period of immigration a decreasing percentage have been returned Irish
and an increasing percentage of migrants have been drawn from non-EU

countries. The Central Statistics Office estimate that in the period from 1997 to 2002 approximately 150,000 immigrants, that is people who are not returned emigrants, arrived in the Republic of Ireland (CSO, 2002). Eighteen thousand and six work permits were granted to non-EU nationals in 2000, 36,436 in 2001, 40,321 in 2002, 47,551 in 2003 and 34,067 in 2004. Following EU enlargement on 1 May 2004 immigrants from the new member states did not require work permits. At the time of enlargement some 60 per cent of such immigrant workers were from EU accession states. Since the enlargement of EU in May 2004 the Polish immigrant community in particular has grown. By 2005 an estimated 75,000 immigrants from China, admitted under a separate scheme, were living in the Republic. Of these some 50,000 were concentrated in Dublin (*Observer*, 3 Apr. 2005). Immigration is likely to be continuing: the Central Statistics Office forecast in 2005 that there will be one million first-generation immigrants living in Ireland in comparison with the 400,000 at the time of the 2002 Census (Punch, 2005: 5).

(iii) The future of dependency

Within the European Union there has been an increasing acknowledgement of the need to compensate for declining birth rates with immigration. Without positive net migration the populations of Germany, Greece, Italy and Sweden would be in decline (Eurostat, 2002: 65). Unlike the United States and Canada,European countries have not traditionally regarded themselves as immigrant societies. Sassen, examining the economic relationship between emigrant and immigrant regions, notes that labour-importing areas experience higher rates of growth. It is better, economically, to be an importer than an exporter of labour. Immigrant countries tend to accumulate advantages in levels of growth over emigrant countries:

> History suggests that this is an advantage which labor-sending areas either a) cannot catch up with and/or b) are structurally not going to be part of because the spatialisation of growth is precisely characterised by this type of uneven development. History suggests it takes several major economic phases to overcome the accumulation of disadvantage and exclusion from the dynamics of growth. One cannot be too rigid or mechanical about these generalizations. But it is clear for Italy and Ireland, even if they now receive immigrants, the fact of two centuries of labour exporting was not a macroeconomic advantage. Only some individuals and localities may have benefited. Today when a whole new economic era is afoot, Italy and Ireland have become part of the new growth dynamics – each in its own specific manner (Sassen, 1999: 140).

Irish society has lagged behind, yet follows the general trend amongst Western European societies of ageing populations, declining birth-rates,

fewer marriages and more couples and unmarried parents living together.
Fewer babies were born in Europe in 1999 than in any year since the end of
the Second World War. In 1999 the proportion of the European Union
population above sixty years of age was twenty one percent. This was
expected to rise to thirty four percent by 2003. Ireland's indigenous population, and hence its age dependency ratio, is low by European standards
but this will change over time. By 2020, 25 per cent of the population as
calculated in 2001 will be over 65, and this percentage is expected to rise
rapidly in subsequent years (Kennedy, 2001: 255). More recent estimates that
take account of immigration trends suggest a figure of 17.5 per cent by 2030
(Punch, 2005: 6). The welfare needs of Ireland's future age-dependent
population will be to some extent funded by the economic and tax
contributions of immigrants. Immigrant children, no less than those of
current Irish citizens, are thus potential contributors to Ireland's future
welfare economy.

New welfare stratifications

Political responses to asylum seekers and immigration have, to a considerable extent, influenced social policy responses. Social policy obligations
to asylum seekers and other categories of immigrant are determined by the
Constitution, under international conventions, EU treaties and Irish legislation. Political responses to immigration have taken the form of legislation,
which has reduced some immigrant welfare rights, as well as constitutional
change. These have resulted in stratifications between the entitlements of
citizens and non-citizens and between various non-citizen categories.

A number of key social rights, such rights to welfare, were not restricted to
citizens under the 1937 Constitution. Article 45.1 of the 1937 Constitution
states: 'The State shall strive to promote the welfare of the whole people by
securing or protecting as effectively as it may as social order in which justice
and charity inform all the institutions of the national life'. The 1937
Constitution emphasised domicile rather than citizenship as the basis of welfare rights and entitlements. Access to welfare goods and services provided by
the state occurred on the basis of means-tested need or as social insurance
entitlements related to paid employment. For example, the Social Welfare
(Consolidation) Act, 1993 set out a statutory right to supplementary welfare
allowance (SWA) not limited to citizens. As stated in Section 171 of the Act,
'every person in the State whose means are insufficient to meet his needs and
the needs of every child dependent of his shall be entitled to SWA'. Under
Section 180 (1) of the Act health boards (Health Service Executive since 2005)
were charged with assessing entitlement to SWA on the basis of the needs
of the person.

International human rights conventions ratified by the Irish state presume obligations to address the welfare of all persons, including non-citizens, on a domiciliary basis. For example, Article 2 of the UN Convention on the Rights of the Child (1989) states that all children should be entitled to basic rights without discrimination. Other articles specify a right to the highest attainable standard of health and to have access to health and medical services (article 24), a right to benefit from social security (article 26), a right to an adequate standard of living with a duty on the state to assist parents, where necessary, in fulfilling this right (Article 27), a right to education and access to appropriate secondary education (Article 28.1) and a right to participate in leisure, recreational and cultural activities (Article 31). The Convention applies to all children within the jurisdiction of the state. In practice, the welfare entitlements of non-citizens set out under national legislation fall short of such obligations. Furthermore, the statutory entitlements of many non-citizens living in Ireland have been eroded in recent years.

In 2000 the government removed the existing SWA entitlements of asylum seekers and means-tested entitlements to rent allowances and replaced it with a 'direct provision' scheme designed as a 'punitive' measure aimed at discouraging asylum seekers from coming to Ireland (Fanning 2002: 103). Under this scheme adults located in hotels, hostels and other reception centres around the country received a weekly benefit of just ?19.05 per week. Children ordinarily received just €9.52 per week plus children's allowance (Fanning and Veale, 2004: 244). Unlike other benefits, which are generally increased on an annual basis, there was no increase in direct provision rates between 2000 and 2006. In effect, the introduction of 'direct provision' in 2000 shifted the basis of SWA entitlement from domicile to citizenship. Further shifts away from domicile-based entitlements occurred as a result of the responses of the government to EU enlargement in May 2004 and the Referendum on Citizenship in June 2004. From May 2004 the entitlements of some new immigrants to a range of benefits including children's allowances, SWA, unemployment benefits and disabilities benefits, were removed for the first two years of their residency in the state (see chapter 5). Others – means-tested entitlements to health care and free primary and secondary education – remained unchanged. As put by the Ombudsman:

> The Referendum was carried by a large majority (80% voted in favour). Some opponents of the proposal argued that it would create a two-tiered society i.e. those who, by virtue of holding citizenship would be entitled to additional rights and benefits and those who, although living and working in Ireland would be denied similar rights by virtue of not being citizens . . . This, in turn, raises wider questions – and not just in Ireland – about the capacity of governments to successfully integrate non-nationals and to allocate to them

heath, education, housing and other benefits on a fair and equitable basis (O'Reilly, 2004).

Immigrant workers, immigrants with Irish-born children, people with refugee status and asylum seekers are all deemed by the state to have different levels of rights and entitlements. In all cases, these are less than the entitlements of citizens. Distinctions between the entitlements of a number of such non-citizen groups are the result of state decisions that categorise and stratify people for administrative and political purposes. A number of studies undertaken in Ireland in recent years have demonstrated how lesser rights and entitlements affect migrants according to the administrative category they find themselves in (Fanning 2004b: 67). The response to EU enlargement has meant that immigrants and their children have been deprived of the safety net of state benefits for an initial two-year period. This loss of entitlement includes loss of entitlement to benefits based on the contributions of those in paid employment. As a result some immigrants and their children face disproportionate risks of poverty in the event of unemployment. Some immigrant children face disproportionate risks of child poverty owing to their lack of entitlement to child benefit. For example, based on 2005 rates, a new immigrant family from outside the EU with three children would be poorer by €283 per month than an equivalent family entitled to child benefit.

A number of Irish qualitative studies have indicated that the experiences of some minority groups in Ireland of discrimination and exclusion mirror, to a degree, those of marginalised minority groups in other western societies. Research undertaken to date in Ireland has found indications of discrimination or exclusion in employment, health and education – areas where non-citizens retain entitlements – and housing, where immigrants are for the most part dependent on the private sector (IBEC, 2000; Comhlámh, 2001; Conroy, 1999; Fanning and Veale, 2004). A number of submissions to the Revised National Anti-Poverty Strategy consultation process identified lesser rights and racism as causes of labour market disadvantage, joblessness, poor health, housing deprivation and social exclusion amongst immigrants (Goodbody, 2001).

The new welfare economy

Within the welfare economy of the early twenty-first century a number of issues can be identified:

• Some aspects of *public sector* provision of welfare goods and services increasingly exclude immigrants and non-citizens at a time when these are forming an increasing proportion of Irish society. As a result immigrants and non-citizens are disproportionately dependent on other parts of the welfare economy. At the same time the *public sector* has come to depend increasingly on immigrant workers and taxpayers.

- In particular, recent immigrants and non-citizens are more dependent on *voluntary sector* provision than citizens. To some extent the most comprehensive changes within the welfare economy have occurred in the voluntary sector through the emergence of new voluntary agencies targeted at immigrant communities and through responses by existing bodies to such communities. As yet, the overall resources and the scale of this response are inadequate to meet the welfare needs of immigrants and non-citizens.

- Immigrants and non-citizens are disproportionately dependent on the *informal sector* at a time when the capacity of informal care to address the welfare needs of children and other dependents has been undermined by increased participation by women in the labour market.

- An increased dependence on *private sector* provision can be identified with the Irish welfare economy particularly in the area of childcare. Immigrants and non-citizens are not exempt from this trend.

Within the welfare economy as a whole the voluntary sector has been particularly affected by immigration. Voluntary providers have the capacity to choose their own clients to a greater extent than statutory services. Access to voluntary provision is not necessarily based upon rights, and therefore not necessarily dependant upon citizenship. The barriers which prevent state agencies from offering a service to non-citizens do not apply to voluntary organisations. At its best the voluntary sector is the bearer of broader definitions of social membership than those institutionalised by the state. The barriers that prevent some state agencies from offering a service to non-citizens do not apply to voluntary organisations. To some extent the voluntary sector chooses its clients. This can be negative where services, ostensibly open to all, are devised and delivered with reference to narrow and exclusionary definitions of community.

There are indications that immigrant communities face institutional barriers both voluntary services and statutory services to which they are entitled. A study by Faughnan and O'Donovan carried out in 2001 examined the responsiveness of voluntary sector to new minority communities with a particular focus on responses to asylum seekers (2002: 6). Just one third of the 174 organisations that participated in the study considered that their work with new minority communities was effective. These organisations included local development associations, information providers, partnership companies, services, resource provision, development education, training, advocacy, campaigning organisations and umbrella or co-ordinating bodies. Partnership

companies were found to be least likely (less than one fifth) to regard themselves as effective in responding to the new communities.

Notwithstanding such institutional barriers, a number of voluntary
organisations have specifically targeted immigrant communities. Some within
the Catholic voluntary sector have developed services for asylum seekers not
entitled to support from the state. For example, the Vincentian Refugee
Centre, established by the Society of St Vincent de Paul, has developed a
range of support services for asylum seekers in Dublin. In addition a number
of new voluntary organisations have emerged to address the needs of immigrants. Integrating Ireland (the national network of refugee, asylum seeker and
immigrant support groups) has a current membership of more than 135
groups. These include advocacy and community development groups, such
as the Africa Solidarity Centre, established by immigrants, sports organisations and asylum seeker support groups. These changes have altered the
predominantly Catholic character of Irish civil society. Immigration has
resulted in increased religious diversity. This can be seen in the expansion of
faith communities including Muslims, the Russian Orthodox Church and
African Pentacostalists. One response to increased religious pluralism has
been the expansion of non-Catholic denominational schools such as the
Muslim schools at Clonskea and Cabra in Dublin.

In the context of (1) lesser rights and entitlements to public provision for
non-EU citizens and (2) of a potentially unresponsive and underdeveloped
voluntary sector, immigrants are likely to be disproportionately dependent on
informal supports. Individual immigrants often rely on the support of family
networks in countries of origin as well as in countries of destination. A significant proportion of immigrants to European countries have been found to be
family members or relatives of existing immigrant communities (Bracalenti,
2002). Family has also been identified as a factor in the capacity of immigrants
to integrate. For example, the presence of family increase levels of contacts
with the receiving society, especially through children (Pumares, 2002).
Conversely, unemployment, economic stress and lack of access to social
support outside the nuclear family are potential causes of relationship break-
downs and divorce amongst immigrants (Corman, 2002). The capacity of
immigrants no less than other groups in Irish society to address the welfare
needs of themselves and their families remains ultimately dependent upon
access to the broader welfare economy.

Conclusion

The dominant conception of Irish society prior to the 1970s, as articulated in
the 1937 Constitution, made distinctions between the rights and duties of
men and women within Irish society. Women had lesser social and economic

rights in ways that resemble, to some extent, the lesser economic and social rights of asylum seekers and immigrants. This could be seen in stratifications within the social welfare system insofar as unemployment benefits and pensions were linked to paid work and women were either formally excluded from paid work (married women were barred from civil service employment until 1973), or could be paid lower rates of pay for the same work as men. Some of the inequalities experienced by women were addressed by legislation during the 1970s. In retrospect it becomes clear that the current prosperity of Irish society would not be possible if the denial of rights and opportunities to women had been allowed to persist.

A key challenge facing Irish social policy in the twenty-first century will be to ensure that the Irish welfare economy adapts to meet the needs of a changing society. In the case of public provision, access depends increasingly upon citizenship-derived rights and entitlements. To a considerable extent stratifications in such rights and entitlements impact upon other areas of the welfare economy insofar as non-entitled groups are disproportionately dependent upon these sectors. Immigrants, no less than other members of Irish society, have welfare needs resulting from their participation in paid employment. Yet immigrants are also providers of welfare, for example in areas such as nursing and health care.

The demands placed on the Irish welfare economy are both immediate and long term, tied into the human lifecycle of childhood dependency, potential adult employment and potential retirement age dependency. For example, people seek to make provision for their retirement age welfare though individual saving and social insurance, but it is also the case that provision for children inevitably addresses long-term societal welfare goals. Over time children cease to be dependents and themselves become providers of welfare and taxpayers. As the Irish birth-rate declines and the indigenous population become older the welfare of Irish citizens may depend more and more upon immigrants and their children. Changes in the composition of Irish society will continue to place new demands upon public, private and voluntary sector providers of welfare goods and services.

Recommended reading

Fanning, B. (2006) *Immigration and Social Change in the Republic of Ireland*. Manchester: Manchester University Press.
Kennedy, F. (2001) *Cottage to Creche: Family Change in Ireland*. Dublin: IPA.
McCashin, A. (2004) *Social Security in Ireland*. Dublin: Gill & Macmillan.

Chapter 2

Governance and social partnership

Martin Geoghegan
Fred Powell

Introduction

This chapter examines the relationship between governance and social partnership in Ireland. It begins with a brief analysis of the concept of governance. This is contextualised in a discussion of the increasingly important involvement of civil society in liberal democracies in general, and in Ireland in particular. The historical forces that have shaped Irish social policy since independence are then discussed, with the influences of Catholic corporatism, nationalism and the 'modernising' agenda of the state being noted. The emergence of 'social partnership' as the product of these influences is then described, as is the form that contemporary social partnership has taken. The inclusion of civil society – through the involvement of the 'community and voluntary sector' – in social partnership is discussed. The work of other writers in assessing social partnership is then reviewed. The chapter concludes with the argument that social partnership has been a totemic influence in shaping Irish social policy, one that has facilitated the Irish state in producing a new form of governance through community.

Governance, government and civil society

(i) The rehabilitation of civil society

During the latter part of the nineteenth century, and throughout almost the entire twentieth century, the predominant focus of social analysis has been on the role that the state does, or should, play in influencing those economic and social factors that impinge on its citizenry. The welfare state, in all its varying guises, has been viewed by many as the apogee of this state-centric period of modernity. However, since the remarkable peaceful revolutions in central and eastern Europe in the late 1980s, there has been a resurgence of interest in the role that 'civil society' has to play in the social, political and economic life of a society. The concept of civil society was once central to political philosophy, and whilst having its origins in the ancient world, it enjoyed its greatest period of usage during the emergence of discussions on civil rights in the works of Locke and Hobbes, with the first explicit use of the term being evident in the eighteenth-century work of Adam Ferguson, who saw civil society as a bulwark against the 'rude society' that was emerging under capitalism, where the scramble for individual wealth was breaking down traditional solidarities. Many more of the great social thinkers of the eighteenth and nineteenth century employed the concept, albeit in differing forms: for example, Hegel saw civil society as inclusive of the 'system of needs' (i,e. the market), which tended towards instability and dysfunctionality because of egoistic individualism, and which therefore needed to be tempered and stabilised through the intervention of a strong state coupled with the solidarity that arises in civil society (see Cohen and Arato, 1992: 102–16). Influenced by Hegel, yet reaching very different conclusions, Marx equated civil society with economic society, thereby seeing it as the arena of commodity production and wealth distribution, and thus the site of class struggle and – in addition to the state – the means of subordination of the proletariat by the bourgeoisie.

Unsurprisingly then, Marx saw the idea of civil society as an objectionable one, and 'an illusion that needs to be unmasked' (Hann and Dunn, 1996: 4). The Italian cultural Marxist philosopher Antonio Gramsci reoriented the Marxian concept of civil society during his imprisonment by the Italian fascist government of the 1920s. In Gramsci's view, civil society was a complex, labyrinthine set of associations and institutions. It was in this complexity that the ideas of the ruling class permeated society and which became inculcated in the population through socialisation. This Gramsci called 'hegemony', which may be viewed as the consensual imposition of the philosophy, values and morality of social elites on society in general. In this way, differences in power, wealth and opportunity between social classes would come to be seen as normal – 'just the way things are' – thereby damping down any potential for social unrest, and thereby negating the possibility of social change. The subordinate social class would be controlled through consent and not coercion (Boggs, 1976: 39). Gramsci stood out not only for the originality of his argument, but also because his use of the concept at all was somewhat anachronistic in the twentieth century, as it had by this time largely disappeared from mainstream political discourse. It would be some sixty years before it reappeared.

The peaceful overthrow of communist regimes in both Poland and Czechoslovakia by their respective 'civil societies' brought civil society back into discussions on the nature of society, and of democracy in particular. In both cases, in contradistinction to traditional modes of political organising, the liberation movements were based not on monolithic organisational units such as a political party, but rather on networks of citizens coming together and associating through voluntary and community groups interacting with, but existing outside, the state. In Poland, the Solidarność movement emerged in 1980 in the Gdansk shipyards initially as a federation of trade unions. However, it quickly transmogrified into a loose affiliation of a variety of social actors ranging from intellectual dissidents, the Roman Catholic Church and the anti-communist left, all united in their opposition to the ruling Communist Party. Many of the key thinkers behind Solidarność – notably Kolakowski, Micknik and Kuron – argued that reform efforts should be directed primarily at civil society, by promoting the free association of citizens (Baker, 2002: 16). In this way, they argued, the state would no longer be viewed as the supreme expression of a society. Social change would come through the marginalisation of the centrality of the state, and not through vanguard politics. This was the very antithesis of Marxist–Leninist organising that had long been the staple in the region. Whilst going through many trials and tribulations, Solidarność eventually won electoral power in 1989, and had succeeded in developing a vibrant civil society.

If Poland led the way in the re-emergence of civil society as a location and vehicle of political change, then it was swiftly followed in no less dramatic circumstances by Czechoslovakia, where in 1989 the ruling Communist Party was ousted by the 'velvet revolution' (in Czech, *sametová revoluce*; in Slovak *nežná revolúcia*). Whilst having a long history of repression and dissidence, the ultimate speed of change in Czechoslovakia accelerated beyond anything imaginable during the Polish experience. In the space of 43 days, the revolution went from a large student protest in Bratislava to the assumption of the Presidency by the dissident and long-time human rights activist, Václav Havel. Havel was one of the founding members of Charter 77, a movement that itself seemed to encapsulate the promise that civil society held out as a democratising force. Formed in 1977, Charter 77 was 'a free informal, open community of people of different convictions, different faiths and different professions united by the will to strive, individually and collectively, for the respect of civic and human rights in our own country and throughout the world' (Charter 77, 1977). It was these dramatic events that heralded the rehabilitation of the concept of civil society.

(ii) The concept 'goes west'
In the early 1990s, the concept of civil society began to re-emerge in western liberal democracies. Whilst conceptions of civil society are manifold, there are two contemporary views that, taken in combination, encapsulate how it has come to be used in this context. Keane has described civil society as

> an ideal typical category that both describes and envisages a complex and dynamic ensemble of legally protected non-governmental institutions that

tend to be non-violent, self-organising, self-reflexive, and permanently in tension with each other and with the state institutions that 'frame', construct and enable their activities (1998: 6).

Keane's definition captures the essence of contemporary conceptions of civil society – a realm of activity where citizens associate voluntarily, and through which they express their identities, needs and interests, occasionally in conflict with others in civil society, and always in a symbiotic relationship with the state. Keane's definition differs, however, in one significant respect from most other contemporary views on the concept, in that he includes the arena of commodity production and distribution – the market – in civil society. Most scholars differ from Keane here, with Young being emblematic, holding a tripartite view of society that sees civil society as one component in three – the other two being the state and the market:

> *Civil Society* refers to a third sector of private associations that are relatively autonomous from both state and economy. They are voluntary, in the sense that they are neither mandated nor run by state institutions, but spring from the everyday lives and activities of communities of interest. The associations of this third sector, moreover, operate not for profit. Most participate in economic activity only as consumers, fund-raisers and sometimes employers. Even those activities of the third sector that involve providing goods and services for fees, however, are not organised towards the objectives of making profit and enlarging market shares (Young, 2000: 158, emphasis in original).

The promise of civil society as a democratising force as exemplified in the east had clearly whetted the appetite of politicians and citizens of the west alike who, for very different reasons, had cause for interest. In what has been often characterised as a 'crisis of democracy', the representative democracy of western liberal societies was by the early 1990s coming under increasing strain. From the perspective of the citizen, the modernist project of the state was in some disrepute – the twentieth century had seen a variety of failed, oppressive statist ideologies such as Bolshevism and fascism; and even the promise of social democracy as a vehicle for the redemption of the identity of all citizens appeared unmade, and perhaps unmakeable. The continued social exclusion not only of those living in poverty, but also of women, ethnic minorities and the disabled came to exemplify the inability of liberal democracy to fulfil its own promises of equality.

In this context, civil society increasingly came to be seen as a potential force for democratisation in liberal democratic societies where the marginalised could find a voice through associational activity. Civil society held out the possibility of holding the state to account, as it did of reinvigorating the public sphere, which could become the realm of the active citizen: where citizens, associating freely, could meet, discuss, march, demonstrate and ultimately organise resistance to injustice. The 'thick democracy' of civil society, typified by citizen involvement and the self-organisation of marginalised groups, was held in contrast to the 'thin democracy' of representative democracy (see Barber, 1984 and Prugh et al., 2000). In the words of Paul Hirst, representative democracy had 'even in the most effective and responsive of political systems . . . become increasingly plebiscitarian in character, the popular vote determining which party or coalition of parties shall have exclusive control of the state machine for a period of years. . . . Such ineffective political systems do not ensure the regular succession of parties in office that is essential to the health of representative democratic political competition' (Hirst, 1994: 3–4). The declining health of representative democracy was typified by citizen apathy, symbolised most clearly in declining voter turnout. Many people simply no longer trusted politics, politicians or the institutions of government. This presented the political leaders of the west with a serious challenge: how to regain this trust, and thereby re-engage the citizenry with politics. From the perspective of liberal democratic governments, the support of civil society came to be seen as a way of encouraging citizens to re-engage in the political life of a society. It is in this context that the idea of 'active citizenship' emerged – where citizenship is re-imagined as the active involvement of the citizenry in the socio-political life of a society, rather than, for example, as the passive recipients of rights. This has been a dramatic shift in the self-understanding of liberal democracies: from *governing* a populace, to involving them in their own *governance*.

The concept of governance, like most concepts in the social sciences, enjoys several meanings and uses. However, in discussions on the nature of democracy, politics and social policy it is commonly held to mean the act, process, administration or power of governing. It is therefore distinct from the concept of governing, which is the exercise of governmental authority. Rather it is the mode by which such governing is achieved. The extent of the re-imagining of democratic governance through the inclusion of civil society is evident when one considers that it currently informs organisations and institutions as diverse as the United Nations, the European Union and states themselves. To exemplify, the UN, itself undergoing internal reflection on its mission and method, has observed:

> The United Nations is, and will remain, an intergovernmental organization in which the decision-making power rests firmly in the hands of Member States. At the same time, however, we live in an international system in which influence is also increasingly wielded by non-State actors, such as civil society organisations, voluntary agencies, interest groups, private companies, philanthropic foundations,

universities and think tanks and, of course, creative individuals. To bring about change today it is necessary to mobilise the support, and cultivate the ideas, of a diverse network of non-State actors. . . . Today, a major United Nations gathering without the involvement of civil society in all its various forms is scarcely imaginable. (UN, 2002: 7)

And the 2002 reflections noted above ultimately informed the UN Secretary-General, Kofi Annan, to say, 'I encourage the Security Council to find ways to strengthen further its relationship with civil society' (UN, 2004: 4).

In Europe, as a result of the Irish 'no Vote' on ratifying the Treaty of Nice, the European Union in 2001 published a white paper entitled *European Governance*, which noted:

people increasingly distrust institutions and politics or are simply not interested in them. The problem is acknowledged by national parliaments and governments alike. It is particularly acute at the level of the European Union. Many people are losing confidence in a poorly understood and complex system to deliver the policies that they want. The Union is often seen as remote and at the same time too intrusive. . . . There needs to be a stronger interaction with regional and local governments and civil society. . . . Civil society plays an important role in giving voice to the concerns of citizens and delivering services that meet people's needs. Churches and religious communities have a particular contribution to make. The organisations which make up civil society mobilise people and support, for instance, those suffering from exclusion or discrimination. The Union has encouraged the development of civil society in the applicant countries, as part of their preparation for membership. Non governmental organisations play an important role at global level in development policy. They often act as an early warning system for the direction of political debate. (EU, 2001: 3, 4, 14).

And in Ireland, the 2000 White Paper on *Supporting Voluntary Activity* stated that:

[t]he State recognises and validates the [community and voluntary] sector as a core component of a vibrant civil society and the effort to build a broader, more participative and more accountable democracy in Ireland. . . . Civil society is coming to play a more active role in shaping socio-economic change and addressing multi-dimensional needs. . . . The sector has a specific role in ensuring that the experiences and interests of marginalised communities and groups are articulated and are heard when decisions that affect them are being made. (Government of Ireland, 2000c: 31, 61, 90).

The inclusion of the community and voluntary sector in decision making referred to above has, in recent years, been only one element in the emergence of what is referred to as 'social partnership'. Underpinned by the national agreements that have sought to secure *inter alia* stable industrial relations, guaranteed wage increases and progressive social policies, 'social partnership' has come to dominate political and policy discourse. Whilst the global renaissance of civil society has clearly been influential in this development, it should not be viewed as the sole factor. This shift in Irish governance has deeper historical roots and influences, and it is to these we now turn.

Partnership: the historical context

(i) Nationalism, Catholic corporatism and embryonic social partnership

The social and economic policies of Ireland have, since independence in 1922, been the historical product of the complex intertwining of many forces, the most notable of which have been the ideologies of nationalism and Catholic corporatism (Lee, 1989; McLaughlin, 2001). According to Hobsbawm (1975, pp. 114–17), Ireland was the only country in Europe during the period of 'nation-building' in the mid nineteenth century that already had an organic, existing sense of itself. This identity, carefully honed during the period of cultural nationalism of the late nineteenth and early twentieth centuries, was the backbone of the struggle against British colonialism. However, the struggle for independence came to be viewed through the optic of nationalism to the point where liberation was constructed as a political project of national assertion, rather than of other possibilities, such as social or economic reform or revolution. Notwithstanding the impeccable socialist credentials of several of the leaders of the nationalist movement, by the time of the 1916 rising the publication of the Proclamation of Independence '[t]here were not even mildly reformist demands for better living and working conditions for the labouring poor in Ireland' (Powell, 1992: 158). Social policy considerations were subservient to the burgeoning sense of nation.

Post-independence politics reflected this, with political parties constructed in terms of their attitude to the degree of completion of the national project, with the legitimacy, or not, of the resultant partitioned state of paramount concern. This orientation to the politics of the civil war meant that parties tended to appeal to the electorate in nationalist terms, however so conceived, thus eclipsing social concerns as the basis for politics, and thereby relegating social policy to a relatively minor concern of the fledgling state. This tendency was exacerbated by the global economic depression of the 1920s and 1930s, in that there was precious little money to spend on social services (Burke, 1999: 25). The money that was available in the state was purposively directed away from social expenditure. Between 1923 and 1927, for example, public expenditure was cut by over 30 per cent in real terms, whilst income tax was halved (Powell, 1992: 166). The fiscal parsimony of the state was not the only reason for the marginalisation of social policy. A profound conservatism lay at the heart of the newly independent Ireland (Brown, 1985). The influence of the Catholic Church in this social conservatism has been well charted (e.g. Connolly, 2002; D'Arcy, 1999; Inglis, 1987, 1998; Powell, 1992; Powell and Geoghegan, 2004; Whyte, 1980). The Catholic social principles enunciated in the seminally influential papal encyclicals *Rerum Novarum* (1983, orig, 1891) and *Quadragesimo Anno* (1936, orig. 1931) became cornerstones of Irish social policy. These encyclicals, and *Quadragesimo Anno* in particular, concerned themselves primarily with what the church referred to as 'the social problem' i.e. the rising class antagonisms that were sweeping Europe. The social Catholicism that the encyclicals promoted sought to protect workers from the worst excesses of market capitalism. Conversely, though, they expressed deep antagonism towards socialism. Social Catholicism became the hallmark of Eamon De Valera's Fianna Fáil party first elected to office in 1932. In 1937 a new Constitution was introduced based upon Catholic social principles, the central tenet of which was subsidiarity.

The concept of subsidiarity reflected the influence of corporatist ideology in 1930s Ireland. It sought to undermine the class appeal of socialism through an alternative system of vocational organisation. The corporate state achieved its strongest endorsement in Fascist regimes, notably those of Italy and Germany. But it was also influential in authoritarian conservative Catholic countries including Spain, Portugal and France (under the Vichy regime). Ireland, with an ostensibly democratic constitution, had incorporated vocationalist elements into its governance. The structure of the Irish Senate, established under the 1937 Constitution, was explicitly vocationalist. However, this enthusiasm for corporatism must be viewed within the context of Ireland's intense loyalty to Catholic social teaching. The concept of subsidiarity was at its core. Subsidiarity refers to a principle of government endorsed by Pope Pius XI in the encyclical *Quadragesimo Anno*:

It is an injustice, a grave evil and a disturbance of right order, for a larger and higher association to arrogate to itself functions which can be performed efficiently by smaller and lower societies.

Of its very nature, the true aim of all social activity should be to help the members of the social body, but never to destroy or absorb them.

The State . . . should leave to smaller groups the settlement of business of minor importance, which otherwise would greatly distract it; it will thus carry out with greater freedom, power and success the tasks belonging to it alone.

> The more faithfully this principle of subsidiary function be followed . . . the greater will be both social authority and social efficiency, and the happier and more prosperous the condition of the Commonwealth (Paras. 79–80).

The implications of the concept of subsidiarity for social policy makers in Ireland were abundantly clear. The state should not assume responsibility for social service provision if help could be alternatively provided through individual initiative, family assistance or voluntary association. Proponents of the concept of subsidiarity grounded its rationale in an appeal to public opinion based on a fear of the totalitarian powers of the state. Catholic social teaching also advocated a corporatist view. In an attempt to maintain social consensus, corporatism stressed:

> that there should be a common set of moral values – provided by Catholicism – which would bond society together. Corporatism also dovetailed neatly with the principles of subsidiarity and family solidarity because 'the collective solidarity of a guild, fraternity or mutuality was clearly closer to the family unit, and hence more capable of serving its needs than was the more remote central state' (Esping-Andersen, 1990: 61).

The Commission on Vocational Organisation which reported in 1944 advocated the establishment of a National Vocational Assembly that would comprise a variety of vocational interests (Government of Ireland, 1944: 442). It was to be the pinnacle of a complex framework of lower vocational bodies that formed a hierarchical structure. Separate representation for labour was conspicuous by its absence. In the corporate scheme of things there was no place for class conflict. Ultimately, the Commission's proposal did not meet with political approval (Varley and Curtin, 2002: 28). This was owing to the concern at the denuding of representatives' power to vocational groups, and also the concern of senior civil servants about the eclipse of ministerial responsibility (Cradden, 2004: 85–6). So whilst social Catholicism had set the conceptual scene for a 'partnership' between the various competing interests in Irish society, it would be the economic modernisation of Ireland that would ultimately bring corporatism to fruition.

(ii) Economic 'modernisation' and partnership

Even by the standards of the day, Ireland commenced the twentieth century as a predominantly agricultural society, characterised by small family farms, owned by a 'stable, conservative, land-owning peasantry' (Breen et al., 1990: 185). Agricultural production was the staple of the economy. This largely remained the case until independence. Kirby identifies three stages of economic development that Ireland went through from 1922 onwards: Comparative

Advantage, 1922–32; Protectionism, 1932–59; and Liberalisation, 1959 to the present (Kirby, 2002: 14–20). In the first of these phases, the perception that Ireland enjoyed an exceptional agricultural base compared to other European states led to a policy of support for farming at the cost of developing industrially. The period was marked by near complete neglect of industrial development. When Fianna Fáil took power in 1932 for the first time, a distinct policy of autarchy was pursued (Lee, 1989: 175–270). Economic and cultural self-sufficiency became the aim of public policy. A more balanced development policy was adopted, encompassing both agricultural and industrial development. Industrial development was largely premised on a policy of import substitution industrialisation, which protected Irish industry from external competition through tariffs, and secured a high yielding domestic market. Whilst ultimately economically unsuccessful, this period saw the first 'national agreement' in 1948, when under a government threat to unilaterally promulgate a pay award, trade unions and employers agreed a pay pact (Cradden, 1999). What was notable to this point was that corporatism, such as it was, was a bipartite affair between employers and unions. The state's involvement was at some remove. This began to change in the third period of economic development as identified by Kirby. This period was characterised by outward-looking economic policies that sought to maximise industrial development by encouraging export business, and by attracting foreign inward investment in the form of manufacturing industry. These policies were initiated by the 1958 Department of Finance Report *Economic Development*, commonly referred to as the Whitaker Report after its main architect, the Department's Secretary, T. K. Whitaker. O'Donnell and Thomas comment that:

> The opening of the economy and the emergence of growth in the 1960s was accompanied by the development of a distinct tripartism in aspects of Irish public policy. Representatives of trade unions and business were appointed to the wide range of public bodies established during those years. While some effort at national pay determination was evident in the 1960s, this approach became dominant in the 1970s, with a series of National Wage Agreements and National Understandings. (1998: 117)

The form of tripartite 'partnership' identified by O'Donnell and Thomas will be recognisable to the student of contemporary social policy as a foreshadowing of what we now refer to as 'social partnership'. Cradden largely concurs with this view. He argues that the term 'social partnership' began to enter industrial relations discourse in the 1970s in centralised bargaining arrangements (1999: 49–57). The road to social partnership and the tripartism on which social partnership is now founded began when the process was joined by the government, drawn in to underwrite the agreements by providing tax and social security guarantees. Notwithstanding that 'the National Agreement phase imploded' (Cradden, 1999: 55), it set the conceptual scene on which social partnership could emerge. Rush is in broad agreement with this analysis, tracing back the emergence of social partnership to the socio-economic effects brought about by the economic modernisation programme launched by the Whitaker Report (Rush, 1999: 157–60).

After the aborted attempts at national agreements in the 1970s, the focus on the potential of social partnership was reignited by the 1986 NESC report *A Strategy for Development 1986–1990: Growth, Employment and Fiscal Balance*, written in the context of the perilous economic and social position that Ireland found itself in the early and mid-1980s. Ireland at this time was characterised by high levels of unemployment, fiscal disarray and significant levels of migration. Clinch et al. note that unemployment peaked at 17 per cent during this period (2002: 27). DeBoer-Ashworth argues that this situation led to 'voter dissatisfaction and a series of collapsing political coalitions' (2004: 6). She further points out that:

> this report [*A Strategy for Development*] insisted on the need for public spending cuts. However, it contained one vital suggestion that would mark out future economic policy in Ireland as quite different from that then being applied by the Conservative government in the neighbouring UK. The NESC report suggested that hard public policy decisions should be taken on the basis of a wide consensus or partnership of economic and social interests. (DeBoer-Ashworth, 2004: 6)

DeBoer-Ashworth's analysis does not go far enough, however. The model of partnership being adopted – one drawing in the state, business (including farmers) and trade union interests and, crucially, civil society (through the conceptual optic of the so-called 'community and voluntary sector') – would come to mark out not only economic policy as she argues, but also social policy, and indeed would come to quietly revolutionise governance in Ireland over the next two decades.

Partnership: the contemporary context

(i) The three levels of social partnership
A series of state-facilitated national agreements between the designated social partners – farmers' organisations, business representatives and trade unions – followed on from the NESC report. These began with the *Programme for National Recovery* (1987–90), followed by the *Programme for Economic and Social Progress* (1990–3), the *Programme for Competitiveness and Work*

(1994–6), the *Partnership 2000 for Inclusion, Employment and Competitiveness* (1997–9), the *Programme for Prosperity and Fairness* (2000–2), and, at the time of writing, the current incarnation, *Sustaining Progress* (2003–5). Civil society, through the 'community and voluntary sector', was formally admitted into the negotiations of these national agreements in 1996 via Community Platform (a composite group of civil society organisations) although it has been a central component of local partnership arrangements (see below) since 1991. Whilst these national agreements have enjoyed the headlines as the purported reason behind Ireland's 'Celtic Tiger' economy, and have therefore become synonymous in the popular imagination with social partnership, they represent only one of three levels of partnership that have evolved. This macro-level social partnership has been described by Larragy as:

> a set of institutions though which pay bargaining is organised, in conjunction with a range of macro-economic policies, management of the state finances, broad guidelines on income and other taxes, on growth of public expenditure on education, health and social services. Two defining features of social partnership can be identified. Firstly, it involves participants other than elected government in shaping policy that otherwise would be decided by the cabinet of the day. Secondly, it involves the government of the day, through its official structures, in the sphere of wage bargaining, which would otherwise be left to the custom and practice of the labour market. (Larragy, 2002: 9)

Larragy's definition is one clearly influenced by the specific shape that social partnership has taken in Ireland, referring as it does to the centrality and proximity of wage bargaining and social and economic policy, and the reciprocity of these components in social partnership arrangements. In less context-specific terms, the OECD offers a more abstract definition of social partnership:

> [a] system of formalised co-operation, grounded in legally binding arrangements or informal understandings, co-operative working relationships, and mutually adopted plans among a number of institutions. They involve agreements on policy and programme objectives and the sharing of responsibility, resources, risks and benefits over a specified period of time. (OECD, 1990: 18, cited in Hughes et al., 1998: 49).

Murphy (2002: 80) has argued 'the social partnership process [has] also been replicated at a local level'. This constitutes the second of its three levels. 'Partnership' is used to describe 72 local development organisations – *partnerships* or *partnership companies* or *ABPCs* (area-based partnership companies) – funded by the EU and the Irish state through an intermediary company, Area

Development Management Ltd (ADM) which is itself modelled on a partnership approach, having a board comprised of members from the various social partners and the community and voluntary sector. Established on a pilot basis in 1991 under the terms of the national agreement Programme for Economic and Social Progress, and subsequently extended as a sub-section of the Local Development Programme (Walsh et al., 1998) the brief of these partnerships is to promote locally based programmes that support integrated local economic and social development. Of these 72 organisations, 38 are fully fledged 'partnership companies', i.e. the localities they serve are officially recognised by the state as being 'disadvantaged', with the other 34 being funded under the moniker *community groups in non-disadvantaged areas.* In many localities, these community groups are often colloquially known as 'partnerships'. That these development organisations are thus referred to is a reflection of the extended conceptualisation of social partnership that has come to suffuse the Irish socio-political landscape. 'Partnership companies' are indicative of the devolvement of 'social partnership' from a purely centralist corporatism in the early years of these new arrangements to a localised version. The third use of the term 'partnership' is in specific social policy programmes, where a 'partnership approach' refers to the coming together of several agencies to deliver, manage and direct specific programmes. The form of this partnership can vary from programme to programme, and from locale to locale, bu usually the delivery agency responsible for the day-today implementation of the programme; local institutionalised state interests such as the Gardaí or the Health Service Executive (HSE); local institutionalised civil society organisations such as Macra na Feirme; and members co-opted for their social status and/or interest in the issue at hand, for example local clergy. This form of multi-agency partnership has become suffused throughout many community interventions – community-based drugs initiatives, Youth Diversion Projects, Community Development Projects, to name but three.

Whilst needing to be set in the historical context outlined above, the involvement of civil society throughout all of these levels of social partnership might be regarded as the potential redemption of the liberal democratic promise discussed at the opening of this chapter, with its renaissance associated with demands for greater participation in the welfare state through the involvement of burgeoning third sector as a partner. In this view, the third sector is perceived as an alternative to state bureaucracy and professional elitism and as a public space between government and market, where the spirit of altruism can flourish. Civil society in its reinvigorated form is presented as a democratic community-based alternative to the dependent status imposed by the social citizenship of the welfare state. Active citizenship and civic republicanism find their most pure expression in the practice of community development, in its ideal form. As the White Paper on *Supporting Voluntary Activity* puts it:

> An active Community and Voluntary sector contributes to a democratic, pluralist society, provides opportunities for the development of decentralized and participative structures and fosters a climate in which the quality of life can be enhanced for all. (Government of Ireland, 2000c: 4)

However, this aspiration needs to be considered firstly in the context of the changing nature of governance in Ireland, which is being fundamentally modernised; and secondly, embedded in an analysis of whether social partnership has indeed enhanced the quality of life of all. A discussion based on these two questions guides the closing section of this chapter.

(ii) Assessing social partnership

Social partnership has been lauded by many, including the OECD, as being primarily responsible for the emergence, development and sustenance of the erstwhile 'Celtic Tiger' economy. In economic statistical terms, social partnership appears to have delivered much. The 2004 UN *Human Development Report* noted that Ireland enjoyed an average of 6.8 per cent growth year-on-year between 1990 and 2002. This was second only to China. It further notes that Ireland now ranks tenth in the world on the Human Development Index (which ranks achievement in terms of life expectancy, educational achievement and real income) (UN, 2004: 150), and that Irish GDP per capita now exceeds that of the USA. Employment has grown significantly during the period of social partnership, with Kirby noting that '[as] recently as 1997, 10.3 per cent of the labour force was unemployed but by late 2000 this had fallen to under 4 per cent' (2002: 32). These indicators suggest a positive appraisal of social partnership, which others too have praised. Sabel has lauded it as 'democratic experimentalism' (1996). Conroy, in an early assessment of local partnership arrangements, was enthusiastic about the potential that partnership could offer in tackling long-term unemployment (1994: 126–7). The government itself is in no doubt as to the success of social partnership, arguing that it has effectively been responsible for eradicating poverty through the National Anti-Poverty Programme (Powell and Geoghegan, 2004: 72–113). Some commentators are more ambivalent. Rush has described the policy landscape that emerged during social partnership as 'participative local and national social partnership', but also offers the more critical description 'convivial corporatism', noting that 'the phase since 1987 has been characterised by subsidiarity and the incorporation and transformation of associational organisations and community activism into delivery of welfare state services on an ad-hoc, non-ideologically or pre-determined basis' (1999: 173). Other commentators' criticisms have been very stringent. Nolan et al. (2000) argue that economic vibrancy through industrial relations stability and increased competitiveness dominates social partnership arrangements to the detriment of issues of social inclusion and equality. Crowley, amongst others, has questioned the legitimacy of co-opting and controlling social unrest through the 'all together' ideology of social partnership (1996: 69–82). Crowley's view of contemporary social partnership is similar to that of Cradden's historical analysis of Catholic social thought described earlier, where drawing on Crouch (1982) he argues that vocationalism was 'vehemently opposed to the liberal objective of widening the choices available to individuals' and its derivative – corporatism – was then a way of maintaining private ownership within capitalism, whilst:

> the stability of the system is ensured through the close integration of political, economic and moral forces, rather than through their separation. And workers (and others) are subordinated not through individualism, but through the very fact that they belong to collectivities/organisations; the organisations which represent them also regulate them. (Cradden, 1999: 50)

Allen's (2000) Marxist account of social partnership is also highly critical. In *The Celtic Tiger: The Myth of Social Partnership in Ireland*, he makes a materialist argument based largely around a concept of class polarisation where:

> [g]overnments of all hues are more likely to help to distribute resources away from the working population and towards the owners of capital. In brief, instead of a trickle-down effect there is a steady stream flowing the other way. (2000: 51)

He goes on to quantify this redistribution of resources to the wealthy since 1987, citing a decline in wages, pensions and social security whilst 'unearned income in the form of profits, interests, dividends and rent' increased; growth in industrial profit outstripped growth in wages by a ratio of two and a half to one; massive reductions in capital gains tax (from 60 per cent to 20 per cent) were enacted, matched only by relatively modest falls in PAYE taxation rates; and an entire raft of economic policies favourable to the wealthy were introduced, such as tax amnesties and tax breaks on property, including urban renewal schemes (2000: 59). Allen sums these developments up thus:

> Here then are some of the main beneficiaries of the Celtic Tiger. The multi-national companies and the Irish corporate elite, the directors of the banks and the growing financial sector, the large property owners and building firms all possessed money to begin with and state policy has been designed to ensure that they made more in the vague hope that there might be a trickle-down effect. (2000: 66–7)

Kirby, from a political economy perspective, is equally withering in his analysis:

> For the growing inequalities in Ireland today reveal in telling form the social consequences of a state which has deferred to the needs of multinational capital and of an emerging transnational class of Irish entrepreneurs. Drawing on its deeply rooted populist reflexes . . . the Irish state has resituated itself not in the militant, ideological way of Thatcher's Britain but in a way that co-opts the trade union movement, and latterly the community and voluntary sector, to its competitive market orientation. Strong on rhetoric about social inclusion, equality and fairness, what these partnership mechanisms have delivered is a 'solidarity without equality' (Ó'Riain and O'Connell, 2000: 239) maximising economic growth alongside a weakening welfare effort. (Kirby, 2002: 187)

The point that Kirby makes here is a vital one: that social partnership has been a means by which the state can quell the potential for social unrest through the development of consensus politics, whilst ushering in neo-liberal economic policies accompanied by a lowered commitment to welfare. How has this been achieved?

(iii) Social partnership, the modernisation of governance and the politics of community

Modernisation in public policy terms is held to be a process which seeks to update the public services in a manner that makes them more responsive to the needs of citizens whilst meeting the market realities of a neo-liberal economy. Newman (2000: 47) asserts:

> Modernisation is a discourse which sets out an agenda for change across different sectors (health, education, criminal justice, local government, the Civil Service). It also denotes a wider political transformation, involving the reform of key relationships in the economy, State and civil society. It offers a particular conception of the citizen (empowered as active, participating subjects); of work (as a source of opportunity for the 'socially excluded'); of community (non-antagonistic and homogeneous); and of nation . . . viewed in this context, the *modern* public management takes on a different inflection: it is a fundamentally political project, to which the rhetorics, narratives and strategies of managerialism are harnessed.

It is very difficult not to view the modernisation of the public sector as essentially a reinvention of governance. The emergence of a partnership between the state, the private sector and the third sector represents this paradigm shift. Landry and Mulgan have been led to ask the question does the whole 'reinventing of government argument really cover a longer-term absorption of the [third] sector into the rules and concerns of government'? (1994: 7). Hulme and Edwards have posed a similar question in relation to the relationship between NGOs, states and donors asking if NGOs are 'too close to the powerful, too far from the powerless' (1997: 275). There are profound concerns arising from the modernisation of governance.

Modernisation in Ireland has been initiated through the Strategic Management Initiative (SMI), which was launched in 1994 and the Public Services Management Act, 1997. The aims of the SMI are set out in the Social Inclusion Strategy of the Department of Social, Community and Family Affairs (Government of Ireland, 1998c: 9):

- The contribution [each government department] could make to national development;
- The quality of services provided to the public;
- The provision of value for money to the taxpayer.

The Public Service Management Act, 1977, which was implemented in September 1997, sought to introduce new management structures, more transparency and greater accountability in government. The Social Inclusion Strategy was prepared in the context of this new government ethos, emphasising the link between government and policy implementation including: 'the provision of quality services, the establishment of a performance management system, the implementation of revised financial management systems and the business planning process' (Government of Ireland, 1998c: 10). Modernisation meant that a core set of values were laid down for the public services: monitoring individual and organisational performance; financial accountability; better customer service and quality assurance. Following a constitutional referendum in 1999, modernisation was extended to Irish local government. Harvey notes that this has had a significant impact on the community and voluntary sector:

> Under the new arrangements, operational from 2002, social, economic and cultural development is guided by 25-strong City (or County) Development Boards (CDBs), comprising councillors, statutory agencies and representatives of local interests and the community sector. CDBs are now an important part of the local authority structures, each headed up by a director of community and enterprise. As part of the reforms, the local authorities are now assisted in their work by Strategic Policy Committees (SPCs) with a similar representative structure. These bodies constitute an important area of work for voluntary and community organizations and set a number or organisational, resource and policy challenges. (Harvey, 2002: 29)

The White Paper on *Supporting Voluntary Activity* discussed the implications of these changes in structures of governance and posed several questions:

- Will civil society be enhanced or undermined by the growth in new forms of governance?
- Can the capacity of civil society be developed to enable the organisations within it to play an effective role?
- How will these organisations evolve to ensure they remain representative?
- Can the institutions of government rise to the challenge of managing increasingly complex, cross-sectoral relationships? (Government of Ireland, 2000c: 39–40)

The White Paper also notes the impact of 'rollback' (the 'hollowing out' of the state through a lower emphasis on welfare), which further heightens the pressures on civil society: 'a parallel development, both internationally and nationally, is a trend in recent years away from State Welfareism towards a more pluralistic system of provision, with many governments looking to the voluntary sector and to volunteers to play a larger role in the direct delivery of welfare services' (Government of Ireland, 2000c.: 14). It concludes that the changes in governance 'require a philosophy reflecting what is sometimes an *enabling state* or *assisted self-reliance* where local globalisation is assisted through the provision of external resources and technical assistance' (Government of Ireland, 2000c.: 43). The concept of an enabling state complements the policy of rollback, with its emphasis on 'a hand up rather than a handout'. The early evidence tends to support the thesis that the state has successfully incorporated civil society in its reinvention of governance (Powell and Geoghegan, 2004) whilst equally successfully lowering welfare commitments (Kirby, 2002). Interestingly, we may also be seeing the beginnings of the participatory democracy of civil society being reined back in by the representative democracy of local government with, for example, some of the community-based initiatives developed in the era of social partnership (notably the Community Development Programme) now having to submit their plans for approval by CDBs. What is emerging is a form of politics where the ideology of community is used to bind social actors together in the name of the national project of partnership. This 'politics of community' perspective underpins O'Carroll's argument that social partnership is 'best understood as [the] state-directed organisation of the economy in the name of the nation', where the 'ideological conflation of economy and society' occurs, in which the state is legitimated, as is the limitation of the demands placed upon it, whilst maintaining the power and health of corporate business (O'Carroll, 2002: 15).

Many of these developments correspond to what Giddens has called 'third way politics'. This now hackneyed term was at the core of his (1998) text on the 'third way' (so called as it was projected as a third way between the extremes of state socialism and unfettered capitalism), entitled *The Third Way: The Renewal of Social Democracy*. Giddens's central argument is that the 'third way' seeks to renew the social democratic project through a process of modernisation (1998: 67). He invokes the language of community when outlining his programme, which he views as a necessity in a globalised world, and argues for a renewal of civil society through:

- Government and civil society in partnership
- Community renewal through harnessing local initiative
- Involvement of the third sector
- Protection of the local public sphere
- Community-based crime prevention
- The democratic family. (Giddens, 1998: 79)

Giddens's 'third way' project describes the character of governance and community development in Ireland over the past decade almost identically. All of the features are present. First, modernisation of governance has been initiated through the Strategic Management Initiative and the Public Services Management Act. Second, the Celtic Tiger economy has linked the welfare of the nation to a policy of dynamic economic growth, creating what is widely referred to as an enterprise culture. Third, the state has embraced civil society, producing a Green Paper (Government of Ireland, 1997a) and a White Paper (2000c) copper-fastening this relationship. Fourth, social partnership has become the connecting discourse in shaping this new form of governance in a manner and on a scale that is unique in Europe. Fifth, the Irish state has sought to proclaim the end of poverty. This has enabled the language of social policy debate to be discursively reinvented in the context of 'the pursuit of social inclusion', which seeks to integrate the marginalised into mainstream society through the provision of 'opportunities'.

It is difficult not to conclude that the Irish state has been particularly adept at co-opting civil society into a partnership governance of Irish society. The boundaries between state and civil society have become both porous and permeable. This is the Irish version of 'third way' politics. Social partnership has emerged as a totemic influence in shaping Irish society as a whole. There is a profound contradiction at the heart of social partnership – the pursuit of social inclusion in a market-led economy that is widening social inequality as an integral function of wealth creation. Part of this contradiction is expressed in the emergence of a social left within civil society that seeks to influence the state outside a parliamentary landscape. Historically dominated by the political right on a scale unimagined elsewhere in Europe, parliamentary democracy in Ireland has had to discover a means of including those social, economic and political elements that would find a voice in a social democratic party elsewhere in Europe. The problem for this social left in Ireland, expressing itself through a vibrant civil society, is that partnership with the state may prove to be Faustian pact in which a state that has embraced neo-liberalism and is replacing welfare policy by an enterprise culture is seeking to incorporate civil society into a project of governance that will fatally compromise its ethical legitimacy and democratising potential. The question that remains is whether the 'democratic experimentalism' outlined herein can fundamentally reshape partnership in the direction of 'governance from the bottom up'. Might it represent the green shoots of a process of 'democratising democracy'? In a globalised society, dominated by the market, that is a task of Herculean proportions, and yet there is ample evidence of citizens willing to try.

Recommended reading

Barber, B. (1984) *Strong Democracy: Participatory Politics for a New Age.* University of California Press, Berkeley.

Kirby, P. (2002) *The Celtic Tiger in Distress: Growth with Inequality in Ireland.* Basingstoke and New York: Palgrave.

Kirby, P., Gibbons, L. and Cronin, M. (2002) *Reinventing Ireland: Culture, Society and the Global Economy.* London: Pluto.

Powell, F. and Geoghegan, M. (2004) *The Politics of Community Development: Reclaiming Civil Society or Reinventing Governance?* Dublin: A&A Farmar.

Sabel, C. (1996) *Ireland: Local Partnerships and Social Innovation.* Paris: OECD.

Chapter 3

The politics of care

Michael Rush

Introduction

Care has emerged as a fresh concept in social policy debates concerning the rights and obligations of social citizenship and the moral foundations of welfare. This chapter contrasts mainstream feminist perspectives on care with communitarian perspectives in Ireland, some of which are deeply rooted in orthodox values about marriage, motherhood and the family. The chapter argues that contemporary perspectives on care can be understood as a critical response to the impact of economic and employment policies on caring relationships and the nature of social interdependence in Ireland.

Welfare theory in relation to the family and the welfare state relies heavily upon feminist analysis from English speaking countries where informal care is generally depicted as a barrier to women's citizenship and gender equality (Gordon, 1990: 20). These debates usefully distinguish between two types of institutional responses to informal care and welfare: in the first approach mothers are treated as full-time carers and entitled to a social wage, and in the second approach they are assumed to be workers and are provided with care through their labour market status (Sainsbury, 1999: 4). Historically, Ireland was a weak example of the first, where mothers were treated as full-time carers but were provided only with a means-tested social wage in the absence of a male-breadwinner, thereby maintaining lone parents in welfare dependency (Richardson, 1995: 134). This chapter argues that the outstanding issues of lone parent benefit reform (NESC, 2005: 183; OECD, 2003: 199) and constitutional family policy reform (Constitutional Review Group, 1996) have become inextricably linked, bringing a renewed relevance for contemporary Irish social policy to an unresolved feminist dilemma. That is whether national welfare arrangements can support equally 'a mother's wage for caring that would allow her to form an autonomous household' and a 'system of services and provision that would allow mothers to be integrated into working life' (Hobson, 1994: 186).

A major development in the comparison of family policies in Europe and OECD countries has been the classification of four different types of welfare arrangements: Scandinavian, Anglo-Saxon, Continental European, and Southern European (Fotakis, 2000; 40, Rush, 2005a). The emerging trajectory of welfare in Ireland is mapped out here in a comparative context by examining the discussion on childcare, elder care and the activation of people with a disability contained in the influential *Developmental Welfare State* report. This report argues that the welfare state in Ireland is a hybrid with disparate elements that resembles, respectively, 'the citizen-based Nordic welfare model, the social insurance Continental European model, and the residual Anglo-Saxon welfare model' (NESC, 2005: xvii). In contrast to the prevailing politics of Anglo-Saxon residual welfare reform where the responsibilities of family and community are 'emphasised so heavily' (Orton, 2004: 185), a fundamental shift in Irish social policy debates is identified here, away from a familial model of welfare towards the 'new caring capacity on the part of the State, non-for-profit agencies and commercial organisations' (NESC, 2005: 36). Any retreat from a familial model of welfare and a social wage approach to full-time care would, in the Irish case it is concluded, serve only to institutionalise a preference for an Anglo-Saxon type of residual welfare system designed primarily to encourage paid employment.

The demography of social care in Ireland

A distinguishing feature of Scandinavian welfare states has been the development of a public social care infrastructure for older people and children which is detached from health and education services (Rostgaard and Lehto, 2001: 165). The emergence of a similar sector in Ireland can be traced back to child welfare campaigns in the 1970s and 1980s which focused on the inadequacy of residential childcare. A raft of reports, including the Task Force Report on Childcare Services (Task Force, 1980), recommended the urgent need for professional training of social care practitioners. The focus of concern in relation to institutional care has since embraced the treatment of women in the past in the Magdalene Laundries for 'unmarried mothers' (Fanning, 2004a: 16). Historically social care in Ireland was provided mainly by the Catholic Church, and the former ill-treatment of adults and children in residential care has been attributed to a legacy of Catholic moral authority in such institutions (Raftery and O'Sullivan, 1999: 200). Contemporary concern, however, is now focused on the quality of care provided in private day care settings for children and the 'chronic conditions endured by old people in private Irish nursing homes' (*Sunday Times*, 28 August 2005). These anxieties notwithstanding, social care is a growing sector of the Irish welfare economy.

The Report of the Joint Committee on Social Care Professionals (2003) counted 2,904 social care practitioners working in a variety of settings including community childcare, residential childcare and intellectual disability services (Gallagher, 2005). Other emerging arenas which have been identified for the practice of professional social care include: community development projects, Garda and community youth projects, county child-care committees and institutional and non-institutional settings for the care of older people (Share and McElwee, 2005: 13).

Older people

The relatively late emergence of a social care infrastructure in Ireland can in part be attributed to a constitutional bias for familial welfare and to a legacy of emigration which left Ireland with comparatively fewer older people. In 2002 only 15 per cent of people living in Ireland were aged 60 or over. By contrast in most European countries, the percentage of people over 60 is well over 20 per cent with the highest percentages occurring in Italy (24.55 per cent), Greece, (23.5 per cent), Germany (24.1 per cent) and Sweden (22.3 per cent) (NESC, 2005: 115). Although people aged 65 or over represent just 11 per cent of the general population this is set to increase to 15 per cent by 2021. The prospect of a higher percentage of older people in Irish society has led to the widely accepted conclusion that more formal social care will be required both in institutional and non-institutional settings (Gallagher, 2005: 289). It is estimated that only five per cent of people (17,000) over 65 are in long-stay residential care, most of whom are over 70 years of age. The number of family carers, however, has been estimated at 149,000, with a lower number of 38,931 being in receipt of the Carer's Allowance (NESC, 2005: 47). Those in receipt of the Carer's Allowance constitute about ten per cent of Care Alliance Ireland's estimate of 300,000 familial carers who provide the 'backbone of community care' mainly to older people and people with an intellectual disability (www.carealliance.ie)

People with a disability

Debates in relation to social care and disability have become centred on advocating a social model of disability which aims to focus social policy initiatives on how society disables people, as opposed to a medical model of disability in which disability is regarded as an individual physical handicap or physical impairment requiring diagnosis and treatment by medical experts (Bochel et al., 2005: 302). Understandings of disability based on the social model can be traced back to disability rights campaigns and the emergence of the Independent Living Movement (Barnes and Mercer, 1996). National organisations such as the Forum of People with Disabilities, People with Disabilities Ireland (PWDI) and the National Disability Authority (NDA) have successfully advocated for the adoption of the social model in Irish public policy. Policies which are at variance with the social model are viewed as generating 'disablism' – the failure to treat people with a disability as active welfare citizens or social agents in their own right (Pierce, 2003: 16).

The estimated number of people with a disability in Ireland is ten per cent of the overall population or 360,000 people (Commission on the Status of People with Disabilities, 1996). The National Intellectual Learning Disability Database (NILDD) established by the Health Research Board (HRB) enumerated 25,557 people in 2003, while the National Physical and Sensory Database (NPSD) enumerated 38,190 people (Finnerty and Collins, 2005: 272). Research into childcare, diversity and early education provision concluded that the availability of such precise and locally available data made the absence of appropriate supports for individual children with a learning disability entering primary school much less understandable (Rush, 2004a: 5). Contemporary policies for adults registered with a disability tend to be focused on promoting independent living through labour market participation (Ellis, 2004: 33). The most recent Census data in Ireland show that the employment rate of people with a disability was 43 per cent compared to an overall employment rate of 68 per cent. Research findings reveal, not surprisingly, that people with a disability, including those from ethnic minorities, regard paid employment in the labour market as a way of contributing to the wider society (Pierce, 2003: 38). An emerging critique of labour market policies in relation to people with a disability, however, is that the focus has tended to be on the individual rather than on the discriminatory barriers to employment that the individual faces, and furthermore that people who cannot fulfil an obligation to work are treated residually (Ellis, 2004: 37). This critique has a strong resonance in the development of social policy in Ireland in which people in receipt of disability benefits are observed '[to] outnumber those who are classed as unemployed in areas of disadvantage' (NESC, 2005: 184).

Childcare

Prohibitive costs translate into low economic demand for childcare in Ireland. According to the National Childcare Census 2000, only 4.8 per cent of children under one year of age were accessing childcare from a total of 48,854. Similarly, from a total of 97,585 children under three years of age only 12.8 per cent were attending centre-based childcare. The highest percentages of children accessing centre-based childcare in Ireland were aged between three and six: from a total of 159,118 children just under about 25 per cent attend centre-based care.

Ireland consequently remains far from compliant with the EU Barcelona Objectives (NDP/CSF, 2003) which propose that 90 per cent of children over three and 33 per cent of children under three should be provided with childcare by 2010. An overarching reliance on informal childminding in Ireland has led some rural County Childcare Committees to challenge a normative Eurocentric emphasis on centre-based care through the pursuit of a combination care approach involving community centres, school premises and informal childminding organised at the administrative level of the parish or village (Rush, 2003). Despite extensive media coverage of a €1,000 a year childcare subsidy for children under six, statutory consideration of the future trajectory of childcare services remains limited to the development of a National Plan for the Development of Early Childhood Services for implementation by City and County Development Boards, the City and County Childcare Committees and Family Resource Centres. This vision for the development of childcare services hinging as it does on existing targeted paid employment measures is not at variance with 'the contention that welfare reform in Ireland should primarily be about increased targeting and travelling further down the road of a residual welfare state' (NESC, 2005: 150).

Despite the overall growth in population in Ireland, the percentage of children in the population has been declining dramatically for several decades. In 1972 children aged 14 and under comprised a staggering 31 per cent of the overall population; by 2002 the number had fallen to 21.1 per cent. In the Travelling community, however, children under 14 represented 42.2 per cent of the overall community, making the issue of childcare of even greater significance than for the rest of the society. In 2002, there were 827,428 children (CSO, 2003a) which was 31,996 fewer children than in the 1996 Census. In addition the Total Period Fertility rate at 1.95 is stable but below replacement level (Vital Statistics, July 2005). It has been argued that the social construction of childhood needs to be understood at a number of different levels and that childhood is institutionalised through family education and the state (Jenkin and Scott, 2000: 153). In case of Irish social policy Catholic social teaching retains a strong influence over the social construction of childhood because 'the particular aspects of social policy of greatest concern to the Catholic Church are those of family and education – those of greatest relevance to the lives of children' (Devine et al., 2004: 211). In relation to the children's rights issue in Ireland, a 'child protection and development perspective' informed the shaping of the National Children's Strategy (Department of Health and Children, 2000a) and the National Childcare Strategy (Department of Justice, Equality and Law Reform, 1999) the latter of which being strongly influenced by trade union and gender equality perspectives (Rush, 2004b: 107).

Comparative social care

A comparative study of 22 countries found that less help was available for childcare in Ireland than in any other country (Bradshaw and Finch, 2002: 139). A major criticism of services for children in Ireland is that they are primarily discussed as a labour market consideration, particularly in relation to female employment (Devine et al., 2004: 225). On the other hand, international studies distinguish between countries which organise children's services in terms of social care such as the Swedish *daghem* (day-home) or pre-school education such as the French *école maternelle*. While they are both primarily focused on children's social and pedagogical development, the former has an implicit latent function of facilitating parents to engage in paid employment which continues to be available after a child commences formal education (Rostgaard and Lehto, 2001: 138). In the Swedish case it would be wrong to overstate the gender equality dimensions of social care services without due regard to the parallel ideological motivation which emphasises childcare as an equal opportunities welfare measure, or anti-poverty measure for children. These motivations are rooted in the Swedish experience of rapid urbanisation and poor housing conditions in the 1930s, which at the time were perceived as offering children an unhealthy playground, with reduced adult supervision and pedagogical support (Bjornberg, 2002: 49). While social services in most countries are not governed by rights criteria, the right to day care for children has been made explicit in several Nordic countries, beginning with Sweden in 1991 when all children over one and half years of age were guaranteed a place in municipal day care. Although less explicit, children in France are in principle entitled to a place in *l'école maternelle* from as young as two years of age, and in Germany children are guaranteed a place in nursery school from three and half years of age. The two English speaking European countries of Ireland and Britain offer the weakest guarantees which consist of early entry into primary school (Rostgaard and Lehto, 2001: 158).

The situation with regard to the service rights of older people is that they are more weakly developed in all countries. Only in Denmark is there a degree of universalism with regard to home help and institutional care. Internationally there has been a universal shift away from institutional care towards more home-like settings, with Finland, the Netherlands and Sweden maintaining the highest proportion of in-patient care beds for older people. Studies into international convergence in relation to social care for older people focus on more means testing, varying standards with the ability to pay, and the observation that some countries such as France and Germany have a legal obligation for families to provide or purchase care. Social care services are depicted within the Nordic social policy discourse as having emerged from the efforts of women, older people and people with a disability to gain more personal autonomy in their daily lives; in the case of women this personal autonomy is strongly linked to wage employment (Anttonen and Sipilä, 1996: 90). It has been observed more recently, however, that policies in relation to care are increasingly framed around support for working parents, reinforcing an economic emphasis on paid work, productivity and national competitiveness, and thus eroding an emphasis on care (Ellis, 2004: 32, Daly, 2002).

Care as employment policy

The most important fiscal policy initiative to assist people in Ireland in maintaining their caring responsibilities for older or disabled family members is the Carer's Allowance which mainly supports women carers at home independent of the labour market. The Carer's Allowance is in essence a social wage approach to the care of older people and people with a disability. The most important fiscal initiative for the care of children at home is the One Parent Family Payment (OPFP), which in a study of similar payments in 22 countries was found to be 'higher than everywhere else save for Austria' (Bradshaw and Finch, 2002: 139). The Carer's Allowance and the OPFP are important forms of social assistance which allow people, mainly women, to care for family members outside the paid labour market. The most important universal childbirth support for mothers within the paid labour market was introduced under the Maternity Protection Act, 1994 which offers 18 consecutive weeks for maternity leave with no obligation on behalf of the employer to pay the employee. The Parental Leave Act, 1998 is more parsimonious, with parents in Ireland entitled to just 14 weeks' parental leave without pay. The OECD have observed that everywhere, 'take-up of existing family friendly measures is predominantly a female affair' (OECD, 2003) therefore any comparative underdevelopment of parental leave regimes primarily disadvantages mothers engaged in paid employment. In the Irish case the Parental Leave Review Group had their primary recommendation in 1998 to attach a payment to parental leave derailed by delegates from the Farming Pillar, the Employers Pillar and the Department of Finance (Rush, 2004b). The following observation from the influential *Developmental Welfare State* report implicitly suggests that a conventional emphasis on economic competitiveness and employment growth within Irish social policy is now seen to be prejudicial to the caring responsibilities of workers in the exponential Irish labour market:

When large numbers of women remained in the home, the family was arguably the single most important pillar of Ireland's national system of social protection. In a large number of instances, the care of young children, older people and other household members with special needs hinged around the full-time presence of a fit and capable household member, usually a woman. Relatively residual roles were played by the State and organisations in civil society, and an even lesser one by commercial bodies. The rise in women's employment rates from the 1970s onwards began to weaken this pillar of caring and, during the 1990s the rates jumped further to open a significant deficit between the diminished capacity of families to provide care and the development of new caring capacity on the part of the state, not-for-profit bodies and commercial interests. (NESC, 2005: 36).

Despite the observation that employment growth has created a care deficit in Ireland the *Developmental Welfare State* report reiterates a commitment to an expanding labour market without providing a convincing strategy to support the diminished capacity of families to provide care.

From caring social wage to 'participation income'

In mapping the future trajectory of welfare in Ireland, *The Developmental Welfare State* report (NESC, 2005) seeks to shape the development of welfare futures in Ireland. It follows on from the publication of the equally far-sighted *Strategy into the 21st Century* (NESC, 1996). Both reports were published by the National Economic and Social Council, the national statutory organisation pledged to analyse and report on strategic issues relating to the efficient development of the economy and the achievement of social justice in Ireland, and they can therefore be read as a statutory engagement with the shaping of Irish welfare futures. The reports reflect two decades of Social Partnership arrangements and a corporatist confidence in an integrated welfare state in which public economic and social policies are closely and explicitly connected (Peillon, 2001). The report effectively demonstrates the institutionalisation of welfare relationships towards a preference for an 'integrated welfare state' in Ireland. *The Development Welfare State* adopts a comparative framework which locates Ireland internationally and compares and contrasts the benefits and drawbacks of varying national approaches to welfare.

In mapping the future trajectory of social protection in Ireland of *The Developmental Welfare State* report cites a strong preference for a paid employment approach to welfare and the ultimate merging of all categorical social assistance payments into a single 'participation income' (NESC, 2005: 219). This move could involve the withdrawal of One Parent Family payment, the longevity and security of which made it a distinguishing feature of the

Irish welfare regime and one which stood it apart internationally from economic liberal welfare to work strategies (Rush, 2004b; Eardley, 1996). The introduction of a participation income could also mean the removal of the Carer's Allowance and the Disability Allowance. Between them, lone parents (25 per cent), full-time carers in receipt of the Carer's Allowance (5 per cent) and people in receipt of Disability Allowance Carers (10 per cent) constitute 40 per cent of all those in receipt of social assistance payments. Entitlement to a participation income would require welfare claimants to understand that only in 'rare circumstances' would society expect people not be more self reliant, and that in return claimants could have an expectation for society to provide them with paid work (NESC, 2005: 219). The argument that social protection or a European social model could be built on high levels of employment is made on the basis that the highest risk of poverty in Ireland is still attached to non-employment. The counter argument that the high risk of poverty attached to non-employment in Ireland is caused by comparatively low social assistance levels is not, however, addressed effectively by the NESC. In Ireland low skilled jobs have grown as part of employment growth, a fact which is depicted as a national economic achievement despite the fact that 'in-work poverty' has grown in significance (NESC, 2005: 24–5). A key variable of welfare state comparison is how low skilled workers are treated. In Ireland they are maintained in poverty by the market in a typically Anglo-Saxon labour market arrangement. This is in stark contrast to the Scandinavian approach where a high minimum wage rate is set for low-skilled jobs in the market and where large numbers of women are employed by local authorities to provide social care services.

The diminished capacity of families to provide care in Ireland owing to rising women's employment rates serves only to reinforce 'the inescapable *fact that it is women who do the housework'* (Kiely, 1995: 148). The inequitable gender division of housework has remained an unresolved and ubiquitous concern of social theory and welfare debates for many years (Orloff, 1993). The failure of welfare provision to constructively acknowledge unpaid care and domestic labour has similarly been a major focus of comparative social policy debates (Lewis, 1992). Women's entitlements as wives have not, however, been a major consideration in such social policy debates and it has been argued that wives' entitlements have been skirted by a gender equality perspective that has helped to shape a normative preference for individualist over familial models of welfare (Sainsbury, 1996: 45). The 'articulation of feminist projects regarding women's employment' has also helped to create a context in which welfare reform from a feminist perspective was always likely to be based on 'employment for all' (Orloff, 2002: 96). However, when employment for all or welfare to work is embraced as a policy goal, the subsequent withdrawal of social assistance programmes can serve to seriously erode the social entitlement and economic capacity of lone mothers and other full-time carers to maintain autonomous households independent of the labour market or male-breadwinning.

The last official review of the One Parent Family Payment (Department of Social, Community and Family Affairs, 2000) pointed out that welfare disentitlement in the USA was preceded by the development of underclass theories and a subsequent 'hardening of attitudes' towards lone parents. Internationally this hardening of attitudes has become a wider trend as governments in Anglo-Saxon type welfare states attempt to resolve communitarian expressions of social solidarity with economic liberal welfare reforms by 'projecting notions of moral disintegration onto welfare claimants' (Harris, 2002: 377), thereby paving the way for welfare disentitlement based on moral advancement.

A mother's wage for caring?

Mapping the future of family welfare in a comparative context has in the past been typically the preserve of English-speaking feminist welfare debates (Sainsbury, 1996: 45). Anglo-Saxon feminism has expressed an ambivalent (Lewis, 1992) or unreceptive analysis to state welfare policies (Wilson, 1977: 9). A contemporary dilemma facing the future trajectory of welfare in Ireland (NESC, 2005: 179) and feminist welfare theory generally (Hobson, 1994: 186) is whether the welfare state should 'support a mother's wage for caring that would allow her to form an autonomous household', that is some form of one parent family payment. In Ireland this dilemma can also be extended to full-time carers in the home whatever their parental or family status. For contemporary social policy it is a dilemma which requires consideration against a background of dramatic changes which are taking place in family formation.

In the Irish case, wives and husbands in married relationships still represent just under two thirds of all families, numbering 692,985 (CSO, 2003a). This is a social situation that still remains far removed from the scenario envisaged in some quarters of British family policy analysis which proclaims the end of marriage in anticipation of a welfare future based on new autonomous and cohabiting relationships (Lewis, 2001). An increase in the number of cohabiting relationships to 84,966 is, however, of contemporary relevance to Ireland as the social citizenship rights of cohabiting couples in 'marriage like' relationships are increasingly coming under legislative review (Law Reform Commission, 2004). Lone parents, however, still remain the second largest family type in Ireland, numbering 153,863 families, of which 23,499 are lone father families. Despite the fact that nearly two thirds of Irish families are constituted in married families, one in three new births are taking place to families outside marriage making the current link between

marriage and childbirth weaker in Ireland (Rush, 2005a). In addition divorce
has become available in Ireland since 1996. The consequential moral dilemma
depicted in statutory social policy debates is suggested here:

> Societies are having to accept that separation and divorce are swelling the
> numbers of lone parents and leaving the social welfare system with effectively two
> choices – to allow poverty among them grow or to enable more of them to
> function as independent households. (NESC, 2005: 179)

The tautological proposition here is that lone parents, whether through solo-
motherhood, separation, divorce or widowhood, will remain in poverty while
in receipt of social assistance. In effect the choice to 'function as independent
households' through entitlement to the One Parent Family Payment, outside
paid employment or the support of a male breadwinner is being sealed off as
a viable social option. The National Women's Council of Ireland has meanwhile launched a rights-based campaign for women's unpaid care-work and
paid employment to be acknowledged legally within the tax and welfare
system and for all women to be treated as individuals.

Paradigms of care

An analytical preference for individualisation is common to English-speaking
welfare debates as is a legacy of idealising a 'yet to be realised shift' in care
provision away from the family towards a universally expanding public sector
(Sainsbury, 1996: 37). The preference for public sector care is most evident
within British welfare analysis where it is argued that informal caring and care
in the community reinforce the economic dependence of women (Graham,
1983). A shift in emphasis away from concerns with gender exploitation in
care debates can be traced back to 1980s with the development of a feminist
ethic of care (Gilligan, 1982). Subsequently a 'political ethic of care' perspective has emerged to balance the contemporary emphasis on paid employment
within welfare reform debates (Williams, 2001: 467). The 'political ethic of
care' perspective which has now become embedded in comparative welfare
theory is related directly to feminist concern with the relationship between
care, gender and employment. Within these debates the concepts of care and
social interdependence have been re-introduced to balance classical liberal
individualistic conceptions of justice based on protecting the freedoms of
rational autonomous independent actors (Ellis, 2004). These political ethic
of care perspectives however remain influenced by an analytical preference for
individualisation and public sector expansion.

An ethic of care in Ireland

In Ireland an ethic of care has been advocated through criticism of state healthcare policies, for example by Fergus O'Farrell, Director of the Adelaide Hospital Society and by Maureen Gaffney of the National Economic and Social Forum. Care Alliance Ireland, a national organisation of over 80 Community and Voluntary Organisations for familial care, has reiterated the call for a revaluation of the ethic of care and for the development of social processes to build the social capital essential for good health outcomes (Gaffney, 2001: 63). The introduction of an ethic of care into Irish welfare debates thus essentially strengthens the argument for greater state investment right across Ireland's mixed economy of welfare.

Organisations campaigning for the care of older people and people with a disability in Ireland have emerged from a community and voluntary sector which is heavily influenced by organised women's participation. For example Caring for Carers, an influential family orientated caring advocacy group, was originally formed with help from the Ennis and District branch of Soroptimist International. Soroptimist means 'best for women' and there are 23 branches of Soroptomist International in Ireland. Soroptimist International gave support to the launch of the Carers' Charter in 1991 which was compiled by Professor Joyce O'Connor, Director of the National College of Industrial Relations. The aim of the Care Alliance Ireland umbrella network is that formal care services should compliment rather than substitute for family-based and informal care and that carers should have a right to a social wage in the form of a Carer's Allowance.

Advocacy of an ethic of care within Irish welfare debates is strongly associated with a project of rebuilding social capital and strengthening voluntarism (Gaffney, 2001). The ethic-of-care perspective has emerged from social dissatisfaction with economic growth in which prosperity is depicted as having negative outcomes on individual health, morbidity and well-being for many in Irish society (Sweeney, 2001: 14). Influential voices of opposition include the Adelaide Hospital Trust, the Irish Commission for Justice and Peace, the Irish Bishops' Council and the Society of St Vincent de Paul. Combined, these voices form the basis of communitarian critiques which are addressed implicitly by the following quote;

> People who believe Ireland's economic development model has sacrificed compassion, social standards and solidarity need to be convinced that the successful pursuit of current economic objectives has inherent social implications that will directly serve social justice and a more egalitarian society. (NESC, 2005: 32)

This can be read as an official acknowledgement that many in Irish society have yet to be convinced that an ongoing emphasis on economic growth and universal paid employment provides the best path to social egalitarianism. In Ireland, advocacy of an ethic of care has become strongly associated with the advocacy of universal health and social care, egalitarianism, voluntarism, and recognition of full-time carers in the home. The advocacy of an ethic of care does not necessarily mean advocacy of public sector expansion but rather greater public investment in the quality of care in Ireland's mixed economy of welfare. Within Irish welfare debates, the perspective of carers in the home and of volunteers generally sits uneasily with social policy depictions of family-based care as oppressive to women and a barrier to the autonomy of people with a disability (Anttonen and Sipilä, 1996: 90).

Familial care and family policy reform

Welfare debates in Ireland concerned with reconciling work and family life have shifted in rhetoric towards individualisation by emphasising the 'work–life balance' rather than family friendly work policies. In this way a focus on the family is eliminated from discussion of employment policies. A parallel shift is evident in a review of the Constitutional Articles dealing specifically with the family which can be traced back to a long-standing request by the Department of Health and Children for the Oireachtas to consider a constitutional amendment to underpin the individual rights of children. Article 41 of the Constitution contains the main provisions relating to the family. The principal criticism of the Constitution in relation to children and the family is that according to Article 41.3 the family in Ireland is founded on the institution of marriage and that children's rights are explicitly absent.

Treoir, the National Federation for Unmarried Parents and their Children has formed part of a broad-based campaign for children in all family forms to be given equal protection under the Constitution and for children's rights and their best interests to be given paramount importance. In contrast to concerns expressed by statutory agencies, NGOs the Constitutional Review Group as well as a broad-based civic and religious agenda to have the Constitution amended, other organisations such as the Irish Bishops' Council and the Mothers' Union Ireland favoured a retention of a definition of the family based on marriage. Furthermore they supported the retention of Article 41.2 quoted below which depicted a societal preference for home based maternal childcare and a traditional reinforcement of the gender division of informal welfare:

1   In particular, the State recognises that by her life within the home, woman gives
      to the State a support without which the common good cannot be achieved.

2   The State shall therefore endeavour to ensure that mothers shall not be obliged by economic necessity to engage in labour to the neglect of their duties in the home. (Constitution, Article 41.2)

In the interests of gender equality, however, and in recognition of the role of carers and care carried out within the home, *The All-Party Oireachtas Committee on the Constitution Tenth Progress Report: The Family* (Government of Ireland, 2006: 127) recommended that Article 41.2.1 and 41.2.2 be revised as follows:

The State recognises that by reason of family life within the home, a parent gives to the state a support without which the common good cannot be achieved

The State shall, therefore, endeavour to ensure that both parents shall not be obliged by economic necessity to work outside the home to the neglect of their parental duties

This report advised the government not to change the definition of the family based on marriage and instead recommended legislative changes to provide for civil partnerships for cohabiting and same sex couples. In a speech to launch the report on 24 January 2006, the Taoiseach, Mr Bertie Ahern TD, declared that on 'the issue of the description of women in the home, it is fairly clear that the existing terms of article 41.2.1 are not appropriate to the modern world'. The speech also proclaimed, however, that any changes in the constitution should not have the effect of 'denigrating or undermining the work of people who choose to work in the home'. In effect, the influence of Catholic social thinking in shaping Article 41 of the Constitution which afforded all mothers social protection from the labour market had created a situation where lone mothers had an implicit social entitlement not to engage in paid work. The proposed amendments to the Constitution have on the one hand failed adequately to accommodate perspectives for change in relation to non-married families, but on the other hand they may have consolidated a degree of insulation from paid employment and market outcomes for all families. Of additional importance for the politics of care in Ireland and consideration for this chapter is the recommendation for research-based improvements in the institutional capacity of the Department of Social and Family Affairs to support the family in its role as a primary provider of social solidarity in the face of a growth of individualisation (All Party Oireachtas Committee on the Constitution, 2006: 128).

In common with other countries the Irish Constitution of 1937 is regarded as the basic or fundamental law of the state and 'a kind of higher law' (Chubb, 1997: 37). The influence of Catholic social theory is to be mostly found in articles 40–4 which are collectively entitled *Fundamental Rights* and Article 45 which is entitled *Directive Principles of Social Policy*. These five articles reflect a traditional state recognition of the family as the 'primary and fundamental unit group of society' which is 'indispensable to the welfare of the Nation and the State'. Under Article 45 the predominant aim of social policy is 'the welfare of the people as a whole' within a system of efficient private enterprise. According to Article 45 the state pledges itself to safeguard with 'especial care' the economic interests of the weaker sections of society and to support where necessary the 'infirm, the widow, the orphan and the aged'. In this respect constitutional social policy in Ireland explicitly advocates the goal of moderating market outcomes, which is the primary characteristic of what Bussemaker and Van Kersbergen identify as Central European social capitalist welfare states – culturally conservative countries with traditional views of the family and gender roles and a commitment to a significant degree of social protection (Bussemaker and Van Kersbergen, 1999: 17).

The constitutional legacy accorded by Article 41 of family-based social policy in Ireland divides those who otherwise share a commitment to an ethic of care and greater egalitarianism within Irish society. In addition, women's organisations are divided on the issue of marriage and the family with many remaining unconvinced by an emphasis on 'liberal individualism within which mainstream feminism is grounded' (Fanning, 2004a: 16). Women's organisations, such as WITH/Curam (Women in the Home) and the Irish Parent and Carer NGO, campaign for public fiscal recognition for the unpaid work carried out in the home, the community and in all aspects of the economy. They are similarly concerned to promote parity for carers at home with men and women in the paid labour market.

Within feminist welfare debates care is considered not only as a moral concept but also as a political concept through which judgements about the public world can made. Care is regarded as a primary political and social concern which offers the basis of a universal paradigm of citizenship and welfare activism operating under the slogan 'It is time we began to change our political and social institutions to reflect this truth'. Ultimately the 'ethic of care' discourse is rooted in feminist opposition to the distribution of political power in the USA and to the international mobilisation of the politically disenfranchised (Tronto, 1993: 180). Women's organisations which maintain a traditional perspective towards marriage and the family share similar concerns, for example groups such as the Mothers' Union (MU) claim a global membership of 3.6 million in 76 countries with special accreditation at the United Nations as a member of the Commission on the Status of women. The MU are active in the campaign to cancel Third World Debt, the Make Poverty History campaign and actively lobby the G8 to support the Millennium Development Goals.

In Ireland there are many organisations engaged in welfare debates and delivery who subscribe neither to an emphasis on liberal individualism nor to a preference for public sector delivery. These organisations can be described as communitarian in that they are loyal to the family, to voluntarism, to egalitarianism and share a moral commitment to welfare egalitarianism. Many of these organisations, such as the Mothers Union, Curam-Women in the Home and the Irish Bishops' Council, are expressly opposed to any constitutional change in relation to the family while at the same time supporting the extension of social citizenship rights and welfare entitlements to cohabiting and same sex coupes. Despite their contrasting perspectives on family and individualisation debates, however, mainstream feminist perspectives and communitarian perspectives on care share a critical view of the impact of employment-led economic growth in Irish society.

Spheres of care versus care in the family

The decreasing percentage of children in Irish society and the increasing number of older people are reshaping the demographic profile of Irish society. The proportion of households formed by people living alone or in couples without children is increasing, which is in itself a reflection of a trend towards greater individualisation in Irish life. As a result it has been argued that concepts of family and community will need adjusting to reflect the realities of Irish life and that new types of social interaction in addition to those generated by children across households will need to be facilitated in neighbourhoods (NESC, 2005: 37). Implicit in this recommendation is the observation that in modern societies children have traditionally provided the principal basis of non-workplace social interdependence and inter-generational social solidarity across households in extended families and neighbourhoods.

The introduction of a care ethic to welfare capitalism has become an imperative aim of mainstream policy debates in Ireland, as in other English speaking countries (Gaffney, 2001; Williams, 2001). It has been argued, however, that any further development of an ethic of care is beyond current liberal thinking and that any change would require a new 'social liberal ideological mandate' (O'Connor et al., 1999: 230). Analysis of the egalitarian potential of the welfare state has placed the role of the family and gender at the centre of comparative studies (Sainsbury, 1999: 40). In Nordic welfare debates the family and the household are conceptually prominent. In Anglo-Saxon welfare debates, however, there is an ideological ambivalence with the term 'family' itself. Therefore a new discourse is advocated 'which is not just about "family friendly" policies but about the work–life balance' (Williams, 2001: 472). Discussion of care provides for a wider consideration 'of the values that are important to people in their relationships of care and intimacy than that which is allowed by the phrase "family values"' (Williams, 2001: 475). Within this new 'ethics of care' discourse the possibility of 'a greater awareness of the realities of intimacy' being linked to notions of 'family' or 'family diversity' is not feasible while the term family is inextricably linked to notions of traditional 'family values' and 'the superiority of the two parent heterosexual family as the site of care' (Williams, 2001, 475). Williams (2001) draws upon a range of perspectives on care which have emerged to challenge the institutionalisation of care in institutional and family settings. These include disabled feminist critiques (Morris, 1993), critiques taking into account race and ethnicity (Gunaratnam, 1990), gay critiques, non-heterosexual families of choice (Weeks et al., 1996) and critiques which advocate friendship as the basis of care (Pahl, 2000).

The mainstream ethic of care perspective views caring responsibilities as belonging equally to all citizens – men and women, parents, and those without children. It embraces a paradigm of difference in which people have caring ties to friends, relatives and neighbours. The place of the family is related to building a society where all citizens can participate equally in the 'sphere of the labour market' and the 'sphere of care and responsibility' (O'Connor et al., 1999, p. 230). A challenge to the hypothesis that we are all obliged to care is the argument that some non-parents may in future challenge the development of family-friendly employment practices on the grounds that parenthood, and by association all informal care work, is now a case of individual choice and therefore an individual rather than a collective activity (Morgan, 2002: 283). In a similar vein, influential debates into the moral, philosophical and legal basis of welfare in the USA have conjectured procreative strategies that might require 'parents to be taxed when they have children' (Burley, 2004: xviii). A contrasting challenge to mainstream social policy ambivalence towards the family has come from feminist political economy where the concept of 'identity as persons-in-relation' has been advocated. Here the focus is on the family and marriage as arenas of social choice in relation to agency, affiliation and standard of living where all members of the family have at 'least some limited area of agency' (Nelson, 1996: 69; Sen, 1984).

Conclusion

Mainstream feminist analysis considers that political and institutional power is crucial for bringing issues such as the gender division and recognition of unpaid work and care labour to the forefront of welfare debates (Lewis, 1992: 171). In Ireland the argument has been made that government policy has ignored care work (Kennedy, 2004: 85). More recently there have been calls to unblock the ideological disagreements which are preventing progress on single issues such as subsidised childcare for parents entering employment. In addition the Government has been strongly urged to respond to the recommendations of the OECD to the Department of Education and Science on how to improve early childhood and education policy (NESC, 2005: 216; OECD, 2004). Furthermore recommendations have been made for the National Disability Strategy to be used as an example of how a Strategy for Older People can be made to tailor attention to the individual (NESC, 2005: 222) in the context of the development of a wider diversity of residential care. The Irish concept of 'tailored universalism', with services delivered by mainstream providers to a more diverse public has echoes of the 'differentiated universalism' which is embraced by the mainstream political ethic of care perspective in critical opposition to third way managerialism in Britain (Ellis, 2004: 44). Importantly the statutory perspective outlined in the *Developmental Welfare State* report on the future of care, employment and welfare in Ireland claims not to be a 'top-down blueprint' but a representation of a 'significant convergence of views' on Irelands welfare state reform (NESC, 2005: 6).

Analysis of the extent to which policies are the result of top-down consideration or bottom-up social pressure has emerged in response to the divide between familial feminism and more mainstream feminists in the Nordic welfare states. It has concluded that in some feminist circles the valorisation of care and motherhood has been recognised as an important part of an ideological critique of the dominant values in industrial societies (Bergman, 2002: 5). In a similar fashion it has been argued in Ireland that modernisation cannot proceed at the expense of family orientation and that more individualisation does not necessarily mean less family orientation. It has also been argued that the concept of security rather than the concept of formal or substantive equality has been at the basis of Nordic welfare development (Kiely, 2004: 71; Abrahamson, 1999: 38).

An overarching emphasis within the statutory discourse of welfare reform in Ireland, for example in the *Developmental Welfare State* report on the labour market activation particularly of women, mothers and people with a disability and other groups, reveals a strong preference for labour market dependence rather than welfare state dependence. This raises a question of terminology. While dependency on the welfare state, particularly by women, is regarded as sign of weakness and a lack of power, de-commodification of mainly male workers by the welfare state is seen as strengthening workers. When income transfers to mothers, lone mothers in particular are described by some feminists as transferring dependence from individual men to dependence on the state, and this lessens the significance of the difference between being dependent on an individual man and being dependent on the state (Nyberg, 2002: 93) Similarly, labour market activation policies lessen the significance of being dependent on an individual employer particularly when variables such as low labour market status, gender, and caring responsibilities are involved. While some feminists have argued that the Nordic states are women friendly or state feminist (Hatland, 2001: 67), others have pointed out that cash transfers to women pass straight through the hands of the mothers to their children (Nyberg, 2002: 93).

Such a simple observation makes clear that policies for child care and child support by necessity require recognition that mothers are in general the primary carers even where there is a more advanced egalitarianism in the gender division of unpaid labour, and where there is an advanced social care infrastructure, for example in the Nordic states. An ethic of care which recognises the caring needs of minority groups and a 'paradigm of difference' cannot also fail to recognise that while married couples and cohabiting relationships are not the possessors of superior family values, they retain a critical importance as subjects of Irish family policy and care policies. Equally lone-parent families retain a significant role, as do an estimated 300,000 home-based carers. In recent decades Ireland has consolidated a commitment to developing an integrated welfare state, yet fresh statutory emphasis on employment for all, increased targeting and a commitment to residual welfare (NESC, 2005: 150) may in the longer term have negative fiscal implications for full-time carers in Ireland and offer nothing more than residual targeted measures to the exponential social care sector.

Recommended reading

Gaffney, M. (2001) 'Rebuilding social capital: restoring the ethic of care in Irish society', pp. 57–64 in Bohan, H. and Kennedy, G. (eds), *Redefining Roles and Relationships: Our Society in the New Millennium.* London: Veritas.

NESC (2005) *The Development Welfare State*, Report no 113. Dublin: NESC.

Sweeney, J. (2001) 'Prosperity and well-being', *Studies* 90 (357): 7–16.

Williams, F. (2001) 'In and beyond new labour: towards a new political ethics of care', *Critical Social Policy* 21 (4): 467–93

Part 2   Change and challenges

Chapter 4

Education, life chances and disadvantage

Tina MacVeigh

Introduction

This chapter examines the effectiveness of Irish policy initiatives aimed at addressing educational disadvantage, and the problems resulting from it. In 1965, an OECD analysis of education found the Irish system to be grossly neglecting the children of poorer classes in society. It reported that over half (53 per cent) of children left school at or before the age of 13 (Garvin, 2004: 152). In 2001, 40 per cent of children did not complete the second-level school cycle in certain parts of Dublin's inner city (Barry, 2001: 6). In 2004, 13 per cent of the population aged 18 to 24 years had achieved at most a lower secondary education (the Junior Certificate) and were not involved in further education or training (Department of Education and Science, 2005: 22). Changes in the nature of work and the skills required mean that the knowledge industry now plays a greater role than the more traditional manufacturing forms of employment. While the probability and duration of unemployment are significantly less for those who complete the Leaving Certificate cycle compared to those who finish their schooling at the Junior Certificate cycle, the probability decreases substantially for those achieving a degree compared to those with only the leaving certificate.

A number of initiatives, particularly the removal of second- and third-level fees in 1967 and 1996 respectively, have been successful in increasing the numbers participating both in second- and third-level education in Ireland. However, there are still a significant number of individuals who do not manage to complete the formal education cycle. It is now generally accepted that educational disadvantage, and disadvantage in general, are associated with a number of factors including unemployment and limited social mobility (Clancy, 2005: 97, Kellaghan, 2002: 17, Smyth and Hannan, 2000: 125) and is often concentrated (but not confined) to urban pockets of social deprivation characterised by high levels of crime, substance abuse, unemployment and family breakdown (Barry, 2001: 4).

Educational disadvantage

The Combat Poverty Agency defines educational disadvantage as 'a situation whereby individuals in Irish society derive less benefit from the education system than their peers' manifested in several ways but particularly in terms of low participation and achievement in the formal education system (CPA, 2003: 2). According to the Department of Education and Science, 'educational disadvantage' means the 'impediments to education arising from social or economic disadvantage, which prevent students from deriving appropriate benefit from education in schools' (Department of Education and Science, 1998, Education Act, Section 32 (9): 32).

Pupils attending schools which draw from disadvantaged areas are more likely to drop out and under-perform, regardless of personal circumstances (Smyth and Hannan, 2000: 111). Structural problems in the education system may also play a role in the maintenance or creation of disadvantage (Kellaghan, 2002: 20). Given the extent to which educational disadvantage is linked to poverty, social mobility, patterns of employment and potential earnings over the life-course, it is important that individuals leave the school system with a formal education so they can avoid cycles of unemployment and low income in their adult years.

The extent to which pupils from disadvantaged areas are disadvantaged in education is reflected in differences in the levels of access to third-level education. The differences are easily demonstrated in the Dublin area, where disadvantage is concentrated in certain postal districts. In Dublin, eight postal districts (Dublin 3, 4, 6, 9, 14, 15, 16 and 18) had admission rates higher than the overall Dublin county average of 0.45 and five postal districts had admission rates of less than half of the county average (Dublin 1, 10, 17, 20, 22). In the Dublin 1 and 10 postal areas, where a significant degree of economic disadvantage is concentrated, 20 per cent and 10 per cent of pupils attend third-level colleges respectively, in contrast to 73 per cent and 79 per cent in the Dublin 18 and 14 areas respectively (HEA, 2005: 39). The most recent analysis of college entrants in 2004 demonstrates that, despite progress in the third-level participation of individuals from lower-income backgrounds, university education in Ireland remains dominated by the children of the professional and managerial classes and farmers, to an extent unmatched in most other EU states (O'Connell et al., 2006: 64). Students from some of the more affluent south Dublin suburbs are still up to eight times more likely to proceed to third level than teenagers from the north inner-city (O'Connell et al., 2006: 107). In 2002, 293 pupils who left primary school neither emigrated nor transferred to another school within the state. For a further 639 pupils leaving primary school, the subsequent destination is unknown (Department of Education and Science, 2004: 21). It would be safe to assume that a proportion of these pupils also failed to transfer to post-primary education. In 1999, 3.2 per cent of the student cohort left the formal education system with no recognised qualification, which means they left school before taking the Junior Certificate examination (NESF, 2002: 32). One in ten children leave primary school with significant literacy problems, despite reductions in class sizes, increases in library resources and in the availability of learning support teachers in recent years (CPA, 2003: 2).

Factors associated with disadvantage in education

Numerous studies have made the link between levels of educational qualifications achieved and earnings potential in working life. Hannan and O'Riain (1993), in their study of pathways to adulthood among Irish youth, found that failure in education almost guaranteed failure in employment and was associated with other problems such as early pregnancy and psychological distress. They also found these factors to be mostly associated with the typical transition for youths from lower income backgrounds and to be linked to fathers' employment status and mothers' educational attainment. Their findings confirmed the results of earlier work (Breen, 1984, 1991), which found level of educational attainment to be a significant factor influencing the ability to gain employment, to establish a household and in determining the length and quality of future employment. In this regard, level of education achieved was a significant factor influencing the life chances of an individual (Hannan and O'Riain, 1993: 44). In the Irish context, educational qualifications are highly predictive of access to employment, social mobility and future earnings (McCoy and Smyth, 2003: 92). There are also substantial differences in the levels of educational attainment achieved and the time spent unemployed after leaving school (Hannan et al., 1998: 60).

Individuals with higher levels of exam performance are more likely to secure access to paid employment (Breen 1991: 37) while higher levels and longer spells of unemployment occur among those who fail their final exams (Breen 1991: 17). Educational attainment, while playing an important signalling role in securing access to paid employment, is also highly predictive of the type of job obtained (Hannan et al., 1998: 80).

Educational attainment is strongly linked to social class and education is highly predictive of labour market outcomes. Social background therefore continues to influence occupational status achieved. Educational choice can be regarded as the produce of the relative costs and benefits of continued participation. Where the cost of schooling varies by social class, the perceived benefits and probabilities of success may also vary across social classes. It follows that if social groups continue to differ in their financial and cultural resources, then differences in education participation and outcome are likely to persist (Smyth and Hannan, 2000: 111).

In addition to the relationship of educational attainment with social class, it is also linked to other aspects of family background. For pupils whose parents have higher levels of education and for those from smaller families, participation rates are likely to be higher. Educational level is also associated with parental employment and educational status, as is employment status (Hannan and O'Riain, 1993: 102). Pupils attending schools which draw from disadvantaged areas are more likely to drop out and under-perform, regardless of personal circumstances.

The policy environment

The Irish education system has bee   ed as highly centralised and standardised. Preparation for schoc   in terms of curriculum and examination, and access to third leve   n are dependent on the grades achieved in the school leaving exa   . Educational outcomes are, however, highly differentiated, depei   he stage at which young people exit the schooling system, the level o   ions they take and their grades (Smyth and Hannan, 2000: 110). W   e are differences in the level of resources available, both financial   ural, between social groups, differences in the degree of educatic   ipation and attainment persist (Smyth and Hannan, 2000: 113). In ireiana, where access to resources and social background are linked to educational outcomes, education is treated as a commodity, rather than a right. The right to be educated is explicitly referred to in the text of the Constitution (Bunreacht Na hÉireann, 42,1: 162) and the 1998 Education Act (Department of Education and Science, 1998a, Part 1, Section 6: 10), but in reality for many individuals it is not realised. In spite of significant progress made in recent years, a considerable number of students each year leave school without any formal qualification (Clancy, 2005: 99). Although there has been some reduction over time in the difference between those from higher professional and unskilled manual backgrounds in the rate of school completion (McCoy and Smyth, 2003: 67), participation rates in third-level education are significantly lower for individuals from lower income backgrounds (HEA, 2005: 62; O'Connell et al., 2006: 65).

In the mid-1960s, free second-level education was introduced in an attempt to counter inequalities in education. In the 1970s and 1980s the focus was on increasing participation in schooling rather than eliminating educational inequalities. More recent initiatives have been focused on tackling under-performance in schooling and examinations rather than addressing broader educational inequalities (Smyth and Hannan, 2000: 112). However, these

The policy response

The education system in Ireland operates within a context of broader socio-economic inequalities and it is understood, as acknowledged by the 1998 Education Act, that inequities result in the under-representation of individuals from disadvantaged backgrounds in the third-level system. It is also well established that patterns of inequality, which are manifested at third level, are the result of a variety of factors stemming from a variety of sources – socio-economic, structural and family life (Kellaghan 2002: 17). That addressing social exclusion, or promoting social inclusion, is central to social policy in Ireland is evident from the degree to which it is addressed in a variety of government strategies and reports. A succession of accords between the social partners from the 1990s, notably the National Anti-Poverty Strategy (NAPS) 1997 and the revised NAPS in 2002, as well as the National Action Plan against Poverty and Social Exclusion 2003–5 prepared for the European Union, emphasise the promotion of social inclusion generally including educational disadvantage specifically (Government of Ireland, 1997b: 9; 2002c: 11, 28). It is generally acknowledged throughout that disadvantage is multi-dimensional and thus requires a holistic and integrated approach. Employability is seen as the route out of disadvantage while both remedial and preventative measures are required to address the problems that arise in situations of disadvantage. To this end, activities are required at all levels of the education system, and require both systemic change as well as services and resources targeted at those most in need (Kellaghan, 2002: 21).

Despite the fact that the concepts of equity, equality of opportunity and social inclusion are, according to Kellaghan, not fully operationalised in Ireland, they have nevertheless become a major aspect of social policy in Ireland. Kellaghan identifies seven principles which he believes underpin the activities in the National Development Plan that relate to education and include adopting a multi-dimensional approach, promoting employability, integrating and co-ordinating services and adopting preventative measures (Kellaghan, 2002: 19). In addition to centralised structures, such as the establishment of the Cabinet Committee on Social Inclusion (chaired by An Taoiseach) and the Social Inclusion Unit in the Department of Education and Science, a number of partnerships have emerged at local level to help communities develop and to provide support for individuals at risk of educational failure. Recently, there has been an attempt to focus on a complementary approach to addressing educational disadvantage, which focuses on the system as a whole. The approach acknowledges the view that structural problems in the system may be playing a role in either the creation or maintenance of disadvantage (Kellaghan 2002: 20). The 1998 Education Act established the Educational Disadvantage Committee to advise the Minister for Education

and Science on policies and strategies to identify and correct educational disadvantage. The National Education Welfare Board, also established in the 1998
Act, has a remit in relation to disadvantage through a network of school and
family mediators, charged with following up incidences of school absenteeism.

While initiatives aimed at reducing educational disadvantage exist at all
levels in the education cycle, this section will concentrate on the pre-school
and primary schemes, considering the evidence supporting the view that early
intervention schemes are more likely to eliminate educational disadvantages
(McCoy and Smyth, 2003: 75). The main schemes targeted at and intended
to tackle educational disadvantage in pre-school and primary are the Home
School Community Liaison, Early Start, the Support Teacher Project and
Breaking the Cycle.

Home/School/Community Liaison (HSCL) scheme

The HSCL was introduced in 1990 as an attempt to strengthen and structure
parent involvement as a means to counteract disadvantage in the education of
young people. It was initiated as a pilot project in 1990 and was mainstreamed
in 1993. All schools designated as disadvantaged are, since 1999, entitled to
make use of the services of a HSCL co-ordinator.

The stated aims of the HSCL include the maximisation of active participation of children, the promotion of active co-operation between home,
school and the relevant community agencies, and raising awareness in parents
of their own capacities to enhance their children's educational progress and
retention in the education system. An evaluation of the HSCL carried out by
the Educational Research Centre (ERC) found the programme to have
expanded significantly since its inception in 1990 but notes that resources at
national level to support and provide leadership to the scheme have not kept
pace with the expansion (ERC, 2003b: 111). They reported evidence of progress
on several fronts including pupil achievement and clear signs of improved co-
operation between parents and teachers. On the negative side, the evaluation
found that literacy was not receiving the attention it warranted and any
further literacy schemes introduced should be facilitated by HSCL. In addition,
the evaluation found that HSCL did not adequately address the need to raise
the expectations of parents and teachers of what disadvantaged children can
achieve educationally (ERC, 2003b: 109). The evaluation findings were,
however, limited, as they were based on the perceptions of those participating
in HSCL and in fact, recommend that deeper evaluation of the impact of
HSCL scheme on pupils, families, schools and communities, especially on
pupil achievement, would be necessary and worthwhile. This would involve
the establishment of more specific performance indicators being linked to the
objectives of the scheme.

Breaking the Cycle

The Breaking the Cycle scheme (BTC) was introduced in 1996 both to urban and rural schools with the specific aim of reducing the class size at junior level, to provide resources for the purchase of books and teaching materials and to provide in-career development for teachers.

The evaluation, again carried out by the Educational Research Centre, found that while schools were experiencing difficulties with staff turnover and shortages, they were, however, better resourced in terms of materials and equipment than before the scheme (ERC, 2003a: vii). All schools participating in the BTC scheme were also in HSCL so greater connectedness with parents and community had developed. This could, however, be more a result of participation in HSCL than in the BTC scheme. The evaluation found that parental expectations for their children in terms of educational achievement were still low although teaching practice and staff morale had been positively affected. While reductions in teacher–pupil ratios had been achieved, the positive effect of the smaller class size was negated when pupils moved on to next phase of schooling.

Of critical importance in evaluating the scheme was its effect on pupils' absenteeism, behaviour and discipline, and changes in attitudes towards school and schoolwork and achievement. Pupil attendance rates (86 per cent in schools participating in Breaking the Cycle compared with 91 per cent attendance in other Dublin City schools) did not improve as a result of participation in the programme, although a general decline in problems of discipline was noted. There was no discernible improvement in average achievement, which is significantly lower than national rates anyway. In fact, there was a statistically significant decrease in literacy and numeric achievements between 1997 and 2000, although there was evidence of improvements in attitudes to school work with more pupils stating they were proud of their schoolwork (ERC 2003a: x). These successes could not, however, be entirely attributable to the BTC scheme as other interventions exist, such as the more child centred curriculum, the establishment of the Education Welfare Board and the National Psychological Service as well as several local, national and community pilot projects aimed at educational disadvantage.

Early Start

The Early Start scheme, a pre-school initiative launched in 1994, aims to provide children in a pre-school setting with an environment that facilitates the development of knowledge, skills and attitudes appropriate to later school success and to increase the involvement of parents in their children's education. Some level of success was evident in the findings of the ERC evaluation. The intelligence of participating children improved over the two years of participation in the scheme and there was some change in parents' school-related behaviour (ERC 2002: 43). The Early Start Programme, however, caters for a small minority of pupils in the educational system, around five per cent of three and four year olds. Public funding available for pre-school provision in Ireland remains very low by European standards and early childhood education provision is highly fragmented falling under the jurisdiction of several departments and agencies (McCoy and Smyth, 2003: 75).

Education and rights

Given the persistence of inequalities in education outlined above, a case may be made for adopting a rights-based approach to education. A right to education is recognised at an international level by the 1948 United Nations (UN) Declaration of Human Rights and the 1976 UN International Covenant on Economic and Social Rights. At a European level, a right to education is contained within article 14 of the Charter of Fundamental Rights of the European Union (EU) (Council of the EU, 2000: 31) and article 17 of the Council of Europe's revised European Social Charter (Council of Europe, 1996: 85). The text of the new EU Treaty Establishing a Constitution for Europe contains a right to education in Article II–74 (Council of the EU, 2004: 44), already established in the EU Charter of Fundamental Rights (above). In Ireland, a right to a primary education is established in the text of the 1937 Constitution (Bunreacht Na hÉireann, 42,1: 162). The right to education could be described as both a right in itself and an indispensable means of realising other rights. It is an empowerment right, the primary vehicle by which economically and socially marginalized adults and children can lift themselves out of poverty and disadvantage and obtain the means to participate fully in their communities (UN Economic and Social Council, 1999: 1). In this regard, the right to education can be considered both to have constitutive and instrumental relevance. It is constitutive because a person's lack of command over material resources can inhibit realisation of the right. At the same time it is instrumental because realisation of the right to education facilitates the realisation of other rights, for example the right to vote or the right to work. So, for example, the right to food informs the instrumental nature of the right to education as under-nutrition inhibits brain cell development, preventing hungry children from concentrating at school (UN OHCHR, 2002). The right to securing adequate food is instrumental to the right to education, health and work and must be secured through adequate distribution.

At the international level the right to education, is protected by two international treaties. The UN International Covenant on Economic and Social Rights (ICESR) devotes two articles to education. Article 13, the longest provision in the Covenant, is the most wide-ranging and comprehensive article on the right to education in international human rights law. In the European Social Charter (ESC) the right to education is contained and protected within Article 17.

In Ireland, article 42.4 of the Constitution obliges the state to provide for free primary education, from which the courts have inferred a constitutional right on the part of children to a primary education (Whyte, 2002: 45).

The Education Act, 1998; White Paper on Education, 1995

The Education Act, 1998 and the White Paper on Education, 1995 present broad and comprehensive principles providing the basis for the provision of education in Ireland. A right to education can be inferred from the text of both documents.

The educational principles outlined in the White Paper on Education, 1995 are based on the premise that 'rights are derived from the fundamental aim of education to serve individual, social and economic well-being and to enhance quality of life' (Department of Education and Science, 1995: 7). The principles identified reflect the principles of a rights-based approach to poverty reduction strategies: pluralism, equality, partnership, accountability and quality. In the document, the state views its responsibilities to the provision of education as:

> The State's role in education arises as part of its overall concern to achieve economic prosperity, social well-being and a good quality of life within a democratically structured society. This concern affirms fundamental human values and confers on the State a responsibility to protect the rights of individuals and to safeguard the common good. Education is a right for each individual and a means to enhancing well-being and quality of life for the whole of society' (Department of Education and Science, 1995: 6).

Thus the state takes the view that not only do individuals have a right to education, but that education is the route to realising other rights, such as the right to work and to participate in society. Additionally, the Department of Education and Science's Statement of Strategy, outlines the mission of the Department 'to provide for high-quality education, which will enable individuals to achieve their full potential and to participate fully as members of society, and contribute to Ireland's social, cultural and economic development' (Department of Education and Science, 2002: 7).

As outlined above, the UN views education as both a constitutive and instrumental right. It is constitutive as a lack of resources can prevent an individual from realising the right and instrumental as a lack of education could prohibit other rights from being realised, such as the right to work. Evidence such as that outlined in previous sections, has established the link between educational attainment, employment status and earnings potential in adult life. In their General Comment on Education, the UN outline what they believe are the essential and interrelated characteristics of a right to education (UN Economic and Social Council, 1999). Where the state explicitly acknowledges a right to education, in this case established in the constitution and various judgements as well as the 1995 White Paper and the 1998 Education Act, then the principles become relevant. They include, among other things, that the state provide free education at all levels for all who have the capacity to participate regardless of access to financial resources, that there be sufficient supply of educational institutions equally accessible to all without discrimination, and that a grant system should enhance equality of educational access for individuals from disadvantaged groups.

Conclusion

This chapter has explored the link between the level of education achieved and the potential for employment and earnings in adult years. It argued that resources at the primary school level are not sufficient to meet the schooling needs of young persons, especially those who come from disadvantaged backgrounds. Apart from resources, other factors such as schooling and family environment are also significant in determining the likelihood of school completion and levels of achievement in the school-leaving examinations. Where access to third-level education is based on academic achievement at the school-leaving cycle, it is clear that for pupils for whom there are difficulties in participating in and completing the secondary school cycle, access to third level is more difficult.

Changes in the nature of work in the knowledge economy necessitate a higher degree of skill or educational attainment to secure access to the labour market. There is an over-reliance on the part of employers on the results achieved in the schooling system as a method of selection. Several initiatives have been implemented at the early or pre-school stage and it is encouraging that these schemes have been the subject of ongoing evaluations. However, as the evaluations themselves highlight, there may be a need for a broadening of the schemes and resources provided through the provision of more funding while maintaining a child-centred focus in determining the successes of the schemes.

Educational disadvantage is a multi-faceted phenomenon, which has, as we have seen, the potential to create, maintain or perpetuate existing levels of disadvantage and exclusion. Unless individuals are afforded equality of opportunity, participation and outcome in the education system, there will be consequences for their ability to participate fully in the institutions and processes, which constitute contemporary social and economic life. Given the extent to which educational disadvantage is linked to poverty, social mobility, patterns of employment and potential earnings over the life-course, it is important that individuals leave the school system with a formal education so as to prevent cycles of unemployment and low income in their adult years.

Recommended reading

Clancy, P. (2005) 'Education policy', pp. 80–114 in Quin, S. et al. (eds), *Contemporary Irish Social Policy*, 2nd edn. Dublin: UCD Press.

HEA (2005) *A Review of Higher Education Participation in 2003*. Dublin: ESRI.

McCoy, S. and Smyth, E. (2003) 'Educational expenditure: implications for equality', in ESRI, *Budget Perspectives 2004*. Dublin: ESRI.

Smyth, E. and Hannan, D. F. (2000), 'Education and inequality', pp. 109–26 in Nolan, B. et al. (eds), *Bust to Boom? The Irish Experience of Growth and Inequality*. Dublin: IPA.

Chapter 5

Immigration, racism and social exclusion

Bryan Fanning

Introduction

This chapter examines racism as a potential contributing factor to poverty and social exclusion in Irish society. It draws on the findings of international research which suggest that poverty and social exclusion are likely to be experienced differently by different minority ethnic groups and to be experienced differently within such groups on the basis of factors such as social class, gender or citizenship status. This chapter emphasises how racism in society and institutional racism can exacerbate other forms of deprivation and serve to deepen experiences of social exclusion. It considers the identification of 'migrants and ethnic minorities' as a specific target group within the Revised (2002) National Anti-Poverty Strategy (Government of Ireland, 2002c: 17). It is argued that goals set out in the strategy of ensuring that 'migrants and ethnic minorities' do not face disproportionate risks of poverty and social exclusion have often been ignored within social policy responses to immigrants. Emphasis is placed on how the experiences by immigrants of lesser rights and entitlements can be a potential contributing factor to poverty and deprivation. The experiences of other countries and mounting evidence in Ireland suggest that factors such as racism and lesser rights and entitlements negatively affect the life chances of immigrants. This can be seen with respect to income poverty resulting from restrictions on employment and racism in employment. However the removal in 2004 of many benefit entitlements for some new immigrants, including children's allowances, for an initial two-year period of residency can also be seen to contribute to risks of poverty and social exclusion.

Racism and ethnicity

It is generally accepted that racism in western societies has detrimental consequences for the lives of people from a range of minority ethnic groups. Yet racism is an imprecise term which is loosely used to describe a collection of interrelated prejudices, beliefs and ideologies, which assume the biological or cultural inferiority of distinct groups. Racism can be expressed through the acts of individuals or in the values presumptions, structures and processes of social, economic, cultural and political institutions. For example, Article 2 of the UNESCO Declaration on Race and Racial Prejudice emphasises the role of structural and institutional barriers in producing racist barriers in society:

> Racism includes racist ideologies, prejudiced attitudes, discriminatory behaviour, structural arrangements and institutional practices resulting in racial inequality as well as the fallacious notion that discriminatory relations between groups are morally and scientifically justifiable; it is reflected in discriminatory provisions in legislation or regulations and discriminatory practices as well as in anti-social beliefs and acts (UNESCO, 1978).

The above definition emphasises how institutional barriers contribute to racist discrimination. Macpherson defined institutional racism in the following terms:

> The collective failure of an organisation to provide an appropriate and professional service to people because of their colour, culture or ethnic origin. It can be seen in processes, attitudes and behaviour which amount to discrimination through unwitting prejudice, ignorance thoughtlessness and racist stereotyping which disadvantage ethnic minority people (Macpherson, 1999: 22).

The consequences of institutional racism include unequal access to services and unequal outcomes on the basis of ethnicity. An ethnic group is generally defined as a socially distinct community of people who share a common history and culture and often share a distinct language and religion. Cornell and Hartmann define ethnicity in terms of shared and subjective feelings of belonging emanating from kinship patterns, geographical concentration, religious affiliation, language, and physical differences (1998: 17–19). *The Parekh Report on The Future of Multi-Ethnic Britain* (Parekh, 2000) defined racism broadly to include the experiences of Jews, Muslims and Irish as well as black people. For instance, it argued that anti-Irish racism has many of the same features as most racisms. The report criticised race equality organisations, academics and other specialists for promoting a narrow definition of racism which tacitly denied the existence of anti-Irish racism within a false belief that the Irish were indistinguishably part of the British white majority (Parekh, 2000: 61). It argued that denial of anti-Irish racism was part of the institutional structure of anti-Irish racism. The experiences of the Irish in Britain illustrate the limits of the black–white dualistic model of racist discrimination (Mac an Ghaill, 1999: 81). Similarly racism in Ireland can be seen to affect a range of groups who are not black such as Travellers, Eastern European asylum seekers, migrant workers or Muslims.

Racism, poverty and social exclusion

Racism can be understood as one potential causal factor – amongst others – of poverty and social exclusion. In practice, when we talk about racist discrimination there are a whole range of complex social, economic and political processes at work. Direct and indirect discrimination are only part of the story. It is important to recognise the role of class, gender and spatial processes in shaping the way in which racialised inequalities are formed and reproduced over time (Solomos and Back, 1996: 66) Racism and discrimination in the provision of welfare goods and services have also contributed to disproportionate numbers of people from minority communities living in poverty. In the past it has taken two distinct forms. The first consists of overt or institutional forms of discrimination experienced by citizens of black and ethnic minorities. One example here would the experiences of Irish Travellers in the areas of health, education and accommodation (Fanning, 2002: 152–68). The second consists of forms of inequality and discrimination experienced by minority populations excluded from citizenship. Non-citizens living in a number of western societies, including Ireland, are disproportionately from minority ethnic groups. Stratifications within Irish welfare and social rights linked to national and EU citizenship tend to exclude people disproportionately on the basis of colour and ethnicity.

All European countries have minority ethnic minority populations that face disproportionate levels of social exclusion and marginalisation. Research has shown that migrant and minority populations in the European Union are disproportionately represented in forms of poor and insecure work and are disproportionately unemployed. Furthermore, these problems have continued with second and third generations of migrant-descended communities who have been born, raised and educated in European member states (Wrench, 1997). Solomos and Back (1999) argue that a large body of research in a wide range of societies has illustrated how racism in society interacts with other social and political processes to produce distinct forms of 'racialised' inequality. They identify a link between societal racism and deeply entrenched inequalities in areas such as welfare provision, employment and housing.

For example during the 1950s Britain recruited workers on a large scale from Commonwealth countries. These were 'skilled, semi-skilled or had the potential to become skilled workers'. However, they experienced discrimination in employment, education and training, and as recently as 1995 the unemployment level of ethnic minority groups was 19 per cent compared to eight per cent for the white majority communities (Solomos and Back, 1996: 65). A UK Cabinet Office report in 2000 noted that minority ethnic groups are more likely to be poor and to be unemployed, regardless of their age, sex, qualifications and place of residence (Cabinet Office, 2000: 7). The report described the experiences of social exclusion of different ethnic minorities as 'mixed, but grim' (2000: 35). An examination of ethnicity, racism and disadvantage in Britain from 1966, when the first major survey was undertaken, to 1994 when the fourth such survey was undertaken reveals disparate experiences of poverty and disadvantage. A picture emerges of shifts in the fortunes of some communities over time and the ongoing marginalisation of others (Mohdood et al., 1997). The British experience suggests that it is unhelpful to generalise about the impact of racism or discrimination on minority ethnic groups. Different communities may experience different barriers. Each is likely to have some distinct needs. Yet research has shown that migrant and minority populations in the European Union are disproportionately represented in forms of poor and insecure work and are disproportionately unemployed. Furthermore these problems have continued with second and third generations of migrant descended communities who have been born, raised and educated in European member states (Wrench, 1997).

Studies of racism and discrimination in Ireland

Notwithstanding the absence of comprehensive data on ethnicity and disadvantage, some recent Irish surveys and qualitative studies have indicated that some ethnic minorities experience distinct forms of discrimination and social exclusion. A number of these have indicated that the experiences of some minority groups in Ireland of discrimination and exclusion mirror, to a degree, those of marginalised minority groups in other western societies. Research undertaken to date in Ireland has found indications of discrimination or exclusion in employment, housing and education. Other studies have examined child poverty, institutional barriers to public services and access to maternity health services (table 5.1).

Collectively these studies suggest that that racism and discrimination may be causes of labour market disadvantage, joblessness, poor health, housing deprivation and social exclusion.

Integration, social inclusion and social citizenship

The National Anti-Poverty Strategy since its inception in 1997 has emphasised the concept of social exclusion. Social exclusion is in effectseen as a consequence of the relative material deprivation that can result from income

Table 5.1 **Some studies of racism and discrimination**

Author and title	Findings
Barry, J., Herity B. and Solan, S. (1989) *The Travellers Health Status Study.* Dublin: HRB.	Travellers experience extreme health inequalities. e.g.; the infant mortality rate for Travellers in 1987 was 18.1 per thousand live births compared with the national figure of 7.4 per thousand.
Begley, G. et al. (1999) *Asylum in Ireland: A Public Health Perspective.* Dublin: UCD.	Enforced unemployment owing to the lack of a right to work seriously affected the psychological, social and general well-being of asylum seekers. Almost all (95 per cent) of respondents identified racial discrimination as a problem.
Clann Housing Association (1999) *From Bosnia to Ireland's Private Rented Sector: A Study of Bosnian Housing Need in Ireland.* Dublin: Clann Housing Association.	Overt dependence on private rented sector, owing to a lack of access to social housing, contributed to welfare dependency. Unemployment amongst Bosnian Programme Refugees registered as available for work was found to be in excess of 40 percent; ten times the national rate of unemployment.
Comhlámh (2001) *Refugee Lives.* Dublin: Comhlámh.	Respondents experienced barriers to integration owing to the segregated nature of accommodation and lack of money. Some respondents experienced severe accommodation deprivation from over-crowding. Racism identified by respondents as a major problem.
Faughnan, P. and Woods, M. (2000) *Lives on Hold: Seeking Asylum in Ireland.* Dublin: Social Science Research Centre, UCD.	Respondents reported racism and discrimination in the private rented sector and in the 'pub and club scene'. Lack of an entitlement to work found to be a source of considerable frustration.
Faughnan, P. and O'Connor, A. (2002) *A Changing Voluntary Sector: Working with New Minority Communities in 2001.* Dublin: Social Science Research Centre, UCD.	Lack of responsiveness by most relevant voluntary sector services to new minority communities.
Fanning, B., Loyal, S. and Staunton, C. (2000) *Asylum Seekers and the Right to Work in Ireland.* Dublin: Irish Refugee Council	Discrimination in employment exacerbated by lesser entitlements to state- funded employment training and support.

Author and title	Findings
Fanning, B., Veale, A. and O'Connor, D. (2001) *Beyond the Pale: Asylum Seeker Children and Social Exclusion.* Dublin: Irish Refugee Council	Extreme child poverty amongst asylum seekers on direct provision resulting from lesser welfare entitlements and accommodation deprivation. Distinct forms of social exclusion amongst asylum seekers resulting from racism and family separations.
IBEC Survey Unit (2000) *Employment of Non-EU Nationals/Refugees in Ireland* (Dublin: Interact Ireland)	Racism identified as the main barrier to employment amongst respondents.
Kennedy, P. and Murphy-Lawless, J. (2002) *The Maternity Needs of Refugee and Asylum-seeking Women.* Dublin: Applied Social Science Research Programme, UCD	The study found that the inadequately nutritious diet available for women in direct provision caused difficulties in breastfeeding. Women in hostels tended to give up breastfeeding within a few weeks of the birth of their babies.
McCarthy, P. (1999) *African Refugees: Needs Analysis.* Dublin: African Refugee Network	75 per cent of respondents had been refused a service on the basis of their skin colour. 72.5 per cent of respondents reported racism from landlords.
McVeigh, R. (1998) *Travellers, Refugees and Racism in Tallaght.* Dublin: European Year Against Racism	Travellers and asylum seekers found to experience racism and to encounter institutional barriers to education, health, accommodation and social services.
Manandhar, S., Friel S., Share, M., Hardy, F. and Walsh, O. (2004) *Food, Nutrition and Poverty Amongst Asylum Seekers in North West Ireland.* Dublin: Combat Poverty Agency	Research in Counties Sligo, Leitrim and Donegal during 2003–4 identified food poverty amongst asylum seekers owing to (low) levels of 'Direct Provision' benefits and inability to address cultural issues affecting diet: 'The role of ethnic differences in people's food habits and practices which affect their nutrient intake, nutritional status and ultimately health and well being, should not be underestimated.'
O'Regan, C. (1998) *Report of a Survey of the Vietnamese and Bosnian Communities in Ireland.* Dublin: Refugee Agency	Indications of high levels of unemployment and underemployment in Vietnamese community.
Smith, S. and Mutwarasibo, F. (2000) *Africans in Ireland: Developing Communities.* Dublin: African Cultural Project	Barriers to participation in Irish society experienced by Africans included racism, cultural and communication style differences and perceived formality of dominant community.

poverty and unemployment. The thesis at the heart of Irish anti-poverty policy is that people may be excluded from activities that are considered the norm for other people in society because of inadequate income and resources Many of the problems faced by socially excluded individuals, families and communities relate to social reproduction. For instance, marginalised communities face greater risks of being failed by the education system than those with above average means and supports.

Debates about social inclusion have increasingly converged with those about integration. This latter concept is usually defined as a form of multiculturalism, which suggests that minority groups should be able to participate fully in society without having to surrender cultural distinctiveness. It also implies the need to remove institutional barriers as forms of structural inequalities that inhibit such full participation. The debate associated with multiculturalism has generally focused on the need for further measures, *in addition to* full citizenship rights (Joppke, 1999: 629). In this context, a number of European-wide studies of social exclusion and social diversity view rights as perquisite for social inclusion. As explained in one such study:

> We understand the problems of social exclusion and the possibilities for social inclusion in terms of the problems and possibilities of access to social rights. For our purposes the key social rights and packages of social goods are those relating to work, income and recognition. We refer to these rights and social goods as 'personal social capital'. . . and as 'forms' of inclusion (Roche, 2000:17).

A family resemblance is to be found between the goals implicit in the concepts of integration, social inclusion and full social citizenship. Each is at odds with the stratification of rights and entitlements and stands in opposition to reproduction of social inequalities by public policies.

Research undertaken by the European Commission on patterns of social exclusion across a number of European countries noted the emergence of a dominant paradigm of social exclusion. This was seen to define social exclusion in terms of poverty, related phenomena such as unemployment, the spatial concentration of multiple disadvantages and discrimination. This perspective is seen to focus upon processes of exclusion and processes of inclusion not just in respect of access to resources necessary to participate in society or the ability to achieve security, but also to the attainment of societal norms (Cremer-Schäfer et al., 2001: 12). It is seen potentially to depict excluded communities as dysfunctional communities. A long history of the stigmatisation of socially excluded communities can be noted within Western social science and social policy. One example of this is the notion of the underclass used in Victorian society to refer to the poor as 'people of the abyss' removed from the standards and norms of proper society. Another is the contemporary use of the concept of an underclass as a code by the American right to depict black urban communities as deviant, dangerous and dysfunctional (Stienberg, 2000: 567). In the Irish case, depictions of Travellers as deviant have been politically mobilised within local politics to legitimise discrimination (Fanning, 2002: 135–7). The experiences of Travellers of racism and discrimination illustrate the potential of racism in Irish society to impinge on the well-being and life chances of other minority ethnic groups. They illustrate some of the ways in which institutional racism can contribute to poverty and social exclusion. Successive reports, including *The Report of Task Force on the Travelling People* (Task Force, 1995) and the *First Report of the Monitoring Committee on the Implementation of the Recommendations of the Task Force on the Travelling People* (Department of Justice, 2000) paint a picture of persistent ongoing social exclusion. The 1995 report made more than 400 recommendations aimed at addressing discrimination in areas such as accommodation, health and education. The 2000 report on the implementation of these recommendations noted a 'lack of real improvement on the ground'. Notwithstanding some successful initiatives – notably in the area of public health (Quirke, 2002: 6–11) – Travellers continue to encounter institutional barriers within Irish social policy (Crowley: 2005: 233).

Migrants, ethnic minorities and social policy

The terms social exclusion and social inclusion are employed in different ways. They can be applied analytically to conditions experienced by groups within society, but they are also used more generally to refer to both political and policy goals. A broad agreement is evident within the Irish and EU context that the terms encompass concerns about 'poverty, deprivation, low educational qualifications, labour market disadvantage, joblessness, poor health, poor housing or homelessness, illiteracy and innumeracy, precariousness and incapacity to participate in society' (Atkinson et al., 2002: 3). The Partnership 2000 Agreement (Government of Ireland, 1996b) defined social exclusion in terms of 'cumulative marginalisation: from production (employment), from consumption (income poverty), from social networks (community, family and neighbours), from decision making and from an adequate quality of life'. This definition emphasised access to employment. At the same time it acknowledged that people in low-paid employment or their dependants could also experience poverty. Income and consumption were seen as linked to social processes. People who experienced material deprivation in comparison with community norms were understood to be liable to exclusion from participation in societal activities. At the same time this definition recognised that exclusion from community, family and neighbourhood networks was not merely a consequence of income poverty. The definition of social exclusion in the Partnership 2000 Agreement allows for other factors, such as racism, to be taken into account. (Government of Ireland, 1996b). Such an understanding was also to be found in the National Anti-Poverty Strategy (Government of Ireland, 1997b) which discussed the problem of social exclusion in the following terms:

> No society can view without deep concern the prospect of a significant minority of people becoming more removed from the incomes and lifestyles of the majority. It is the tackling of the structural factors that underpin this exclusion which requires the strategic approach set out in this documen (Government of Ireland, 1997b: 4)

The strategy included the following definition of poverty:

> People are living in poverty, if their income and resources (material, cultural and social) are so inadequate as to preclude them from having a standard of living which is regarded as acceptable by Irish society generally. As a result of inadequate income and resources people may be excluded and marginalised from participating in activities which are considered the norm from other people in society (Atkinson et al., 2002: 3).

It set a global target for poverty reduction over the period 1997–2007 aimed at considerably reducing the numbers of those who were 'consistently poor'. In recognition of the multidimensional nature of poverty, particular attention was given in the strategy to a number of key areas, namely: educational disadvantage, unemployment, income adequacy, disadvantaged urban areas, and rural poverty. As well as setting a global target, the National Anti-Poverty Strategy set targets in each of the key areas identified. In addition, it placed a focus on specific groups suffering from multiple disadvantage and at risk of social exclusion – Travellers were identified as one such group.

Amongst the principles which underpinned the strategy was one of 'guaranteeing the rights of minorities, especially through anti-discrimination measures' (Goodbody, 2001: 4). This commitment, in principle, to responsiveness to the needs of minority communities within the context of an express focus on the relationship between poverty and discrimination, was not always evident in the 1997 strategy. The need for such a focus was amplified within the framework document for the Review of the National Anti-Poverty Strategy published in November 2001:

> There are limited data on the economic and social well-being of ethnic minorities in Ireland. Nevertheless, experience in other countries shows that ethnic minorities

experience racism, tend to suffer discrimination, disadvantage, marginalisation and poverty. In particular, racism may limit people's access to resources and services. Migrant workers and refugees, particularly the unskilled are also vulnerable. If Ireland is to be a successful modern intercultural society, it must integrate foreign-born residents in ways that respect their social, economic and cultural rights (Goodbody, 2001: 4).

A commitment was made under the Programme for Prosperity and Fairness (PPF), which succeeded the Partnership 2000 Agreement, to review the existing targets under the original National Anti-Poverty Strategy framework and introduce possible new targets. A report by the National Economic and Social Forum (NESF) arising from this commitment outlined a number of steps were required to enhance the 1997 strategy (Government of Ireland, 2000a: 79). One of these was to address the links between racism and poverty within the strategy through the inclusion of a new target area (NESF: 2000b: 32). The consultation process undertaken during the review of the National Anti-Poverty Strategy undertaken in 2001 similarly identified the importance of a focus on migrants and ethnic minorities (Goodbody, 2001: 4). The result of this consultation, in keeping with the commitments under the Programme for Prosperity and Fairness was the inclusion of 'migrants and members of ethnic minority groups' as a distinct target group with the Revised National Anti-Poverty Strategy (Government of Ireland, 2002c) and the establishment of a goal of ensuring that 'that members of ethnic minority groups resident in Ireland are not more likely to experience poverty than majority group members' (Government of Ireland, 2002c: 17). However, the revised strategy did not set targets to address these goals. The stated reason for the omission of targets was that; 'very little quantitative information is available about the socio-economic situation of foreign-born residents in Ireland' and 'it was not possible, therefore, to define specific targets for this group as a whole or for a particular ethnic group at this state' Government of Ireland, 2002c: 18) The absence of systematic data on ethnic minorities has been identified as a barrier to the development and implementation of social inclusion policies to meet their needs (Fanning and Pierce, 2004: 11–17).

Exclusion from social inclusion

The identification of 'in principle' goals of ensuring that that 'migrants and ethnic minorities' do not encounter disproportionate risks of poverty and social exclusion have had limited impact on specific social policy responses to immigrants so categorised. Since 2000 immigrants – including asylum seekers but also immigrant workers and their families – have become increasingly

marginal within anti-poverty policy as a result of lesser entitlements. A number
of distinct factors that contribute to the exclusion of immigrants from social
policies aimed at combating poverty and social exclusion can be identified.

Within the community development and voluntary sectors, a picture
emerges of efforts being made to rapidly come to terms with new forms of
societal diversity. At the same time, organisations were self-critical of their
current inabilities to meet the needs of migrants to the same extent as indigenous client groups. For example, the Dublin Inner City Partnership (DICP,
2001: 9) has observed that those working within the networks on multicultural
issues are mostly white and Irish. A study by Faughnan and O'Donovan
carried out in 2001 examined the responsiveness of voluntary sector to new
minority communities with a particular focus on responses to asylum seekers.
Just one third of the 174 organisations that participated in the study
considered that their work with new minority communities was effective.
These organisations included local development associations, information
providers, partnership companies, service, resource provision, development
education, training, advocacy, campaigning organisations and umbrella or
co-ordinating bodies. Partnership companies were found to be least likely
(less than one fifth) to regard themselves as effective in responding to the new
communities (Faughnan and O'Donovan, 2002: 6–7). Some organisations
considered that government policies towards asylum seekers have hampered
their ability to work in this area. Faughnan and O'Donovan (2001: 25) cited
some examples of such responses:

> The fact that we are restricted in how we utilise members of the refugee
> community – we cannot work with and pay asylum seekers who do not have the
> right to work.

> The fact that state agencies have informed us that as their applications are not
> processed, we should not be dealing with asylum seekers.

In 2000 a system of lesser benefit entitlements for asylum seekers, known
as 'direct provision', was introduced as political response to a perceived
asylum crisis. This removed existing entitlements to social assistance and rent
allowances administered since 2005 by the HSE. Direct provision weekly
rates of payment at just €19.05 per adult and €9.53 per child were far less than
those for other categories of welfare recipient in equivalent circumstances,
such as benefit recipients accommodated in hostels. Unlike other state benefits
these were not increased on an annual basis and remained unchanged in 2005.
A 2001 study undertaken on behalf of the Irish Refugee Council identified
extreme child poverty and social exclusion amongst asylum seekers on direct
provision as resulting from lesser welfare entitlements and accommodation

deprivation (Fanning et al., 2001). Another study undertaken the same year found that the inadequately nutritious diet available for women in direct provision caused difficulties in breastfeeding. Women in hostels tended to give up breastfeeding within a few weeks of the birth of their babies (Kennedy and Murphy-Lawless, 2002). Both studies identified instances of malnutrition. Research undertaken in Counties Sligo, Leitrim and Donegal during 2003–4 similarly identified food poverty amongst asylum seekers (Manandhar et al., 2004).

In May 2004, to coincide with the enlargement of the European Union, the Irish government decided to remove many benefit entitlements from new immigrants and their families for an initial two-year period. Under the Social Welfare (Miscellaneous Provisions) *Act* (2004) immigrants not habitually resident in Ireland for two years were deemed not entitled to Unemployment Assistance, Old Age (Non-Contributory) and Blind Pension, Widow(er)'s and Orphan's (Non-Contributory) pensions, One Parent Family Payment, Carer's Allowance, Disability Allowance, Supplementary Welfare Allowance (other than once-off exceptional and urgent needs payments) and Children's Allowances. The removal of welfare safety nets and the loss of entitlement to children's allowances place immigrants at disproportionate risk of poverty. During the 1990s children's allowances became a central element of the response to child poverty (Nolan, 2000: xix). Universal children's allowances were identified in the National Children's Strategy as 'an important means of reducing child poverty (Department of Health and Children, 2000a: 63). Subsequently, in February 2006 the government clarified that EU law (EU 1408 of 1971) imposed reciprocal obligations on EU states to recognise the entitlements of citizens from other EU countries resident in their own countries. This meant that the removal of entitlements set out under the 2004 Act could not apply to immigrants from EU countries. However, the two-year residency eligibility criteria introduced by the act continues to apply from immigrants from non-EU countries.

Conclusion

Racism in Ireland is expressed in a specific setting of distinct interrelationships between the dominant majority (itself an ethnic group), and an evolving continuum of immigrant ethnic minority communities. The degree to which racism is experienced by specific minority ethnic groups and the extent to which racism in Irish society impacts upon the life chances of members of those groups can be expected to vary from group to group. For example, the risks of poverty amongst Travellers who have experienced intergenerational social exclusion, discrimination and racism in Ireland, will be different from immigrant non-citizen members of minority ethnic groups. Minority ethnic communities predominantly comprised of non-EU citizens are likely to encounter barriers to participation and social inclusion not encountered by minority communities comprised predominantly of Irish citizens. These include, in the case of migrant workers, specific risks of discrimination and exploitation in employment. Furthermore, the impact of racism can be expected to vary within groups, for example on the basis of gender, social class, or educational attainment. Women's experiences of racism are constituted differently from those of men (Crickley, 2001: 93). The intersection of inequalities on the basis of gender and ethnicity or social class and ethnicity may also differ from one ethnic group to another. The risks of poverty are therefore likely to experienced differently by different ethnic groups. The relationship between racism and poverty is a complex one.

Recommended reading

Fanning, B. (2002) *Racism and Social Change in the Republic of Ireland.* Manchester: Manchester University Press.

Fanning B. (2006) *Immigration and Social Change in the Republic of Ireland.* Manchester: Manchester University Press.

Joppke, C. (1999) 'How immigration is changing citizenship: a comparative view', *Ethnic and Racial Studies* 22 (4): 629–52.

Chapter 6

Social research and immigration

Alice Feldman

Introduction

This chapter examines the development of a research agenda in relation to immigration and increasing ethnic diversity against the backdrop of a new and evolving area of social policy. It considers research methodologies and emerging best practice in Irish research that have been developed to respond to the problems associated with the 'politics of research' as they play out in this particular arena. Bulmer (1986: 3) observes that social science research has become part of the policy-making process in an unprecedented way. Policy research is no longer simply a matter of a social scientist or 'expert' administering a survey, particularly as the process of policy making includes a variety of information gathering techniques, such as consultations or focus groups, needs assessments, benchmarking, programme evaluation and monitoring. The arena in which policy research is carried out has become more complex, with an increasing variety of stakeholders who commission, conduct and participate in research. This dynamism reflects the potential of research to advance positive social change. It also highlights the 'politics of research' – that is, the ways in which the power relations among research producers, participants and consumers, and the institutions within which they operate, mediate the research process, its effects on those who are researched and the policy outcomes to which it contributes.

Those who are most often the focus or 'subjects' of social policy research are typically from communities experiencing the greatest levels of marginalisation and disadvantage. Because they seldom have opportunities to participate directly in the policy process or in the provision of services to their communities, they typically have little control over how their experiences and interests are represented. As such, researchers – and the policy their work informs – wield great power to define the nature of the 'problems' and 'target groups' (i.e., the designated beneficiaries of a policy or programme) to be addressed, and to specify the types of responses and resources to which they are entitled. The situation is made even more complicated by the conflicts of interest and competition that often characterise relations among the different producers and funders of research. Academics, civil servants, community organisations and consultants all have different backgrounds and training, and approach their research with different objectives, guiding principles and methodologies. Each of these groups has its own particular interests, obligations and available resources with respect to undertaking research. The lack of effective collaboration among these different constituencies, however, poses serious problems for the generation of accurate, representative information and effective policy.

Such dilemmas are particularly evident in the case of policy development with respect to immigration to Ireland, which has proven to be a highly contentious and politicised issue. The recent and rapid increase in immigration to Ireland has seen the emergence of target groups and the formation of communities wholly new to Irish society, along with new issues and new needs not previously incorporated in or addressed by the existing system. Because issues such as immigration, ethnic diversity and multiculturalism have not been historically central issues of concern with respect to Irish society, the government has had, for the most part, to 'start from scratch' in terms of responding to new and diverse needs and circumstances and integrating these responses across the entire system of policy and provision.

Immigration and social change

Ireland has rapidly become a multi-ethnic society, transforming within the past two decades from a country historically characterised as one of emigration to one of notable in-migration (see chapter 1). Between the years 1996 and 2004, almost 63,000 applications for asylum were made, the annual numbers of which peaked in 2004 at over 11,000, compared to only 31 in 1991 (Moran, 2005: 268). According to the 2002 Census, 'non-nationals' accounted for more than seven per cent of the population (Fanning and Pierce, 2004: 3). Persons from as many as 160 countries of origin currently live in the Republic of Ireland (Mutwarasibo, 2005: 3). It is estimated that in 2030 one in five persons living in the Republic of Ireland will be an immigrant. Diversity has become and will remain a defining feature of Irish society (Punch, 2005: 5).

These changes have posed challenges, given the absence of a well-established policy infrastructure or expertise in Ireland in relation to immigration, race equality and multiculturalism, and the government's slow – and often negative – response. Until recently, the government has focused on asylum issues rather than the broader spectrum of immigration (for example international students, foreign medical staff, EU/accession citizens), and the well-documented labour shortage that would require ongoing immigration to the country. Immigration has thus been treated as a temporary phenomenon, whereby asylum seekers would eventually leave either following the failure of the application or when it was deemed 'safe' to return home. This approach has led to a focus predominantly on the processing and reception of asylum seekers, and ad hoc and reactive development of policy and provision rather than more mainstreamed responses to increasing ethnic diversity or integration.

Divisive and discriminatory policies – such as those limiting the right to work or the repeal of the right of asylum seekers to apply automatically for leave to remain on the basis of their Irish-born children – have contributed to the marginalisation and disadvantage of immigrants and to the growth of racism (Comhlámh, 2001, Fanning, 2002: 87–109). There have been instances in which government representatives have either actively promoted or failed to intervene in the construction and dissemination of negative stereotypes and images of asylum seekers (often taken to stand for all immigrants) as 'spongers', 'bogus' and so on. Recently, however, there has been a shift to more substantial and long-term focus in policy development including: steps towards the development of an immigration and residency bill; the establishment of a centralised agency, the Irish Naturalisation and Immigration Service; and more sustained consideration of the need to 'mainstream' integration principles and practices within Irish policy and provision.

Yet it is also important to note that the population of those emigrating to Ireland is itself exceedingly heterogeneous. Different legal statuses and categories (for example 'asylum seeker', 'programme refugee', 'migrant worker') and different circumstances (whether an international student, Irish-born child, spouse of someone working for a multi-national corporation) create varying entitlements, opportunities and experiences. Moreover, there are vast differences across nationalities and within cultural or ethnic affiliations (according to age, gender, occupation), and the nature of the communities that are in the process of formation is unclear. For example, some people emigrating from Africa who have settled in Ireland feel they are part of an 'African' community. Some prefer identifying themselves more specifically according to their national origin (for example, the Ghanaian or Rwandan community). Some people, or perhaps the children they are raising here, might consider themselves African-Irish. Their views in turn may differ from those coming from China, or for existing or new accession states of the European Union.

Even the terminology used in this chapter is contentious, as different people prefer different terms depending on their experiences and circumstances. On one hand, people who have been in Ireland for many years or who have chosen to make Ireland their home might reject the term 'immigrant' because it denotes temporariness or outsider-status, preferring the term 'minority ethnic', which denotes a diverse community that is part of the wider society and nation. On the other hand, some feel the term immigrant or migrant is more accurate as these communities have not yet taken root. And still others find it necessary to make the distinction between these newer groups and other 'indigenous' Irish ethnic minorities such as Travellers, Jews and Black Irish, whose circumstances have different implications for the issues at hand, which helps explain why the term new minority ethnic communities is often used. Beyond their entry into the state, the label 'immigrants' may not be sufficient terminology for this evolving 'target group', particularly in terms of the development of policy around social inclusion, cohesion, equality and integration. All of these issues have implications for both the research and policy processes.

Immigration-related research in Ireland

As a comparatively mono-cultural society that has only recently become a destination for in-migration, Ireland is undergoing significant social and institutional changes. Immigration and its many related issues are essentially 'new' areas of policy and provision, for which there is little existing infra-structure or information base. There have been rapidly increasing demands for research in order to provide: (1) baseline data for policy development, reform and implementation, (2) a foundation for use by civil society actors in campaigning and advocacy, and (3) a vehicle for new scholarly approaches to familiar topics of national identity, ethnic conflict and social exclusion in Ireland, the analysis of which has been shaped by preoccupations concerning the Catholic–Protestant divide and Ireland's status as a poor, post-colonial, peripheral European nation (Feldman, 2003; 2006). This trend is also reinforced by the increasing demands for research resulting from European and international conventions and initiatives, such as the development of a common EU agenda for integration, and requirements stemming from the United Nations Committee on the Elimination of Racism.

Despite the fact that increasing immigration was an established trend by 2000, a question on ethnicity was absent from the national census until 2006. There is therefore a dearth of accurate demographic or baseline data, that is, the basic inventory upon which policies and programmes may be developed and their impacts measured. This undermines the effective development of the necessary policies and services, and the ability to ascertain and respond to the levels of social exclusion and patterns of inequality that have emerged with respect to this population (Fanning and Pierce, 2004: 17). The absence of an adequate information base combined with the ad hoc development of policy and provision have contributed to a situation in which a considerable amount of research has been undertaken in a piecemeal and fragmented fashion. In order to respond to the demands of their mandates, different government agencies have been commissioning their own research without co-ordinating across departments. Local groups and authorities have had to carry out smaller projects in order to assess the needs of the communities in their catchment areas. Many larger NGOs have done research that can contribute to policy and advocacy at national level. University-based researchers have responded to a variety of factors, both internal and external to their institutions, and which reflect their individual interests, disciplinary background and particular areas of specialism. While this has generated a rich knowledge base, it has also led to duplication, inconsistent quality and findings that are too incommensurate (i.e., information that cannot be adequately compared or brought together) to be usefully applied in a more comprehensive way.

Types and topics of research

A report published in 2004 by Integrating Ireland catalogued the proliferation of (primarily policy-related) research done in the areas relating to immigration and asylum, from 1998 to 2003 (the years marking the peak in the numbers of asylum applications) (Cotter, 2004). In that five-year period, the report identified about 275 research reports and papers, conducted across 30 different thematic areas by contract researchers, academics, NGOs, and government agencies. Although the report focused on 'applied' rather than 'basic' research (the latter constituting the majority of university-based publications), the fact that over 100 master's theses on these issues were reported to have been completed during that time indicates the level of academic activity generated by these topics.

The research included in this report falls within three general areas. The first addresses immigration and asylum policy, which includes analyses of asylum/refugee, immigration and human rights law, the asylum application process and the programmes to provide for asylum seekers while they await the outcome of their applications. Research in the second area focuses on service provision and local governance, which covers needs assessments and recommendations concerning community development, education and training, health, housing/accommodation, criminal justice, social exclusion and poverty, social work, spatial development, work and employment. Some of these projects focus on immigration generally, while others are specific to groups like children and unaccompanied minors, migrant workers, women, international students, returned Irish migrants. The third central area of work relates to racism which, in addition to experiences of racism, public attitudes towards immigrants and the role of the media, also addresses the social and political circumstances relating to equality, multiculturalism, interculturalism and integration, as well as understandings of race/ethnicity and religion in the formation of 'new' individual and community identities.

Research over the past ten years has only recently shifted from a focus on target groups like asylum seekers and refugees to a concern with 'migrants' and 'immigrants', reflecting a much broader constituency, legally, economically and culturally. Research and policy topics have also expanded. Work on racism and service provision has become more specific, according to the diversity of circumstances, ethnic differences and community heterogeneity (addressing differences in age, gender, occupation and so on). Moves towards the development of an immigration and residence policy and related government commitments to mainstreaming integration indicate that research activity in these areas will also increase.

Criticisms of research and the research process

In light of the copious amount of research activity taking place it is not surprising that asylum seekers, refugees and immigrants are becoming increasingly critical of the process and its consequences (Feldman et al., 2002: 4). An exploratory study examining this issue confirmed that, in some cases, participants reported that research could provide challenging and exciting opportunities to gain and showcase skills, learn about Irish society and institutions, and serve as a way of giving back to their communities. Yet, overall, interviewees across sectors shared the view that refugees and asylum seekers are 'sick to death' (2002: 12) of being researched, particularly as they rarely receive copies of the final report or other outcomes. Many who were interviewed felt exploited by the lack of inclusion and consultation in all stages of the research and knowledge-production process, particularly as they often felt they were 'doing all the work' without compensation or training in return. Because most were well aware of the importance and influence of research in identifying needs and contributing to social change, and the implications of the ways in which researchers represent their needs on 'their behalf', this exclusion proved particularly frustrating: 'it's like a doctor saying "you have a headache . . .", without even asking you what's wrong' (2002: 12). Paradoxically, those who constitute the most valuable sources of information in the research process are nonetheless treated as expendable and ancillary: 'We are considered ignorant, very limited people. They think we are all the same, a group with problems, an unwanted group to be researched' (2002: 12).

Both Feldman (2003) and Cotter (2004), identify problems occurring in three key areas relating to the research process.

1 *Poor research skills and implementation of the research process.* This includes deficiencies in researchers' level of preparation and familiarity with the topic and target communities and their failure to draw existing work, as well as their narrow conceptualisation of the research process as a whole (i.e., as just data collection). Other problems stem from the lack of co-ordination among institutions undertaking research and failure to consult with target groups and compensate participants.

2 *Insufficient capacity of researchers and those commissioning research.* Problems in this area were related to the lack of contacts, relationships and co-ordination between researchers and relevant stakeholders, organisations, gatekeepers, and communities, as well as inadequate training in research methods and practice. The absence of codes of research and other best practice to guide this work contributes to chronic difficulties in this area.

3 *Poor or ineffective application of research output.* Although valuable, research, particularly with regard to needs analyses, tends to be general, predictable and repetitive. More specialisation is needed particularly with regard to the diversity of communities and groups within communities. The politics of research funding often curtails the level of critique of government policies and practices that can be asserted in research find-ings, and the focus on 'emergency' rather than longer-term issues, the lack of application and follow up limits the extent to which the findings can impact the policy process.

Such criticisms and recommendations apply to the full range of those commissioning and carrying out research – including academics and students who do research as a regular part of their working life, as well as NGOs and community groups, statutory and semi-state agencies, partnerships and local authorities. For many people working in these contexts, research is one task among many or a new or add-on responsibility for which they may not be properly trained (Feldman, 2003: 17). Insufficient resources and rigid dead-lines can often prove too constraining to allow adequate time for building relationships and gaining community trust or for following an emergent, participatory research design. Research contracts often arise from a pressing government or agency demand, and therefore have short lead-in times and imminent deadlines. Because of this, marketing and other similar consultancies increasingly have been awarded research contracts on the assumption that their larger staff and large-scale survey methods yield better 'value for money' – a service for which they charge premium if not exorbitant prices. They have not proven immune, however, to the negative consequences of target group burnout, and their lack of any connections with the communities or the Third Sector has, in some cases, yielded poor data and missed deadlines (Feldman, 2003: 15).

There was a general feeling that, the more mainstream or majority-led organisations and NGOs were funded to undertake research and deliver services with respect to their communities, the more this circumvented the establishment of their own, community-led organisations (Feldman et al., 2002: 20). This concern was particularly significant in light of the 10-year struggle on the part of immigrants to be recognised as valuable and legitimate members of Irish society, to cultivate a modicum of means through which to represent themselves, and to gain acknowledgement of their vast administrative, technical and leadership skills. Despite the substantial efforts of this constituency to mobilise effectively as civil society actors, it is constrained by the lack of a national cross-community or minority ethnic-led council or federation. This has created a critical gap in these groups' ability to participate directly in key policy fora, which is therefore filled by other experts, agencies and NGOs which continue to represent their interests for them and control the development of policy that will shape their futures (Feldman et al., 2005).

And while both the involvement of this constituency as well as the central role of social science research in immigration and integration would now appear to be essential to the development of policy in these areas, they have yet to become standard elements of policy making and implementation in these areas. For example, while the recently published National Action Plan Against Racism is permeated by calls for research, there is no university-based researcher included on the Steering Group (Department of Justice, Equality and Law Reform, 2005: 73). The Steering Group does not include a research sub-committee and the Plan does not mention the need to develop minimum standards or codes of research practice, although the concerns across sectors with regard to research in this area are well documented. Similarly, there are no representatives from immigrant-led organisations on the Steering Group, and no steps thus far by any state agency or social partner to fill the gap left by the absence of a national level minority ethnic council or to initiate support for its development. It appears that, despite the breadth of activity and wealth of information that has arisen through the efforts of stakeholders involved in these social and policy sectors in the past decade alone, relations among them continue to be characterised by a lack of trust in, and perhaps commitment to, building sustainable working partnerships.

This brief overview of the state of immigration-related research in Ireland highlights important issues arising from the impact of research on target communities as well as the influence of wider institutional factors that mediate the use and impact of the research on the policy-making process. Two areas of research methodologies have been developed in response to these concerns, and are discussed briefly in order to further understanding of how the dilemmas raised in the previous section might be addressed. Both place a high premium on the role of good relationships in policy research and on the importance of participation of all stakeholders. The first – what is commonly referred to as participatory or action research – focuses on the researcher–community relationship, and the second – what is termed evidence-based policy making – primarily addresses relationships between university and statutory sectors.

Participatory and action-based approaches to research

Oliver (1992: 102) argues that because of the nature and power dynamics of social science in general, and the policy research process in particular, the needs and experiences of target groups are typically misunderstood and misrepresented. He observes that because the process has proven so alienating and oppressive for those who have been the subjects of research, the research generated is often irrelevant and fails to impact positively on either the policy process or the lives of the target group members (1992: 103). Such issues have come to the fore in debates about methodology in recent years, leading to the development of a variety of methodologies that are often referred to as participatory, emancipatory or action research (Reason and Bradbury, 2001; Truman et al., 2000; Hood et al., 1999).

These methods emphasise the necessity for research that contributes to changing the power relations between the researchers and the researched, and create opportunities for target groups to cultivate the resources and capacity necessary to contribute more directly to policy making through the research process. The different methodologies that fall under this rubric include a wide continuum of practices, from those that may include research participants in advisory roles, to those that actively train and employ them or that create research partnerships with a number of individuals or organisations, and those that work towards the establishment of ongoing organisations or community development structures as part of the research process itself. These issues are not new in Ireland, and actors such as the National Disability Authority (NDA, 2002), Pavee Point Travellers Centre (1997) and statutory youth workers (Byrne et al., 2003) have done extensive work in responding to their constituencies' negative experiences of research and community development by developing codes of practice and participatory methodologies necessary to overcome them.

The aspirations and objectives of participatory research are, however, notably difficult to achieve, and the literature is replete with discussions of the many obstacles and dilemmas that mediate their success. The substantial length of time required to undertake such projects effectively often makes this method undesirable if the policy process participants seek to influence is moving too quickly. Research funders are not typically inclined to commit the level of funding necessary to implement them – which may require funds for participants' travel, childcare and extra administrative responsibilities. Group development work may be required before the participants are able to work together, and a substantial amount of training may also be required before they are qualified to carry out the designated research tasks.

Yet complex structural and material difficulties also undermine the participation of target groups in such work and their overall success (Feldman 2003: 5). For example, at community level, there exists a problem of 'gate-keeping', whereby key NGOs or individuals who are either well known or purport to 'represent' the community may control the types of research questions that can be pursued and the community members researchers have access to. In many cases, those who are able to participate in the research are not democratically appointed representatives, and so have no structures of accountability to guide their activities. Moreover, obligations and capacities for consultation are not evenly distributed within the community, and if the number of people or organisations available and able to take part is limited, such opportunities, despite their benefits, also contribute to the creation of research fatigue. In this way, this type of research is dependent upon commu-nity members' capacity to participate and sustain it. Circumstances change, and individuals or organisations may be unable to complete the project for any number of reasons. Finally, participatory projects cannot avoid the problem of power relations within the research process. For example, even if all participants are invited or expected to review and approve the final research report, if such feedback is not forthcoming, a decision to proceed with its publication must typically be made, usually by a designated project member who is responsible to the management or funding structure for the completion of the project.

Evidence-based policy making

In addition to providing voice and building community capacity building, research is an essential tool for policy development in terms of its ability to identify new social problems, inform policy rationales and priorities, measure and assess policy impacts, improve implementation, and help generate 'ownership' and public support. The practice of what is called evidence-based policymaking has come to the fore in recent years in order to augment the application of academic research to policy development (Solesbury, 2001; UNESCO, 2001). Central to this objective is addressing the misconceptions and negative attitudes held by both policy makers and academics towards their respective research needs and undertakings that have hindered the development of collaborative working relationships across these two sectors

(Cross et al., 2000: 16). Those employing this approach advocate the use of both applied and theory-driven research that is informed by a variety of different disciplines and the direct participation of people from different sectors who have complementary skills and expertise (2000: 35).

Within this approach, developing quality relationships among the participants is considered even more important than technical expertise, because they play a key role in creating the environment necessary for maximising research-policy partnerships (Cross et al. 2000: 19). This demands sustained interaction and structures of engagement, which are typically absent from the course of participants' regular work or remits. These elements are essential, however, for cultivating the shared aims and ownership, common vocabulary, mutual trust and self-reflexivity required to maintain good working relationships. Further, ongoing opportunities for research-policy dialogue provide the opportunity for participants to develop their different roles, complementary skills, experience and management styles and how they fit into the overall project.

Despite the fact that migration has always been a defining element of global life, it is now acknowledged as being one of 'the' defining issues of the twenty-first century, and occupies a central place on the policy agenda of the European Union in particular. The complex transformations brought about by contemporary migrations have galvanised substantial innovations in international best practice in cross-sector, collaborative policy research, which is increasingly seen as part and parcel of integration policy work (Niessen and Schibel, 2004). However, the development of close university–policy research links and the particularly close relationship between the evolution of the migration research agenda and public policy concerns are problematic in a number of ways (Koenig, 2005: 1).

In this context, researchers run the risk of reproducing the perspectives of the state by undertaking research that is designed and funded by government and which, for example, uses the categories, language and concerns of the state, which may differ substantially – and even be seen as anti-immigration or discriminatory – from those of practitioners working on the ground or the communities themselves (Florence and Martiniello, 2005: 4). University researchers must also face strong competition from the media and non-academic experts whose views are much more easily incorporated into popular discourse and policy debates; as a result, academic work tends to be 'disqualified because it is "disenchanting", complex and even critical' as a result (2005: 3). Perhaps most importantly, in a case study of research-policy impact of immigration in the Netherlands, Penninx showed that the impact of research lessened once the issue became highly politicised (2005: 44–5).

Emerging best practice in Ireland

In Ireland, one of the first cross-sector policy research projects was the Southern Integrated Research Partnership (SIRP), comprising a variety of local and regional authorities in Cork, along with the NASC, the Cork-based immigrant support centre. SIRP undertook baseline research on the community of asylum seekers and analysis of the Voluntary Sector in Cork City and County. It also provided a programme of European study visits for SIRP members to explore best practice in integration and service provision. The Reception and Integration Agency has since sponsored further development of this initial research.

The Migration and Citizenship Research Initiative, established in 2004 in the Geary Institute at UCD, is the first national multi-disciplinary, inter-university and cross-sector research infrastructure that supports research, dissemination and training activities and collaborations addressing im/migration and integration. Its research focuses on identity, citizenship and civil society; social policy and institutional change; and global trends and transformations. In addition to UCD staff and postgraduate students, its affiliates include other research centres such as the Internationalism, Interculturalism and Social Development Programme (Dublin City University) and the Women and Belonging Research Group (University of Limerick), NGOs such as the Immigrant Council of Ireland, the Irish Refugee Council and Cáirde (an organisation addressing ethnic minority health inequalities) – each of whom are engaged in a variety of innovative initiatives with respect to community development and policy-making processes – and agencies such as the Integration Unit (Reception and Integration Agency).

Dublin City University also hosts the Intercultural Workplace Project, which forms part of the work of the Internationalisation, Interculturalism and Social Development strategic DCU theme, with the specific aim of increasing understanding of the complexity and breadth of workplace diversity issues and the trends that are emerging in the field of diversity and inclusion. This project draws upon researchers' specialisms in education, business studies, law, psychology, sociology, health studies and intercultural specialists as well as strategic, cross-sector alliances with other stakeholders.

Two participatory/action-based projects are located at Dublin Institute of Technology. The Centre for Transcultural Research and Media Practice is a research and postgraduate unit dedicated to the enrichment of scholarly and public understanding of transnational migration and globalisation, to new forms of citizenship and transcultural relations and histories. The Centre's aim is to develop an interface between media-led research, public policy/education and civil society activism. Combining production in social documentary film, photography, radio and new media with applied, action-based social research, the Centre identifies media practice as a catalyst for opening dialogue about social inclusion in collaboration with organisations and representatives of civil society.

Another interdisciplinary initiative, the Immigrant Entrepreneurship Project, has been established through the collaboration between the Centre for Transcultural Research and Media Practice, the Graduate Business School and the Legal Studies Programme at DIT, along with *Metro Éireann*, Ireland's first multicultural newspaper. It examines immigrant entrepreneurship as an emerging phenomenon in Ireland, signalling an important shift in the social integration of immigrants into Irish cultural life. It has recently undertaken the project, 'Immigrant Entrepreneurship: An Investigation of the Business Culture of the "New Irish"', which examines the concrete initiatives made by immigrant business in the last decade and the cultural codes and knowledge transmitted through everyday business transactions and the local and global networks created through immigrant entrepreneurship.

Challenges and opportunities

Penninx observes that the quality of a nation's democracy is best measured by the extent to which public debate is used as an instrument to build consensus and compromise, especially in the case of recent immigrant communities, whose needs are not reflected in existing infrastructures and who have limited means to participate in the policy process (2005: 34). He emphasises that politicians have a responsibility to actively seek out all the information necessary upon which to develop the best policies, and researchers to provide that information, thereby contributing to the robustness of public debate. Ultimately, both of these constituencies have an obligation to support target groups, in this case immigrant or 'new minority ethnic' communities to participate in both the research and policy-making processes.

There have been many positive developments emerging in Ireland in recent years that have created a promising foundation and momentum neces-sary to help support and advance such mandates. First, the infrastructure, knowledge base and expertise in relation to immigration-related issues and policies have matured, and there is a discernable (albeit precarious) shift in the political arena towards the acknowledgment of the permanency of immi-gration, the multi-ethnicity of Irish society, and the need for effective, long-term and integrated policy responses. This has been accompanied by the strengthening of the mobilisation of immigrant-led community and voluntary organisations and the growing participation of members of their communities in the political system. And, while the problems of racism are still significant, opportunities for social interaction and the integration at local and community levels are slowly increasing. Finally, a growing number of students from immigrant/'new' minority ethnic communities are being awarded postgraduate degrees and who are undertaking participatory, community-based research as part of their qualifications. There are no doubt numerous challenges ahead. However, overcoming the obstacles to the collaboration necessary for exploiting the wealth of knowledge, experience and expertise in Ireland with respect to immigration and integration to ensure the country's successful transition to a vibrant and equitable multi-ethnic society has never been more important, or more possible.

Recommended reading

Bulmer, M. (1986) *Social Science and Social Policy.* Boston: Allen & Unwin.

Cotter, G. (2004). *A Guide to Published Research on Refugees, Asylum-Seekers and Immigrants in Ireland.* Dublin: Integrating Ireland.

Cross, M., Henke, R., Oberknezev, P., and Pouliasi, K. (2000). *Building Bridges: Towards Effective Means of Linking Scientific Research and Public Policy: Migrants in European Cities.* Utrecht: Netherlands School for Social and Economic Policy Research.

Reason, P. and Bradbury, H. (eds) (2001) *Handbook of Action Research.* London: Sage.

Truman, C., Mertens, D., and Humphries B. (eds) (2000) *Research and Inequality.* London: UCL Press.

Chapter 7

Sustainable development, social policy and the environment

Kevin Murphy

Introduction

Sustainable development offers new challenges for social policy analysis and evaluation. It allows traditional social policy concerns to be placed in the context of the ever increasing tension between economic development and environmental degradation. Sustainable development means that short-term economic development, which funds welfare provision, must not compromise long- term economic development which funds future welfare provision. It also means that defining success by economic means alone is no longer appropriate, especially when such success is often accompanied by unacceptable levels of environmental degradation and social dislocation. This chapter examines what sustainable development is, and the context of its emergence. It looks at its international and national dimensions and comments on why the concept is far from being unproblematic. It then examines the relationship between sustainable development and health policy, housing policy, education policy and anti-poverty initiatives in Ireland. It does this, both by looking at the aspirations outlined in two central policy documents, *Sustainable Development: A Strategy for Ireland* (Department of the Environment and Local Government, 1997) and *Making Ireland's Development Sustainable* (Department of the Environment and Local Government, 2002), while it also examines particular policy initiatives. It then examines Irish sustainable development indicators to see how progress is being measured.

The emergence of sustainable development

Sustainable development emerged as a result of a growing belief that industrialisation was reaching its ecological limit, and that within a short space of time the planet would no longer be able to cope with the strain of ever increasing growth rates. It was the product of an increasing awareness that greenhouse gas emissions were heating the earth, and a growing belief that the fossil fuels, which had propelled industrialisation, were becoming exhausted. There were also fears about nuclear fuels, nuclear wars and the increasing differences in wealth between the developed and developing worlds. As regards a timeframe, the concept of the need for sustainable development became increasingly articulated from the early 1970s, and can be said to have entered popular political discourse following the publication of the Brundtland Commission report in 1987 (WCED, 1987). Holmberg and Sandbrook (in Elliot, 1994: 6) identify more than seventy definitions of sustainable development, which illustrates the diversity of interpretation that exists as to what the essence of sustainable development actually is. The Brundtland Commission, an international think tank, which was assembled to asses the extent of the environmental and developmental challenges facing the international community, defined sustainable development as 'development that meets the needs of the present without compromising the ability of future generations to meet their own needs' (WCED, 1987: 43). The concept encompasses many different components, which are said to belong to either the economic, social or environmental pillars of sustainable development.

Debates about sustainable development have consistently been couched in the language of alarm. This heightened sense of risk has seen a sense of urgency enter national and international policy documents, academic discourse and popular discourse. For example, the report of the Brundtland Commission stateD that 'if we do not succeed in putting our message of urgency through to today's parents and decision makers, we risk undermining our children's fundamental right to a healthy, life enhancing environment' (WCED, 1987: xiv). Trevor Sargent, leader of the Irish Green Party claimed that 'The catastrophic effects of unfolding climate change are worse than any terrorist attack' (*The Irish Times*. 21 Aug. 2004), while James Lovelock, author of the seminal Green text, *Gaia: A New Look At Life On Earth* (1979) warned that the dangers presented by a nuclear accident, paled into insignificance when compared with the potential negative effects associated with global warming (in Comby, 2000). The chief scientific adviser to the British government, Sir David King, claimed that the only place on earth that would be habitable for humans in 100 years' time would be Antarctica (*The Guardian* 13 May 2004), while the environmental social policy writer Meg Huby wrote of the inevitable social crisis 'and even societal breakdown' (1998: 2). A recognition of the importance of global warming found expression in the 2002 Irish sustainable development document *Making Ireland's Development Sustainable*, in which a national response to climate change was seen as a priority area (Department of the Environment and Local Government, 2002: 95). It was against this backdrop of perceived global ecological crisis that Irish environmental policy began to emerge.

For some the essence of sustainable development is relatively straightforward and narrow, while for others it represents something far broader and holistic. The contrasting interpretations of Pearse on the one hand, and Christie and Warburton on the other, are instructive in this respect. For Pearse, sustainable development is about ensuring that enough resources exist for continuing economic growth. He refers to 'an enduring flow of output', . . . sustainable yields', which should be reaped at 'a rate less than or equal to the growth rate of the bio-mass' (Pearse, 1993: 3). Both output and the resource being exploited are being sustained, while he also points to the need to develop renewable sources of energy (1993: 4). For Pearse, defining sustainable development is really not a difficult issue', but what has to be done to achieve it? (1993: 7) Although it also 'embraces social goals other than GNP' (1993: 5), we are essentially talking about sustaining economic development (1993: 7). On the other hand, Christie and Warburton present sustainable development in a much more complex light and place a much heavier emphasis on social factors. For them the concept is to be understood in terms of closing gaps: the poverty gap, the development gap the democracy gap and the security gap; as well as environmental sustainability (Christie and Warburton, 2001: 5–6). So for them, the Belfast agreement, a framework for ending conflict in Northern Ireland, represented a move closer to sustainability (2001: 11). Such an approach obviously presents sustainable development in very broad terms. Although the former interpretation is relatively narrow and the latter very broad, both can be said to embody the ethos of sustainable development. It could therefore be argued that such flexibility of interpretation, weakens the potential for translating policy aspiration into action.

The framework of sustainable development allows for a holistic approach to conceptualising social policy. This commitment to holism finds clear expression in the Brundtland Report which recognises that 'The challenges we face require a holistic approach but the policy-making process tends to be fragmented' (WCED, 1987: 310). Ill health from industrial pollution therefore needs to be as much a concern for the minister of industry as it is for a minister of health (1987: 11). In practice, such an approach means that all government departments must take cognisance of the social and environmental implications of their policies. In addition, issues pertaining to sustainable development are social policy issues, and therefore have a direct relevance for Irish social policy. For example commitments to combat pollution are healthcare commitments; sustainable urban planning policy has very direct consequences for Irish housing policy; the anti-poverty aspirations associated with the social pillar of sustainable development have implications for Irish income maintenance policy; Irish education policy attempts to engender in Irish citizens the behavioural changes deemed necessary for a sustainable future. Although the principles of sustainable development have relevance for all aspects of social policy, I shall look at what their implications might be for health policy, housing policy, education policy and anti-poverty initiatives in Ireland.

Health policy and the environment

Economic development has both positive and negative consequences for physical and mental health. Economic development is currently based on production forms which are dependent upon environmental degradation. The resulting pollution is detrimental to physical health, while an increasingly competitive and consumerist oriented society is often characterised by increased social isolation. Hill sees environmental concerns as being important to health, housing, and income maintenance although he says that perhaps the link between environment and health is the most important. For example he says that 'it is known that incidence of certain diseases (asthma, for example) is affected by air quality' (Hill, 1996: 247). He also notes that modern ecological problems are the result of human activity, in particular economic development (1996: 233). Similarly, Heidenheimer et al. note that the advent of the industrial revolution was accompanied by dramatic increases in environmental degradation, as pollution caused by industry in Europe and the USA resulted in tons of industrial waste finding its way into rivers, streams, and groundwater (1990: 308). Mannion has pointed out that the risk posed by the depletion of the ozone layer owing to the presence of increased CFC gases presents 'significant implications for human health as well as for the earth's ecosystems', as the ozone layer is important for filtering out ultra violet radiation which can lead to skin cancer and cataracts (1991: 171). We can therefore see that increased economic development is not without negative social consequences. Against this kind of background, Christie and Warburton (2000: 38) appear justified in calling for the clear articulation of rights to environmental health.

In the Irish case, for most of the twentieth century environmental threats were not perceived as being significant, primarily because of the low levels of industrial development up to the 1960s (Department of the Environment and Local Government, 1997: 21; Whelan, 2001: 3). Although the Air Pollution Act was introduced in 1987, Mullaly considered that it was the publication of the Department of the Environment's first *Environmental Action Programme* in 1990 which represented the first expression of policy coherence (Mullaly, 2001: 137). In the same year the Irish government banned the marketing, sales and distribution of bituminous coals within the city of Dublin which was one of the most significant actions in Irish environmental policy. Clancy et al. (2002: 1210) have argued that the fall in respiratory and cardiovascular death rates coincided with the ban on coal sales: 'Average black smoke concentrations in Dublin declined by 70 per cent after the ban on coal sales. Adjusted non-trauma death rates decreased per year after the ban by 5.7 per cent, respiratory deaths by 15.5 per cent and cardiovascular deaths by 10.3 per cent' (2002: 1210).

In May 2005, a report published by the Institute of Public Health in Ireland, *The Health Impacts of Transport: A Review*, cited evidence pointing to the short term health effects of air pollution, noting in particular its impact upon susceptible groups such as the elderly, and those with underlying health problems, such as heart or lung disease (IPHI, 2005a: 6). The report called for a reduction in traffic volumes, which are a leading source of air pollution, and noted that such a reduction 'could have potential benefits to health by improving air quality' (2005: 6). The institute recognised the link between transport, health and employment, that almost a fifth of Irish workers spent between one and two hours in daily transit to work, the second highest commuting time in the EU, and that increased commuting times means more stress and less physical activity (www.iphi.ie). The report called for a reduction in car use, and the promotion of more environmentally friendly transport methods such as walking and cycling, which would reduce pollution and lead to improved health (IPHI, 2005: 27). It also recommended switching from the present mode of transporting goods, since larger vehicles produced more pollution (2005: 27). Furthermore, a report published in February 2005 for the European Commission argued that human health was seriously threatened by particulate matter and ground level ozone, that exposure to such substances had caused several thousand premature deaths in Europe and had decreased life expectancy on average by approximately nine months (Amann et al., 2005: 4). It also indicated that this situation would deteriorate if current levels of CO_2 emissions continued (2005: 5).

Thus far we have examined how the unintended negative effects associated with economic development may threaten physical well-being. The pressures accompanying an increasingly dynamic economy may also have consequences for mental and emotional well-being. Fitzpatrick and Cahill argue that increased materialism has been accompanied by increased fear, risk and moral panic (2002: 6), while, Conroy points to trends of increasing stress and alienation across Europe (2005: 39).

Cullen's analysis of survey data relating to mental health trends in Ireland undermines the simplistic premise that increased wealth is beneficial for mental health. Although she notes that between 1989 and 2002, the population's average income has doubled, she questions whether or not increased well-being accompanies increased income (2004: 9). While accepting that it is very difficult to measure quality of life factors such as happiness, the evidence she presents suggests that 'Ireland's high growth years have been accompanied by a deterioration in many of the factors that make up the quality of life' (2004: 10). She points to a survey carried out on behalf of the Mental Health

Association of Ireland in 2001, which found that 73 per cent of the 1,000 people interviewed found life more stressful than five years previously. Nineteen per cent of the respondents said that they were smoking more and 17 per cent said that they were drinking more' (2004: 10).

She highlights a National Health and Lifestyle Survey of 6,539 people in 1999, which sought to ascertain how people felt that their health could be best improved. The survey found that the majority reported 'less stress' regardless of their age, sex and social background. A follow up report in 2001 also reported that stress was the most common answer for both males and females' (Cullen, 2004: 10). Cullen points to another online survey in 2001, in which a sample of 2,000 students were asked if they thought that the level of stress experienced by the general Irish population had increased. Over two thirds said that it had increased a lot, 30 per cent said it had a little, and only three per cent said not at all (2004: 10-11). The influential 2004 Amarach report found that between 2001 and 2004, the proportion of people who said they suffered from stress 'often' rose significantly (Amarach, 2004: 9), while a 2002 study in the workplace found that 77 per cent of respondents claimed that the economic boom had not improved their quality of life. Stress was identified as the main cause of absenteeism while almost a quarter said that they suffered 'great stress from bullying, back biting and other forms of aggressive behaviour and intimidation' (Cullen, 2004: 11). Cullen also points to an increase in depressive disorders. For example, a survey comparing four European countries in 2003 showed that women in Dublin were most likely to be depressed, and that in fact one in three suffered from depression (2004: 11).

This deterioration in well-being for some is not noted in Irish sustainable development policy documents. Such trends suggest that economic development can be at odds with social development, and represents an imbalance between the economic and social pillars. This imbalance violates the basic principles of sustainable development. For the principles of sustainable development to find real expression in Irish social policy, initiatives must be developed which ensure that mental and emotional well being are not compromised by economic development. For example, employment policy needs to tackle the bullying and forms of aggressive behaviour in the workplace which are alluded to by Cullen.

Sustainable development and Irish housing policy

With respect to the question of sustainable housing policy, it is important to re-emphasise the mutually reinforcing nature of the three pillars of sustainable development, which is at least nominally at the centre of sustainable development, and also that development must be cognisant of the needs of future generations. In other words we need to ask, (1) how will the needs of future generations benefit from housing policy actions taken now? (2) Are there any negative social consequences attached to housing policy? (3) Is the contribution of the building trade to the *economy* (the spin-off effect being the delivery of strong GNP levels to future generations) to be prioritised? (4) Are the future *environmental* effects of present Irish housing policy to be prioritised as the primary focus of analysis, or (5) does sustainable Irish housing really mean designing policy now with a view to creating communities for the future that are characterised by *social* stability, that is with less social segregation, less crime and less tension. As we shall see, housing development in Ireland presents clear contradictions between economic, environmental and social imperatives.

Bhatti and Dixon point to the link between housing and environmental and social justice; environmental damage; energy consumption and the use of natural resources; urban form and sustainability; green design and the greening of household consumption (Bhatti and Dixon, 2003: 503). Such links appear to have and echo in *Sustainable Development: A Strategy for Ireland*, which, for example, said that 'to avoid unhealthy and unsustainable growth of human settlements it is necessary to promote land-use patterns that minimise transport demands, save energy and protect open and green spaces' (Department of the Environment and Local Government, 1997: 149). This appears to be an unambiguous pledge to promote housing, which does not cause environmental degradation. The 1997 strategy notes the need to ensure 'a clear demarcation between urban and rural land use, to prevent urban sprawl'. Yet the CSO predicts that the greater Dublin area will increase in population to 2,063,000 by 2021, an increase of 51 per cent and that this development will spread into neighbouring counties (CSO, 2005b: 6). *Sustainable Development* goes on to pledge that 'There will be closer co-ordination of transport and land use planning so as to increase the use and efficiency of public transport, rather than private cars, especially in larger cities' (Department of the Environment and Local Government, 1997: 149). However, in the ten years from 1994 to 2004, the number of new private cars registered per annum, has increased from 77,773 in 1994 to 149,635 in 2004 (CSO, 2005b), an increase of almost 50 per cent.

Such population expansion is necessary to boost economic growth and looks set to continue. This policy maximises rather than minimises transport demands. It also contradicts a central aspiration in the *Sustainable Development* report which states that policy needs to encourage 'housing that is nearer the centre' (Department of the Environment and Local Government, 1997: 156). However, Friends of the Earth claim that the average car in Ireland travels 24,000 KM a year, which is 70 per cent higher than Germany, 50 per cent higher than Britain and 30 per cent higher than the USA (Friends of the

Earth, 2005). Planning which encourages housing developments created for their proximity to Dublin locks residents of such communities into car dependence. This in turn increases carbon emissions, which in turn further destabilise the climate, which in turn presents more environmental risks to future generations. Therefore it could be argued that such an approach to housing policy is unsustainable. It represents economic development unconcerned with environmental degradation and social dislocation. Winston argues that a lack of political will at local and national level has underpinned this lack of commitment to sustainable housing policy in Ireland (Winston, 2005: 2).

A 2005 report by the Institute of Public Health in Ireland links housing policy to health effects. It states that 'all Ireland research supports the positive effect of social networks and aspects of social capital on the health of people living across the island. For example, poor perceived neighbourhood quality, one of a number of measures of social capital, has shown association with poor health' (IPHI, 2005a: 7). The report also points to the beneficial physical and mental factors which would result in transport policy which de-prioritises car dependence and encourages active transport (such as cycling and walking), along with developing public transport. It points to a recent study carried out in Galway, which showed that those who lived in areas which were 'car dependent' localities (those which are designed to be negotiated in cars, with amenities spread out over a large area and emphasis on roads and parking over pavements), were less likely to know and trust their neighbours and to participate in local organisations than those who lived in 'walkable' pedestrian-orientated localities (those with pedestrian areas, footpaths, meeting spaces, and local shops) (2005: 36). It also points to studies which claim that increased community contact has beneficial consequences for mental health (2005: 35). Therefore it suggests that transport policy can cause community severance, which contributes to isolation, which in turn contributes to increased mental health problems.

The *Sustainable Development* report also states that 'In the housing context, the concept of sustainability has a social as well as environmental dimension. Positive measures to counteract social segregation and to promote tenant participation and involvement contribute to this social dimension' (Department of the Environment and Local Government, 1997: 154). The document points to the regeneration of Ballymun in Dublin as an opportunity to put the principles of sustainable development into practice. The regeneration of Ballymun did see increased tenant participation in designing an alternative. However, how compatible the development has been with the principles of sustainability has been questioned as it takes up so much space (McDonald, 2000: 254–6). Furthermore, *Making Ireland's Development Sustainable* states that housing policy must combat social segregation, which is unsustainable (Department of the Environment and Local Government,

2002: 52). To achieve this it points to part 5 of the Planning and Development Act, 2000, amended in the 2002 Planning Act, which obliges developers to make 20 per cent of land available for social and affordable housing (Silke, 2005: 71). However, progress in this area has stalled, and the housing unit concedes that part 5 has had very limited impact on the number of units completed to date (Housing Unit, 2005: 4). Therefore when economic, environmental and social development are examined in relation to housing policy, it is economic concerns which appear to be prioritised. This perhaps suggests that policy makers consider that high GNP levels represent a more appropriate inheritance to bestow upon future generations, than a healthy environment or social stability.

Alternative housing policy, 'The Village': a sustainable development housing project, Cloghjordan in County Tipperary

The evidence above suggests that sustainable housing policy and Irish housing policy are at odds in many ways. However, the aims of 'The Village' appear to have a closer relation to the principles outlined in sustainable development documents. The Village is set to be Ireland's first sustainable community and will be established in County Tipperary. The Village, which has now been accepted as part of the county development plan for North Tipperary, is a development that seeks to build affordable ecological homes and generate local enterprise. The Village will have 130 serviced sites, an organic farm, an orchard, a wildlife area, and members are committed to developing renewable energy systems. The population of Cloghjordan was 431 according to the 2002 Census (CSO, 2003a) and The Village will add approximately another 400 members to the community, thus doubling the population of Cloghjordan. This project is the largest of its type in Ireland and one of the largest in the world (Village Ireland, 2005). The environmental charter of The Village states that 95 per cent of annual energy use should be met by renewable sources, while members believe that they can reduce the CO_2 emissions of Cloghjordan by 50 per cent. The stated aims of The Village are: 'To provide a place that can down-size the institutions that provide housing, food, waste disposal, health care, education, social interaction and democracy, and contain these systems in a community where direct human involvement in the institutions is promoted' (Village Ireland, 2005). It also aims to provide as many as possible of the services and products itself which are required by the residents. In this it aims to encourage human activities which, it claims, will be harmlessly integrated into the natural world, and to provide a place, supportive to healthy human development. (Village Ireland, 2005).

The Village thus claims to be embracing the concept of mutuality between economic, environmental and social development. On the one hand its environmental charter contains specific commitments to the use of renewable building materials and has relatively ambitious plans to increase energy efficiency. On the other hand, we also see a commitment to promoting emotional, spiritual and mental welfare, although it is not specified how this will be achieved. Health care, education, and social interaction also receive only a passing mention, while the difference in price between the cheapest site (17,000) and the most expensive (90,000) suggests that equality is not central to how The Village views the social pillar of sustainable development. As planning permission was granted only in July 2005, it will take time to appraise how The Village measures up to the principles of sustainable development, to which it has attached itself.

Sustainable development and education policy

There is a growing belief that education systems need to change in order to reflect the challenges associated with new environmental realities. An awareness of environmental issues must be engendered in citizens, and the negative aspects associated with increased consumption must be highlighted. Many writers see a vital link between education and sustainable development (Irvine and Ponton, 1988; Christie and Warburton, 2001; Pepper, 1986), while the UN has titled the decade 2005–15 as the decade for sustainable education. Irvine and Ponton see education as essential in the engendering of self-restraint, especially regarding consumption, and family size, in order to protect the interests of future generations (1988: 6). Therefore they believe that education must develop in citizens an innate understanding that over-consumption has negative consequences for future generations, and that keeping family size small is part of civic responsibility (1988: 23). Christie and Warburton also argue that the public needs to be informed about the environmental effects of consumption (2001: 145). They call for the introduction of education for citizenship and sustainable development to be put on the curriculum (2002: 149) and call for 'a revolution in education to link moral and civic rights and responsibilities with sustainable development' (2001: 150). George and Wilding consider that green education policy supports replacing the values associated with the logic of industrialism with ecological ones (1994: 182). *Sustainable Development A Strategy for Ireland* states that education is central to changing attitudes and behaviour in relation to solving environmental problems (Department of the Environment and Local Government, 1997: 164). In the non-formal sector the report cites the establishment of ENFO an environmental library service in Dublin as a successful initiative, and in the formal, it notes the introduction of the green schools scheme in 1997.

The green schools initiative

In 1998 the green schools initiative was launched. This is an international programme, which aims to engender responsible attitudes in primary school-children towards environmental protection. As well as creating awareness and responsibility, participants in the programme actively contribute to significantly reducing the schools' energy usage. By the end of the school year 2002–3 there were 1,390 schools registered in the programme (An Taisce, 2005). This represents 35 per cent of Irish schools of which 269 have achieved the green flag award. The Young Reporters for the Environment programme is aimed at secondary school students, and its aims are broadly in line with the general green schools ethos, while it also allows students to identify a local environmental issue, and to inform the local community about it (An Taisce, 2005). However, the emphasis appears to be on energy saving methods, pollution clean ups, awareness and recycling as opposed to an investigation of the link between consumption patterns and their environmental effects. The green schools project is also non-obligatory, and is not part of the formal examination curriculum.

A recent initiative seeks, however, to place ecological principles into certain second level exam subjects. ECO–UNESCO in association with Comhar, have begun looking at incorporating sustainable development principles into geography, science and CSPE. Science is seen as offering opportunities to explore the scientific arguments regarding environmental problems, while CSPE is seen as offering potential to develop critical thinking on sustainable development. Geography is seen as offering an opportunity to explore cultural and economic systems, and perhaps offers the best opportunity to explore the link between consumption and environmental risk. This initiative is at an early stage, and it is therefore too early to evaluate its effectiveness. However, survey data exist which assess the effectiveness of the green schools project.

Can environmental education impact on education?

A survey of 47 schools was undertaken in 2001 by the Environmental Education Unit of An Taisce, to investigate the social impacts of the green schools programme in Ireland. It primary aim was to ascertain whether or not the programme is having any success in improving students' attitudes and behaviour towards the environment. The research compared students from awarded green schools with students from non-green schools (O'Mahony, 2001).

Environmental knowledge/awareness levels were found to be very similar for the two groups (O'Mahony, 2001: 32). As regards positive behaviour towards the environment, the green-schools students scored significantly higher, meaning that overall, the Green-Schools students are less likely to drop litter and more likely to participate in local clean ups and environmental projects, conserve water and electricity and consider the environment when making a purchase (2001: 33). Environmental opinion leadership levels relate to how likely students were to encourage others to act in an environmentally friendly way and green school students scored much higher than non-green school students in this respect. Discussions about the environment were far more common among Green school students, though it must be said that such conversations were mostly held in the classroom (2001: 33). Environmental problems were seen as more of an urgent problem among Green-Schools students; whereas Non-Green-School students felt environmental problems were more of a problem for the future. The levels of recycling of paper/ cardboard, aluminium and glass were higher within the homes of Green-School students (2001: 34). The study also found that the schools that had fully adopted the programme were diverting, on average, 45 per cent waste away from landfill (2001: 32).

So environmental education in Ireland is at a relatively embryonic stage, and its present focus appears to be on creating environmental awareness rather than facilitating a debate about whether or not the business-as-usual approach to economic development and the environmental rights of future generations are compatible. Again, this appears to suggest that Irish education policy does not see the economic, environmental and social pillars of sustainable development as mutually enforcing, but rather views the latter two as being subservient to the needs of the first.

Sustainable development and poverty in Ireland

Some of the links between service provision and sustainability mentioned above, appear quite clear cut. Low-density urban sprawl creates car dependence, which increases CO_2 emission levels. Pollution causes ill-health to present and future generations while education may in theory inculcate behavioural habits promoting sustainability. The implications of sustainable development for income maintenance are perhaps less clear-cut. What is not in doubt is that those who live on lower incomes are confronted with more environmental threats than those living on higher incomes (Bhatti and Dixon, 2003, Heidenheimer et al., 1990; Huby, 1998). Heidenheimer et al. point to 'A significant body of economic research [which] suggests that environmental policies have regressive effects on the distribution of personal incomes' (1990:

334), adding that there has never been more than an uneasy alliance between trade unions and environmental movements (1990: 334–5). There is also ample evidence illustrating how pollution taxes get passed on to the customer by the producer, and these are costs are more of a burden to those on lower incomes (Heidenheimer et al., 1990: 334–5 and Huby, 1998: 34). Therefore environmental degradation re-enforces poverty. However, Irish sustainable development documents do not clearly define what the relationship between Irish poverty and environmental degradation in Ireland is and it is this lack of clarity, which we will examine now.

Aspirations regarding income maintenance policy are outlined in *Making Ireland's Development Sustainable* (Department of the Environment and Local Government, 2002) and draw heavily on the review of the National Anti Poverty Strategy (Government of Ireland, 2002c). Such aspirations include:

- Reducing to two per cent, and ideally eliminating, consistent poverty
- Building an inclusive society
- Developing social capital, particularly for disadvantaged communities
- Eliminating long-term unemployment as soon as circumstances permit, but in any event no later than 2007.

The document also points to progress in this respect, which it says includes:

- A reduction in consistent poverty from 15.1 per cent in 1994 to 6.2 per cent in 2000
- A halving of consistent poverty from 17 per cent in 1997 to 8 per cent in 2000
- A fall in unemployment over the period (Department of the Environment and Local Government, 2002: 94)

There is no mention here of how such actions will address the needs of future generations, though it could be inferred that the need to be free from poverty is being addressed here. However, the three pillars of sustainable development are said to be mutually re-enforcing, but the above document makes no mention of a link between poverty and environmental degradation. Furthermore, it could be argued that the aspirations and achievements listed above refer as much to a *successful* society as to a *sustainable* one, and we shall see later that the concepts of success and sustainability appear to mean the same thing in some Irish sustainable development documents. This interchangeability of qualitatively different concepts represents a conceptual weakness. Furthermore *Making Ireland's Development Sustainable* states that reducing economic inequalities is essential for sustainability, but again no explanation is provided explaining why this is the case, and in particular why income inequality is linked to environmental degradation (2002: 3). It should also be noted that this document, ignores the increase in relative poverty noted by Coakley (2004: 112) over this time.

National progress indicators for sustainable economic, social and environmental development

An examination of sustainable development indicators allow us see how aspirations measure up to outcomes. In February 2002, *The National Progress Indicators for Sustainable Economic, Social and Environmental Development* were published by National Economic and Social Council (NESC, 2002). The central ethos driving the initiative was the stated belief that economic measurements (per capital GNP/GDP rates) alone are no longer to be seen as adequate measurements of progress. For development to be deemed sustainable, growth and rising incomes must be accompanied by a balance in family and work life, as well as a decrease in economic inequalities (NESC, 2002: 3). Sustainable development also implies that future generations must be able to enjoy a level of well-being that is at least as high as that of the current generation (2002: 12). However, although it concludes that Ireland has experienced positive change in relation to economic indicators, little or no change has been experienced in relation to a number of the social indicators, and the environmental indicators have moved in a negative direction (2002: 20).

To measure progress in areas the document sees as key to a successful society, it lists 18 headline indicators and 12 background indicators, which it relates to the 'broad goals of economic, social, and environmental sustainability, thereby mirroring the three dimensions of sustainable development' (2002: 4). Examples include levels of per capita GDP growth rates, the proportion of population with access to a PC/Internet, labour force participation rates, percentage of households or persons living in relative income poverty, participation in adult and continuing education and training, and greenhouse gas emissions (2002: 14). Some indicators are deemed to be relevant to one pillar of sustainable development, for example per-capita GNP/GDP rates are deemed only to be economically significant. Percentages of households and persons experiencing relative income poverty are deemed to be of relevance to both the economic and social pillars, while greenhouse gas emissions are deemed relevant to all three pillars – the economic, social and environmental.

What is of interest is that of the 30 indicators listed, all are deemed to be economically important, 20 are socially relevant and six are deemed to be environmentally relevant. It could be argued that this may be indicative of the relative importance government policy attaches to economic development over social and environmental welfare. This appears to contradict the document's earlier stated belief articulated in the report, that 'The indicators should be *horizontally coherent,* that is each set of indicators should be related to and supportive of each other. Indicators of economic development should have a relevance to those of social and environmental development, and vice versa, rather than each set being considered in isolation' (2002: 7).

We also see a much different emphasis in this document from the one presented in *Making Ireland's Development Sustainable,* which was published in the same year. For example that deocument concedes that economic growth contributes to environmental degradation (Department of the Environment and Local Government, 2002: 90). However *Progress Indicators for Sustainable Development* (NESC, 2002) considers increased GNP/GDP as not environmentally relevant. Again these are seen as having only economic relevance. There are also conceptual problems, primarily related to whether or not, government policy has a clear conception of what sustainability means. The NESC (2002) document alludes both to a successful and sustainable society. However, sustainable and successful are different concepts. A sustainable societal feature may not be a successful societal feature. Communal conflict in Ireland has proved to be an extremely sustainable societal feature but it can hardly be deemed a successful one. Similarly, social inequality has been sustained for centuries, yet it can be interpreted both as being both successful and unsuccessful, depending on one's ideological standpoint.

Conclusion

The benefits which accompany a booming economy are plainly visible in Ireland. However, sustainable development is about ensuring that economic development is not self-referential – is not an end in itself. Economic development must not, therefore, be achieved at the expense of unacceptable environmental or social costs, and it must be cognisant of the needs of future generations. We can see from the National Progress Indicators, that success is visible only in relation to economic development. We see that there have been negative as well as positive health aspects associated with increased economic development, though the negative aspects tend to be overlooked in Irish sustainable development indicators. We see that housing policy looks set to increase car dependence, which has negative implications for social well-being and the environment, while we also see initiatives to combat social segregation through housing policy being diluted. We see that the green-school programme is becoming more popular in Irish schools. However, we see that its emphasis is upon creating environmental awareness, rather than examining the link between increased consumption and the consequent environmental and social threats posed to future generations. 'Common-sense' assumptions regarding economic development are left unchallenged, again suggesting that the economic considerations prevail over social and environmental considerations.

We also see an ambiguity in Irish policy documents in relation to what sustainable development actually is. Such ambiguity is undoubtedly rooted in the flexibility of interpretation associated with definitions of sustainable development. It tends to mean different things to different people, while these differing interpretations are often framed in line with differing interests (Middleton and O'Keefe, 2001: 2). In other words, it is a concept which can mean whatever it suits one to believe it means. Sustainable development assumes that its three pillars are mutually reinforcing. Arguably this suggests that it accords equal importance to all pillars. But again such an approach is open to flexible interpretation and therefore vulnerable to the spin of competing interests. If sustainable development means everything and nothing, it can be seen as merely a reflection of the values of those with the most power to interpret it, in a way favourable to their interests.

Recommended reading

Department of the Environment and Local Government (2002) *Making Ireland's Development Sustainable*. Dublin: Stationery Office.

Fitzpatrick, T. and Cahill, M (2002) *Environment and Welfare: Towards a Green Social Policy*. New York: Palgrave

McDonald, F. (2000) *The Construction of Dublin*. Dublin: Gandon.

NESC (2002) *National Progress Indicators for Sustainable Economic, Social and Environmental Development*. Dublin: NESC.

Chapter 8

Sport, health promotion and social capital

Michael Rush

Introduction

This chapter examines the relationship between sports policies, obesity and physical education, at a time when a decline in the physical fitness of both children and adults has become of major concern. The role of sport and health promotion in Ireland is related to broader debates about individual and collective social capital in Irish social policy (Fanning, 2004c: 55–9). The title of Robert Putnam's influential *Bowling Alone: The Collapse and Revival of American Community* (2001) suggests that the extent of communal bonds, including those fostered through participation in sports, can be an index of societal health just as participation in sport by individuals potentially contributes to physical health. Putnam's arguments have struck a chord within a society that has long emphasised the role of sporting organisations, notably the GAA, at the heart of national and local identity. This chapter explores the relationship between sport and Irish social policy as part of a mixed economy of welfare that includes voluntary provision, a role for schools, government regulation and state funding. A faltering relationship between health promotion and Irish sports policy can be traced back to Dáil debates in 1958 when the then Minister for Health rejected the establishment of a National Fitness Council. A more interventionist role for the state ensued which was consolidated with the establishment of a special section in the Department of Education for 'Youth and physical recreation' in 1969 (Liston and Rush, 2005b: 77).

The Department of Education presided over the development of sports policy for the next three decades. During this period the name of the national governing body of sports was to change in 1977 from COSAC (An Chomhairle Sport agus Caiteamh Aimsire/National Council for Sport) to Cospóir, although both organisations were at the end of the day administered by the Department of Education. Full recognition of sport as a distinct area of social policy finally came about in 1999 with the establishment of the independent Irish Sport Council (ISC).

The establishment of the Irish Sport Council as the first statutory governing body of sport followed a recommendation from the influential report *Targeting Sporting Change* (Department of Education, 1997). Publication of this report coincided with the establishment of the Department of Tourism, Sport and Recreation and the appointment of a Minister for Sport. In addition, a Women in Sport Taskforce was established to make recommendations regarding all aspects of sport and recreational activity, including participation, coaching, administration and decision making. These developments took sports policy beyond concerns with physical education and health promotion through the introduction of a much wider goal, that of making a contribution 'to the economic and social progress of Irish society by developing an active culture in sport and recreation, including the achievement of sporting excellence' (Department of Education, 1997: 6).

A research focus on sporting excellence and one on the experiences and attitudes of men and women who play sport on Ireland now provide 'enormous scope' for contemporary studies into sport and social life (Bairner, 2005: 4) and for the development of Irish sports policy. Recognition of athletes as active agents and policy subjects is a new phenomenon in Ireland and one which can serve only to enlighten the conventional view that Ireland has produced a 'sporting culture arguably more varied than any other' and one which is bound up with the meaning of 'being Irish and the relationship of Irish people with each other and the world beyond'. (Bairner, 2005: 1). Traditionally sport was almost universally written off by social scientists as part of the less serious side of life (Dunning and Rojek, 1992: xiv). This chapter argues therefore that a wider recognition of the importance of sports policy research offers new insights for the overall development for Irish social policy.

Sports policy recognition

Empirical research findings in the report, *The Policy Implications of Social Capital*, revealed that a quarter of Irish adults were members of a sporting or recreational communities compared to an average of one in six on across 32 countries (NESF, 2003b: 62). These findings strengthen the conventional view that sport is a distinguishing feature of social life in Ireland. The potential social and economic significance of sport and associational life to Irish social policy and Irish welfare futures was previously acknowledged in the influential *Strategy into the 21st Century* report,

> Ireland has displayed considerable vitality in the continuation, formation and
> vibrancy of associations in sport, culture, voluntary action, self-help and other

areas. The Council considers the vitality of associational life as key sources of the trust and capacities which are necessary for successful economic and social life in the modern world. (NESC, 1996: 8)

Sports policy reports published by the Department of Education have consistently called for appropriate research data to inform the development of sports policy (Department of Education, 1994, 1997). Specific recommendations included the need for census data and household budget surveys to differentiate the importance of sporting activities from other leisure and recreational activities. From a comparative European perspective Irish sports policy embraced a much wider and radical consideration of the contribution of sport to the national economy than elsewhere. A broader definition of sport *per se* was adopted which included Gaelic games, horse-back riding, fishing, darts, snooker and golf under four categories of game sports, fitness sports, survival sports and national games (Department of Education, 1994: 33).

Such a wide-ranging, wide-encompassing definition of sporting activity in Ireland can be traced back to the nineteenth century when tenant farmers became the largest social group in rural society and when the first dedicated sporting paper was fittingly entitled the *Irish Sportsman and Farmer*. It was a weekly paper that 'was dominated by news of hunting and other horse-related activities, while also carrying reports on the corn and cattle markets' (Rouse, 2005: 9). This was an age when the term sport was a reference to 'hunting, fishing and other such activities enjoyed by Irish gentlemen'. In the same way that that Irish social policy traces its foundations back to the nineteenth-century poor laws, modern understanding of sport in Ireland can be traced back to the social conventions of the last century. Such conventions might help to explain why today horseracing at the Curragh carries the same sporting cachet as the competitive games played in Croke Park or Lansdowne Road (Bairner, 2005: 1)

Gender, feminism and sports policy

The origins of modern sport in the social conventions and gender relations of the nineteenth century partly explain why the participation of women in sport has in Ireland as elsewhere in the world been relatively limited. Tremendous gains have, however, been made in athletic and sports by women athletes, particularly since the 1970s. A growing interest in female sporting experiences led to the development of an exponential body of sports medicine and sports psychology literature which challenges the myths and social conventions surrounding the differential physical and emotional consequences of athletics for men and women (Renzetti and Curran, 2003:

391). A distinct feminist perspective on sport and sports policy emerged. A major criticism of Irish sports policy is the ongoing channelling of girls and boys into gender appropriate sports based on social convention, for example skipping, netball and ice skating for girls and rowing, rugby and football for boys (Liston, 2005: 21). Feminist researchers in the USA and Ireland have focused on the extent to which education, school and the formation of gender identity impacts on gender equality and the increasing levels of female participation in competitive athletics and sports. The implementation of Title IX of the Education Amendments Act in the USA to prohibit sex discrimination in schools is widely credited with the rise to prominence of women in Sport (Renzetti and Curran, 2003: 389).

In Irish sports studies, the traditional dominance of sex segregated team sports, such as gaelic games, hockey, rugby, and soccer in the physical education curriculum is cited as reinforcing existing gender stereotypes (Liston, 2005: 215). Analysis of any continuity in sporting preferences shown by boys and girls in Ireland must, however, take in the important role played by family life and social convention. In Ireland the State gives full recognition to the role of the family as the primary provider of children's education as guided by Article 42 of Bunreacht na Éireann, the Irish Constitution (1937), and this applies equally to their physical education. Children today in Ireland as elsewhere in the world can study physical education as a formal subject at secondary school level; in the Irish case it is offered as part of the optional Leaving Certificate programme.

A growing research interest in the role of sport in school, for example in the relationship between gender and educational achievement in Ireland (Loughrey, 1999), has in recent years been given further momentum by the growth of concern in relation to children's health. A survey entitled 'Take Part' carried out for the Irish Heart Foundation in 2004 found high levels of obesity among teenagers and revealed that girls were less likely to engage in strenuous physical exercise than their male counterparts. The survey was conducted by Dublin City University and funded by the Irish Heart Foundation, the Health Service Executive and the Northern Area and Fingal Sports Partnership. At the other end of the demographic spectrum, research into sports participation and health among adults concluded that older females were at a higher risk of leading desk-bound or sedentary lifestyles than their male counterparts (Fahey et al., 2004). National Health and Lifestyles Surveys in 1999 and 2003 revealed gender differentials in levels of strenuous physical activity and vigorous exercise that are increasingly being raised as a serious social issue, as are findings that reveal that the strong variance in physical activity levels between boys and girls doubles by the age of 15–17 (Liston, 2005: 214).

Health promotion: obesity, cardiovascular problems and diabetes

Social conventions in relation to gender, strenuous exercise and physical health are now being challenged as the relationship between sport and health comes under increasing scrutiny from feminist and health promotion perspectives, (Liston, 2005; Fahey et al., 2004: 2). The shift towards a health promotion emphasis within sports policy has emerged in the context of obesity becoming a major public health problem (Liston and Rush, 2005:73). The National Taskforce on Obesity was established on 10 March 2004. It reported that nearly one in five people (18 per cent) could be considered obese and nearly every second person was classed as being overweight (39 per cent). A 30 per cent increase in obesity levels have been reported over the last four years, and obesity in Europe is now five times more common than it was in the period following the Second World War. It is a problem that is becoming increasingly prevalent among children and young people. The report claims that 300,000 Irish children are overweight and has predicted that the figure will increase by 10,000 a year unless drastic action is taken (Department of Health and Children, 2005b: 2). The Irish Health Promotion Unit has linked the causes of obesity to food habits and physical activity levels, and its key recommendations include changes in diet and regular moderate physical exercise. Recommendations specifically targeted at children include the promotion of active lifestyles, restriction of pre-packaged foods and sweet drinks and the promotion of fruit and vegetables in their diets.

Endemic obesity in children, particularly among young girls, is a challenge to the traditional convention that strenuous physical exercise and sporting activity are principally male preserves. Physical education in school is now widely regarded as essential for instilling the health promotion message that 'healthy habits begin young' (Irish Sports Council, 2003: 3). The contemporary emphasis on health promotion has to some extent recast Irish sporting activity back to being regarded as a diversionary solution to the modern problems of drug abuse, drug related crime, marginalisation and disadvantage and as an remedy in an age of 'increased prosperity' to increasing levels of obesity and diabetes (2003: 2). The health promotion emphasis within Irish sports policy stresses that 'sport improves the quality of our lives' and that sports participation 'sharpen our minds' and 'strengthen [s] our bodies'. A *Code of Ethics and Good Practice for Children's Sport* was launched in November 2000 which has been extensively targeted through the National Governing Bodies of Sport (NGBs) at meetings throughout Ireland of parents, teachers, and coaches.

Health promotion and citizenship

Welfare states are responding in varying ways to the risks to society posed by modern consumption habits and sedentary lifestyles. The everyday ordinariness of addiction, obesity, diabetes and heart diseases, has allowed health promotion to step into the public domain 'as a virtuous activity not only promoting health but also the person' (Higgs, 1998: 179). Health promotion contributes to a prevailing depiction of the welfare subject as an independent agent who cam mould himself or herself according to freely taken lifestyle choices. It provides the basis for a new understanding of social citizenship where individuals are required from very young age to learn to engage with the risks of consumption constructively because there is no collective safety net that can undo the damage of failing to lead a healthy life, or that can adequately compensate for failing to make the adequate economic insurance provision for ill-health and frailty later in life (Higgs, 1998: 179).

In Ireland sports policy is being planned in a context of social change where for the first time the country is 'enjoying net immigration' through the return of emigrants and through migration from Eastern Europe, Africa and Asia. Not only is Ireland undergoing demographic change through migration, it is experiencing change in relation to family type and labour force composition. Young people are increasingly engaging in part-time work while they are still in full-time secondary education and there is an increase in one-parent families, cohabiting families and people living alone. These changes are precipitating speculative changes in sports policy which are seeking to compensate for the difficulties faced by many young people in making time for sports and in receiving the ongoing support and encouragement which has traditionally come from their families. The virtues of sport, health promotion and sports policy and their importance are clearly identified by the Irish Sports Council which warns of the future cardiovascular risks facing Irish primary schoolchildren today:

> We are required to do more to reduce the burden of poor health, disease and disability which reduction can come through involvement in sport. Research is showing a disturbing lack of health giving exercise in children still attending primary school. Inappropriate eating habits coupled with a sedentary lifestyle are leading to the onset of cardiovascular and related illnesses in adults who are still quite young and there is now increasing evidence of the onset of diabetes in children. There is a rise in obesity with 18 per cent of Irish adults now rated obese. The role of sport can play a part in helping to reverse these adverse trends is already reflected in public policy but it is clear that the order of effort required, including the cohesiveness of policies, programmes and implementation between sport, education and health, is much greater than now expended. (ISC, 2003:10).

The clear failure of most western states to reach the enormity of 'the order of effort' required to transform public policy into positive social health outcomes has been criticised by the International Obesity Taskforce in a report to the European Union Obesity Summit (2003) in its conclusion that health promotion schemes advocating improvements in diet and activity levels over many years have had no tangible impact. In most of Europe more of its citizens are overweight and up to one in three adults is clinically obese. Moreover, an emerging research focus on children by the International Obesity Taskforce is highly critical of the failure of government internationally to effectively tackle the child obesity epidemic and the attendant threat of diabetes (International Obesity Taskforce, 2003).

Welfare States are responding in varying ways to the societal risks posed by modern consumption habits and sedentary lifestyles. The everyday ordinariness of addiction, obesity, diabetes and heart diseases, has allowed health promotion to step 'into the public domain as a virtuous activity not only promoting health but also the person' (Higgs, 1998: 193). Health promotion contributes to a prevailing depiction of the welfare subject as an independent agent that can mould himself or herself according to freely taken lifestyle choices, and it provides the basis for a new understanding of social citizenship where 'the new citizen learns to engage with risks constructively because if he or she doesn't there is no collective security net waiting to make good the damage' (Higgs, 1998: 193). In other words, state welfare effort cannot be relied upon as a viable alternative to private insurance arrangements against ill-health and frailty over the life course.

Social capital and public health

A major dilemma for communitarian inspired health promotion campaigns is that comparative studies into the relationship between social capital and population health support the blindingly obvious hypothesis that the higher the level of income inequality in a society the 'steeper the gradient in health inequality' (Kennelly et al., 2002: 2). Population health studies show that people in Sweden live on average longer than people do in Britain or the USA. It is interesting to note therefore that obesity levels of Irish children estimated by the National Task Force on Obesity are extrapolated from UK data in the absence of agreed criteria in Ireland (Department of Health, 2005: 1). The modern paradox that wealth does not equal health is explained by the argument that egalitarian redistribution in less wealthy countries works to improve the psycho-social conditions of people's lives and thereby provides a source of individual self-respect which is essential for well-being (Kennelly et al., 2002: 2). Social capital has emerged in public health research debates as a potential variant for interpreting differential health outcomes in and between advanced capitalist countries (Williams, 2003: 56).

Two major interpretations of the relationship between income inequality and health are emergent. Neo-materialist interpretations argue that societies which tolerate greater income inequality under-invest in human, physical, health and social infrastructure and therefore undermine medical and social care systems. By contrast the psycho-social environmentalist interpretation argues that increased income inequality reduces social cohesion and social capital and that income inequality acts a barrier to the development of communitarian health-inducing social capital relations. It can be argued, however, that it is difficult to generate comparative research measures of social capital that incorporate effects such as the extent of interpersonal trust, norms of reciprocity, voluntary groups membership, and membership of social networks that maintain health improving behavior (Kennelly et al. 2002: 2). Despite these difficulties, the challenge of moving beyond individual level studies to explore population health inequalities has been taken up in Northern Ireland. Anthropological studies of culturally and religiously contrasting rural communities found positive associations between social capital and health outcomes in rural Catholic communities which – of significance to this chapter – were strongly associated with sporting activity and sporting organisations such as the Gaelic Athletic Association (Moore, 2004: 130). The research dilemma of whether to focus on individual level studies or population-based comparative studies remains common to contrasting interpretations of health inequalities. What is not in doubt, however, is that people who live in countries such a Sweden live on average two or three years longer than those in the USA and Britain where income differentials are wider (Kennelly et al., 2002: 2).

Social capital and sports policy

A major development since the publication of *The Economic Impact of Sport in Ireland* (Department of Education, 1994) and the establishment of the Department of Tourism, Sport and Recreation in 1996 has been that the social dimensions of sport have attracted growing attention in the context of a growing interest in the concept of social capital (Delaney and Fahey, 2005: 1). The concept of social capital is applied to sports policy debates in the same way as it is applied to public health debates. It refers to the nature of social interdependence between people in social networks which affect individual and collective well-being.

The OECD (2001) has advocated that social capital should be included as a dimension to be explored in addressing poverty and social exclusion (Liston and Rush, 2006: 73). The OECD define social capital as the social networks, norms, values and understandings that facilitate co-operation among and between groups (OECD, 2001: 41). More recently the American sociologist Robert Putnam has emerged as an influential advocate of the concept in shaping social policy debates in Ireland. The decline of collective participation in sport in the USA provides the central metaphor of *Bowling Alone*, Putnam's best-known book (Putnam, 2001), which is widely credited with stimulating contemporary public interest in the concept of social capital. Irish public policy debates have proved a fertile ground for Putnam's stark communitarian message that unless new forms of social engagement and social interdependence are shaped, our precious 'stock of social capital' will decline and with it all hope for 'a good society'. (Gillespie, 2005)

The crossover of social capital from being an exclusively academic concern to a popular concept of mainstream public policy and media debates in Ireland owes much to the promotion of social capital as a solution to a collapse of civic and community values (Fanning, 2004c: 58). In addition, official publications such as *The Policy Implications of Social Capital* (NESF, 2003b) have made social capital a central theme of public policy discourse in Ireland. An article in *The Irish Times* reporting on an address by Robert Putnam to the Fianna Fáil parliamentary party meeting sums up the popular appeal of social capital:

> So where did it all begin to go wrong? Materialism, individualism, the fall in Mass attendance, two career families, commuting, soulless suburbia. They've all been blamed on the gnawing feeling that, despite our economic success, our quality of life is declining. It's an observation shared by governments who are mindful that the key to retaining political power isn't just about the economy. Citizens also want a society that is compassionate, caring and supportive. There is a pervasive fear, that Irish society is going the way of the US, where life is increasingly characterised by urbanisation, individualism and disconnection. (Gillespie, 2005)

Social change and individual responsibility

The pitfalls of the US welfare system are well documented elsewhere in Irish health policy discussions concerning the application of social capital to analysis of health inequalities (Kennelly et al., 2002: 2). There are have been calls in Ireland from the medical profession for overweight Irish adolescents to follow their US counterparts down the controversial path of surgical and prescription drug treatment. Adolescents in the USA are treated with powerful weight reducing medication such as Xenical, which work by blocking the absorption of fat into the body. Some overweight adolescents do not respond to drugs and for those who do the average weight loss is modest, between five and ten per cent. Nevertheless endocrinologists in favour of surgical and medicinal responses have publicly argued that 'we are not treating obesity as aggressively as we should be' (McDonald and Tallent, 2005). In terms of treatment, health promotion and the scale of the obesity problem, it is argued that Ireland is eight years behind the USA. Yet in the USA practising health promoting behaviour 'is seen to represent individualism and upward mobility' where the pursuit of public health can be achieved by individual agency (Higgs, 1998: 182). Irish social policy whilst placing an emphasis on environmental support ultimately follows a not dissimilar strategy of social change based on individual action:

> The taskforce's social change strategy is to give people meaningful choice. Choice, or the capacity to change (because the strategy is all about change), is facilitated through the development of personal skills and preferences, through supportive and participative environments at work, at school and in the local community, and through a dedicated and clearly communicated public health strategy (Department of Health and Children, 2005b: 3)

In contrast to an emphasis on the pursuit of public health through individual action in the Republic, the Task Force on Childhood Obesity in Northern Ireland has argued that it is time to face up collectively to the harmful consequences which certain products can have on large sections of the population. The argument for a collective regulatory approach is made on the basis that that individuals, particularly children and parents cannot be continually burdened with option of poor choices and to 'constantly carry round a calculator' to establish food safety or non-safety levels (Northern Ireland Taskforce on Childhood Obesity, 2004: 8). In most western welfare states however a collective regulatory approach falls far short of the Finnish gold standard approach which involves extensive economic, agricultural and welfare restructuring.

In Ireland the importance attached to communitarian approaches and the concept of social capital within the public policy discourse can be gathered from the publication of reports such as *Inequalities in Perceived Health* (IPHI, 2005b) and *The Policy Implications of Social Capital* (NESF, 2003b). At a conference on social capital held in Dublin in March 2001, the Taoiseach Bertie Ahern stated that 'Social capital has potential to be a very positive influence in public policy development', and the Agreed Programme for Government (Government of Ireland, 2002c: 27) states 'We will work to promote social capital in all parts of public life'. The Institute of Public Health in Ireland report on perceived health inequalities focused on lifestyle behaviours (smoking, drinking, exercise and body mass), and social capital indicators included views about problems in the local area, views about services, social contacts, trust of neighbours and civic engagement. The report findings high-lighted that education, employment, income and housing tenure all impacted on health outcomes as did people's relationships with their neighbours and their frequency of contact with friends. Interestingly those who viewed their neighbourhood negatively were less likely to be healthy as were single people, who were more likely to smoke, drink excessively and less likely to exercise. In Ireland as elsewhere the relationship between sports policy and social policies aimed at promoting health have become increasingly emphasised (Fahey et al., 2004: 2) at a time when social capital has emerged a central concept for the analysis of habitual behaviour.

A major advantage for the pursuit of communitarian and social capital strategies in Ireland is that Irish social policy can produce empirical evidence to support the claim that organised sporting activity and associational life remains a vital part of Irish society which in turn can contribute to Irish welfare futures (NESC, 1996: 8). In contrast to the USA where the focus of studies such as *Bowling Alone* (Putnam, 2001) charts the decline of collective community-based sports activity, the official public policy discourse in Ireland argues in relation to sports policy development that 'social capital is one resource among others which can be used in support of community develop-ment' (Delaney and Fahey, 2005: 1; NESF, 2003b). This raises the question which has emerged within media debates in Ireland as to whether the erosion of civic life in the USA is a 'manifestation of American exceptionalism' rather than a universal trend (McDonald and Tallent, 2005). A universal link between increasing wealth differentials and reduced social cohesion (Kennelly et al., 2002: 2) would suggest that Ireland may be in serious danger of following an American trajectory in an erosion of social capital.

Communitarian Sport: The Gaelic Athletic Association (GAA)

The Policy Implications of Social Capital report found 'that over a quarter of Irish adults are members of a sports or recreation community or voluntary organisation compared to only just one in six on average across 32 European countries' (Liston and Rush, 2006: 82; NESF, 2003b: 62). The GAA plays a unique role in this distinguishing feature of Irish social life. The exceptional significance of sport to life in Ireland was given additional empirical analysis in the *Social and Economic Value of Sport in Ireland* report (Delaney and Fahey, 2005). The report relies on data from the Survey of Sports and Physical Activity which was carried out by the ESRI and the ISC in 2003 using a national sample of 3,080 adults. The report concludes that the Gaelic Athletic Association 'is by far the largest sports body in the country, and is the strongest representative of the voluntarist, community-based model of sporting organisation', with 2,595 affiliated clubs and an estimated membership of 700,000 people or 15 per cent of the population. (Delaney and Fahey, 2005: 110). The Ladies Gaelic Football Association launched a three-year strategic development plan at the Ladies Association Annual Congress 2006, entitled *Enhancing Lives and Communities for 100,000 players* (LGFA, 2006). The development plan reflects a massive growth of female interest in playing Gaelic football at all levels.

The GAA and the LGFA have over 20,000 active teams, 12,686 Gaelic football teams and 6,850 hurling teams. Staggeringly for a community and voluntary sports organisation, the GAA has physical assets in lands and buildings worth over €3 billion. In 2003 total attendance at inter-county championship games held in the summer months amounted to 1.9 million. This is an immense achievement for any voluntary organisation but it remains only a minor fraction of daily and weekly attendance at Cumman or club levels at team games played by male and female players aged from under 8, under 10, under 12, under 14, under 16 minors, junior B and seniors for the games of camogie, hurling and gaelic football. An average club or cumman will be organising some 20 teams of all ages, and each team will draw spectators, most of which are of course from the same families and extended families.

The aims of the GAA are historically overtly nationalistic and it is strongly allied to the Catholic Church (Delaney and Fahey, 2005: 12). A contemporary analysis of the relationship between Church life and sporting and community life is offered with reference to the predominantly Roman Catholic village of Ballymacross in Northern Ireland where the Gaelic Athletic Association is seen to reinforce social links in the local community and which distinguish it from other Catholic villages (Moore, 2004: 130). The description offered by Moore could be applied to the vast majority of rural Irish towns and villages, and the GAA also 'has a strong presence in urban areas' (Delaney and Fahey, 2005: 12). The GAA is not only committed to civic nationalism but also to the tenets of community voluntarism and amateurism. The danger of oversimplifying the complex relationship between the GAA and nationalism has been cautioned generally (Bairner, 2005: 2), and more specifically by studies which explore links between GAA and Cricket in County Westmeath (Hunt, 2005). A cross tabulation in the Survey of Sports and Physical Activity of membership of sporting organisations would probably reveal similarly that many adult members of GAA cumann are also involved as parents in rugby clubs, soccer clubs and community games. The distinguishing feature of the GAA, however, is the sheer scale of its membership and organisation.

Competitive team games

In comparison with the GAA, support for soccer is modest and there is no adequate record of community-based organisations and networks. While 'there is no systematic information on either the number or strength [of amateur soccer clubs in Ireland]' (Delaney and Fahey, 2005: 14), a clear indication of the scale of their organised competitive fixtures is evident from regional and local newspapers which show the various leagues organised between schoolboy, youth and adult fixtures. Informal soccer playing in similar sense to what Putnam refers to as 'Bowling Alone' – involving low levels of civic organisation and therefore lower levels of social capital – is reportedly higher than any other sport in Ireland, although because of the informal nature its contribution to social capital or levels of individual physical activity is hard to quantify. In Ireland the community organisation of the game of soccer at an amateur club level for adults and children is undoubtedly not sufficiently captured. A major weakness with regard to capturing the data on the many thousands of children and teenagers who play organised soccer on a weekly basis in leagues throughout the country is that the Football Association of Ireland is focused almost exclusively on support for the professional game and the national team. The amateur football league of Dublin does, however, offer a modest enumeration of 119 teams (Delaney and Fahey, 2005: 14).

In contrast to organised soccer's inability to offer concrete data on the amateur game, the Irish Rugby Football Union can boast a national affiliation of 205 clubs and the ISC reports that, despite its popularity in elite private schools, it has pockets of support from lower down the social class scale and from the emergence of the fun version of the game 'tag rugby' which is played in some schools and in mixed gender teams. (Delaney and Fahey, 2005: 15). With the ISC reporting only 115 amateur soccer clubs and 205 rugby clubs, and an implicit suggestion of low organised community involvement, it emerges that with over 2,500 affiliated clubs the Gaelic Athletic Association is totally unrivalled in Ireland, and probably internationally for the sheer scale and depth of its immersion in a society as a voluntary sporting organisation.

Non-team sports

Outside field-based competitive team games, golf involves the highest degree of organised membership. The Golfing Union of Ireland has 408 affiliated clubs with an estimated 350,000 members including junior players. Golf clubs are usually run on a voluntary basis with membership. Golf involves much less organised voluntarism in relation to team organisation and coaching although greater efforts are being made within the sport to generate data which capture the social organisational aspects of the sport and the contribution of golf to social capital in Ireland. For example, studies by the Club Managers Association and the Michael Smurfit Business School are helpful in this regard (Delaney and Fahey, 2005: 16). Swimming and soccer are reportedly the highest participant sports in Ireland with an estimated 17 per cent of male adults and two per cent of female adults playing on an informal basis. However the informal nature of soccer playing in non-league arrangements with colleagues and friends in five-a-side groups means the social capital contribution of informal soccer participation is difficult to capture. It is equally difficult to quantify the numbers of people who regularly go swimming alone or with friends on a regular basis. These activities contribute to individual physical fitness levels and to some extent to the maintenance of social capital through the provision of publicly owned swimming pools. Activities such as aerobics and weight training in private leisure clubs and gyms similarly contribute to individual fitness levels but operate on a commercial basis and contribute little to social capital.

Organising sport in Ireland

Organised sport in Ireland at the highest level falls under the responsibility of the Department of Arts, Sports and Tourism and the Irish Sports Council. The Irish Sports Council funds 64 National Governing Bodies of sport (NGBs). The Federation of Irish Sports which was founded in 2002 has 70 affiliated national governing bodies for sport. In addition Special Olympics Ireland organises year-round sporting activities and the organisation of Special Olympics World Summer Games 2003 involved 7,000 athletes, 3,000 coaches and 14,000 family members.

The Irish Sports Council Budget for 2004 was €29 million of which €8 million was allocated to 68 eligible NGBs. Funding is also allocated to groups such as the Older People and Sports organisation, the Special Olympics and the Irish Adventure Training Trust and the newly established local sports partnerships.

Sport, social life and well-being

Concern has been expressed about the relationship between team sports and alcohol consumption (Delaney and Fahey, 2005: 52,). In previous reports published by the ESRI it was concluded that 'ritualised behaviours' associated with some team sports such as hurling, Gaelic football, soccer and rugby could lead to higher alcohol consumption, higher risk of depression and mental health problems in later life (Fahey et al., 2004: 8). In relation to the benefits of social contact, over 50 per cent of males and females in the Survey of Sports and Physical Activity classified sport as important as a way of meeting friends and, importantly for public health debates, sports were classified as important for relaxation, health and fitness. Research findings from the SSPA suggest that older members of sports clubs drink more than the general population but also that they have higher levels of mental and physical well-being. Overall the conclusion offered by the *Social and Economic Value of Sport in Ireland* report in relation to competitive sports clubs and well-being is that

> We can say that sports club membership is part of a lifestyle package which is associated with healthier living, whatever the causal mechanisms maybe . . . members of sports clubs report higher levels of physical and mental well-being throughout the life cycle than the rest of the population. . . . Sports club membership seems to be part of a package that, relative to patterns in the rest of the population, is bound up with healthy living and successful ageing. (Delaney and Fahey, 2005)

The physical education programme: a communitarian approach

Research findings from the Institute of Public Health in Ireland (2005) report based on the Social Capital and Health Survey highlighted that people's trusting relationships with their neighbours and their frequency of contact with friends were important indicators in relation to high levels of beneficial social capital. The highly social nature of team sports, especially at a voluntary amateur level, stems from the simple axiom that competitive games bring people into social contact with each other (Delaney and Fahey, 2005: 69)

Overall the *Social and Economic Value of Sport in Ireland* report goes to great lengths to bring meaningful recognition to the wider contribution of competitive sports in Ireland to public health and well-being. The emphasis on the contribution of competitive sports to social capital in Ireland contrasts starkly with a research emphasis in Britain where a preferential emphasis is placed on the heath benefits of physical exercise rather than sports *per se* based on the assumption that the promotion of an active lifestyle may be a more useful strategy than the promotion of sports. Health promotion policies in Britain tend to focus on the negative aspects of competitive sports. The tendency to contrast the health benefits associated with regular physical exercise against the health risks associated with participation in competitive sports is now virtually ubiquitous within British welfare debates (Rush and Liston, 2006: 76)

A renewed emphasis on physical activity and physical education is being conceptualised in Ireland as a health promotion project that can to some extent rely on the social capital resources of competitive sports rather than seek to replace them. A good example of this approach is the physical education module in the transition year programme in secondary schools which has four modules that include a gaelic games module, a health, fitness and well-being module, a psychology for health and well-being module and a functioning of GAA club module. The physical education programme is offered on a pilot basis to six schools through a partnership by the GAA in conjunction with the sport support service. If it proves to be successful it will be offered free of charge to all schools. The benefits for the school are that the modules are delivered free of charge and therefore bring additional resources into the schools; the benefits for the GAA are that the course will enhance local volunteerism, for example though the provision of new young referees.

Conclusion

A close relationship between health promotion and voluntary competitive team sports is now emergent within Irish sports policy. The sheer depth of the society's immersion of Gaelic games and the Gaelic Athletic Association and competitive games in general is being revalued as a beneficial public health resource as opposed to a 'ritualised' threat. In order to appreciate the full extent of sports participation in Ireland, however, social survey data would benefit from the addition of 'user' data from National Governing Bodies – from records of individual and family membership and from league records kept throughout the country. The recent introduction of public funding to NGBs from the Irish Sports Council and the introduction of Local Sports Partnerships should accelerate data availability.

In relation to the wider conceptual development of sports policy in Ireland, the contribution of the disciplines of anthropology, sociology, economics and public health is invaluable. A greater emphasis on the relationship between sporting activity and health promotion in Irish social policy has emerged, however, at time when social theory and health studies are beginning to recognise that 'the body – remains theoretically elusive within many sociological narratives – constantly gliding out of analytical view' (Williams, 2003: 55). In relation to the social sciences these contemporary critical observations are compounded only by the more basic observation in relation to modern social theory that 'habit was progressively discarded from the language of sociology' (Camic, 1986: 1076). A new emphasis on habitual behaviour and social life has become central to the analysis of public health and the 'good society'. If the social science influence within social policy is to compete adequately with the natural science influence within public health debates then the academic research focus on 'habit' needs a long overdue revisitation.

This chapter began by welcoming a new emphasis within sports policy analysis on the experiences of people who play sports and those who achieve sporting excellence. A distinguishing feature of Irish society is that more than anywhere else people belong to sporting associations, and sports of all kinds play a large part in the organisation of social life in Ireland. There seems little doubt, therefore, that Ireland has a wealth of organised membership-based social capital although to date it has failed to prevent a dramatic rise in levels of obesity and public ill-health. To what extent social capital and associational sporting life in Ireland can survive a continuing neo-liberal economic trajectory towards greater income inequality remains to be seen. To what extent deepening income inequalities are reflected in the social division of sporting association membership also remains to be seen. In the meantime research reports suggests there are many in Ireland who engage in sports and many more who do not, an over-concentration on the latter to the exclusion of the experiences of the former may ill serve the development of sports policy and health promotion. Internationally, however, there seems little empirical doubt that whatever the social and economic value of sport, the goal of health promotion is best served by a reduction of income inequalities and a healthy degree of market regulation.

Recommended reading

Bairner, A. (2005) *Sport and the Irish: Histories, Identities, Issues.* Dublin: UCD Press.

Fanning, B. (2004c) 'Communitarianism, social capital and subsidiarity', pp. 42–61 in Fanning, B. et al. (eds), *Theorising Irish Social Policy.* Dublin: UCD Press.

Putnam, R. D. (2001), *Bowling Alone: The Collapse and Revival of American Community.* New York: Touchstone.

Part 3   Care

Chapter 9

Family policy and reproductive work

Michael Rush
Valerie Richardson
Gabriel Kiely

Introduction

The two main aims of European social policy are to improve the quality of life and to increase the employment rate for all, including for families with young children, because families remain the cornerstones of social solidarity in Europe (Cuyvess and Kiely, 2000: 12; Krieger, 2004: 1–11). There is, however, a paradox in public policy debates in Ireland and in the USA that 'the deepest anxieties of this prosperous age concern the erosion of our families' (NESF 2003b: 23; Reich, 2002). This chapter argues that social policy perspectives on the family in Ireland as depicted in the Final Report of the Commission on the Family, *Strengthening Families for Life* (Commission on the Family, 1988) bear similarities to a communitarian paradigm in the USA where the 'marriage benefit' argument equates the strength of the family with the strength of marriage and advocates that not only is marriage beneficial for children's welfare but that the 'erosion of marriage carries a price for both individuals and society' (Waite, 2004: 1, Lillard and Waite, 1995).

This chapter contrasts recent depictions of lone parent households and cohabiting families as a threat to the social status of marriage within the Irish policy discourse with findings from Census data and ISSP attitudinal data which show that attitudes as well as families are changing in Ireland. Data show that although radical changes are taking place in family arrangements and in the paid labour market where married women are increasingly active (Richardson 2003), there is a stubborn lack of change in the gender division of unpaid labour in the home. Here, by way of contrast with ongoing social capital frameworks of analysis in relation to the life–work balance (Willemsen, et al., 1998), the gender division of unpaid labour is explored in a comparative context to discuss an ideological continuum of care (Rush, 2005).

A major development in the comparison of social policies in Europe and OECD countries has been the approach which includes the classification of four different institutional types of welfare state: Scandinavian, Anglo-Saxon,

Continental European, and Southern European (Fotakis, 2000: 40). This chapter contrasts recent welfare reforms in the USA, a strong Anglo-Saxon type, where the conditional right for lone parents to care for children full time in the home has been eliminated (Orloff, 2002: 99), with the approach in Ireland, a weak Anglo-Saxon type, where the traditional policy strategy has been one of 'supporting poor lone mothers at home and maintaining welfare dependency' (Richardson, 1995: 134).

The chapter discusses cohabitation, marriage and lone parenthood in Ireland in the context of social citizenship and individualisation debates where it contrasts the Anglo-Saxon approach of individual equality, labour market participation, and male-bread-winning with the Scandinavian approach where the emphasis is on engendered labour market equality, social security, and the social inclusion of children through support for 'reproductive work' irrespective of family form (Sommerstad, 1997; Montanari, 2000; Kiely, 2004; Rush, 2004).

The chapter concludes that an ongoing commitment to social protection combined with a nascent commitment to limited social rights for cohabiting couples and a mixed economy of childcare (Richardson, 2003; Rush, 2003) serves to confirm Ireland's weakening Anglo-Saxon status within an enlarged Europe Union.

Social protection in Ireland: a weak Anglo-Saxon variant

Welfare states in Europe aim to secure social solidarity and social integration within systems of competitive capitalism. There is, however, what Stoesz (2002) refers to as an emerging morality of independence from the welfare state. The values of this morality of independence from the welfare state are most strongly expressed in the Anglo-Saxon model which is limited in Europe to the Irish and UK systems. (Taylor-Gooby, 2001: 137). Outside Europe a particularly strong variant of the model can be found in the US where an increasing significance of the labour market to social policy is driven by the traditional 'Anglo-Saxon separation of the deserving and undeserving poor', a distinction which Handler argues 'is creeping over western Europe' (Handler, 2003: 40). Within such systems, welfare is primarily organised to reinforce work incentives rather than as a response to needs.

As one of only two Anglo-Saxon countries in Europe, a distinctive feature of the Irish welfare system as a weak variant of this particular model is a strong societal commitment to social security and social protection. While the social security system within the United Kingdom is being altered to become more market reliant, by contrast in Ireland social protection is undergoing a gradual expansion within an overall commitment to social inclusion. (Daly and Yeates 2003: 95). In addition, analysis of International Social Survey Project attitudinal data by Peillon shows that a further distinguishing feature of attitudes to welfare legitimacy is that in Ireland there is high societal support not only for quality welfare services, as in Britain, but also for social transfers and social assistance (Peillon, 1996: 185). Further distinguishing evidence emerged from comparative research which showed that Ireland's One Parent Family Allowance stands out as a social benefit payment which is furthest removed from the Anglo-Saxon employment-based approach along an international continuum of social assistance payments (Eardley, 1996)

A continuing distinguishing feature of Ireland as a country within the Anglo-Saxon family is the exponential nature of the welfare state, particularly with regard to the development of public services, which are considered a central feature of economic development. The National Economic and Social Council (NESC) is the national statutory organisation pledged to analyse and report on strategic issues relating to the efficient development of the economy and the achievement of social justice in Ireland. In a report entitled *The Developmental Welfare State*, the NESC argued that Ireland's strong economic performance offers a new context for major improvements in social protection (NESC, 2005: xiii). The NESC regards the radical development of public sector services, in a mixed economy of welfare, as the most important route to improving social protection. *The Development Welfare State* report makes a case for 'tailored universalism' to accommodate social diversity in the context of knowledge based economy and a more egalitarian society (NESC 2005). The extent to which Ireland can improve welfare outcomes for poorer families, particularly those with young children, independent of labour market participation, in the midst of an international neo-liberal consensus which views social protection from labour market participation not only as illogical but also as immoral (Rush, 2005), is one of the major challenges facing the exponential Irish welfare state.

An ongoing commitment to social protection, independent of labour market participation, remains a core principle of the continental corporate system of central economic and social policy formulation known in Ireland as Social Partnership. Social partnership was born out of the economic crisis of the 1980s and it has been attributed to helping to generate a positive view of social policy and the welfare state in Ireland (Peillon, 2001; Daly and Yeates, 2003: 94). Social partnership is a feature of Continental Europe, which further distinguishes Ireland from other Anglo-Saxon regimes. Critical analysis of Ireland's reluctance to introduce models of employment-based social citizenship, particularly in relation to lone parents, argues that it stems from Ireland's willingness to maintain women and children on welfare as part and parcel of the general subordination of women as secondary earners and beneficiaries within the Irish welfare regime (Jackson, 1963; Richardson, 1995: 130; Conroy, 1998: 94; Rush 2004).

Lone parents and social protection

The introduction of a payment without time limits specifically to support lone mothers was introduced to Ireland in 1973 following a recommendation from the Commission on the Status of Women (1972). The latest official evaluation of the payment explored a variety of international approaches to social citizenship rights of lone mothers including the labour market approach of the USA (Department of Social, Community and Family Affairs, 2000: 42–50). In the USA eligibility to a cash assistance payment specifically for lone parents was replaced with the Temporary Assistance for Needy Families (TANF) which is time limited to five years over parents' lifetimes, thereby increasing the significance of the labour market to welfare, in particular for lone mothers and their children.

The Review of the One Parent Family Payment observed that the end of lone parent entitlement in America was preceded by 'a hardening of attitudes' which occurred following the development of 'influential underclass theories which held that the emergence of the lone parent family in the USA had made a significant contribution to social ills' (Department of Social, Community and Family Affairs, 2000: 47). Social policy theorists in the USA have argued that the social right for lone mothers to care for their children on a full-time basis was eradicated because 'wage work is the penance for illegitimacy' (Orloff, 2002: 99; Mink, 1998).

Instead of recommending the 'wage work' approach, the Review of the One Parent Family Payment (Department of Social, Community and Family Affairs, 2000) clearly stated that any introduction of time limits for lone parents, similar to those that exist in the USA was considered impractical and unacceptable for Ireland 'because the childcare infrastructure required to support such a condition is not in place yet' (2000: 83). A second major consideration in introducing time limits and work incentives would be the traditional depiction within Irish social policy that 'mothers of children should work full time at home' (2000: 34), and the strong body of opinion which believes 'the State should recognise the position of those who choose to stay at home' (2000: 84). In support of the case that time limits would be impractical for Ireland, the report cited the Minister for Justice, Equality and Law Reform who at the launch of the Equal Opportunities Childcare Programme (EOCP) 2000–6 reiterated that whether a parent decides to enter or 're-enter the workforce outside the home should be a matter of choice' (2000: 86).

Strong opinions along similar lines were expressed at the Irish Bishops Conference in 2004 that children who are in full day-care from two or three months of age are 'basically spending their childhood in care' (IBC, 2004). In contrast to the prevailing Anglo-Saxon concern of increasing the relevance of the labour market to the welfare of lone mothers, the traditional concern in

Ireland is the exact opposite, a position which is made categorically clear in Article 41.2 of the Constitution: 'The State shall, therefore, endeavour to ensure that mothers shall not be obliged by economic necessity to engage in labour to the neglect of their home duties'.

Births outside marriage to lone parent families and cohabiting families

More recently the traditional concern to protect all mothers from the labour market has been overshadowed by new concerns depicted in the Final Report of the Commission on the Family, *Strengthening Families for Life*, that the trend towards births outside marriage to lone parents and cohabiting families is eroding the social status of marriage (Commission on the Family, 1998: 182).

Although *Strengthening Families for Life* acknowledges that lone parents and cohabiting couples are legitimate objects for welfare, the report concluded that the family in Ireland should continue to be defined by marriage in accordance with 41.3.1 of the Constitution by which the state pledges to guard with special care the institution of marriage and to protect it against attack (1998: 191). The implicit policy goal of the Commission on the Family to halt the trend toward lone parenthood and cohabitation and to bolster the social status of marriage seems to have been overwhelmed by social change, as table 9.1 clearly demonstrates.

Table 9.1 demonstrates that non-marital families are increasing at a greater percentage rate than married families, and the most dramatic increase is in cohabiting couples with and without children. It is worth noting that the number of cohabiting families with children does not necessarily indicate shared biological parenthood, and until parents of children in such unions are obliged to register their shared biological children jointly it will be difficult to obtain accurate data in this regard.

Table 9.1 **Types of family in Ireland, 1996 and 2002**

Family Categories	1996	2002	Actual increase	% increase
Husband and wife without children	154,854	184,950	30,096	19
Cohabiting couple without children	18,640	47,907	29,267	157
Married couple with children	491,567	508,035	16,468	4
Cohabiting couple with children	12,658	29,709	17,051	134
Lone mother with children	108,282	130,364	22,082	20
Lone father with children	20,834	23,499	2,665	13

Sources: Census data, 1996, 2002

Strengthening Families for Life (Commission on the Family, 1998) argues that cohabitation throughout Northern and Western Europe is a 'relatively youthful practice' which is a transition towards marriage rather than a permanent widescale rejection of marriage (1998: 189), although analysis of the 1996 Census data led the Commission to conclude elsewhere that cohabitation in Ireland is in many cases a more permanent form of union (1998: 188). The increase in the amount of cohabiting families with children in the 2002 Census shown in table 9.1 would seem to confirm this.

Despite clear anxieties expressed in relation to the social status of marriage, recommendations for a greater recognition of family diversity within Irish family law have come from both the Constitutional Review Group (1996) and the Commission on the Family (1998). More recently the *Consultation Paper on the Rights and Duties of Cohabitees* published by the Law Reform Commission (2004) introduced a wide-ranging set of recommendations in relation to the legal, policy, property, succession, maintenance and social welfare rights of cohabiting couples.

The recommendations of the Law Reform Commission met, however, with stout criticism from the Irish Bishops Council. Although the IBC recognised those families in 'difficult situations' as legitimate welfare subjects, it argued strongly that any recognition of de facto unions otherwise described as 'forms of cohabitation of a sexual kind which are not marriage' and in particular 'legal recognition of homosexual unions would obscure certain basic moral values and cause a devaluation of the institution of marriage'. For the IBC what is at stake is 'the natural right of children to the presence normally of a mother and a father in their lives'. Equally worrying to the IBC as the 'looming debate' on de facto unions were official statistics on children born outside marriage that show 'more and more children are being born to single mothers, some of whom are very young' (IBC, 2004).

In contrast to the ongoing concerns of the Irish Bishops Council in relation to births outside marriage to very young mothers, findings from research commissioned by the Vincentian Partnership for Justice into young mothers and social inclusion showed that births to teenage mothers have been declining steadily in Ireland since 1980 (Richardson, 2001a: 26, Commission on the Family, 1998: 108). The data presented in table 9.2 confirm this trend and show that while more children are being born outside marriage the number being born to very young mothers is continuing to decline.

Table 9.2 shows that the demographic profile of non-married mothers in Ireland is changing and the higher percentage increases in births outside marriage are taking place in the older age groups from 25 to 44. Mothers aged forty and over had six times more children outside marriage than young mothers of 15 or under. It can be argued that a continuing emphasis on strategies to prevent unplanned teenage pregnancies, including relationship

Table 9.2 **Number of births outside marriage, 1994, 2002**

Age of mother	No of births outside marriage 1994	No of births outside marriage 2002	% increase
15 and under	67	59	–12
Under 20	2,218	2,721	23
20–24	4,023	6,458	60
25–29	1,811	4,839	167
30–34	828	2,926	253
35–39	379	1,399	269
40–44	83	321	386
45–49	5	12	140
Age not stated	103	139	34
Total	9,450	18,815	98.99
Overall Total	47,929	60,521	26.27

Source: Vital Statistics, 1994 and 2002

and sex education in schools remains critical for children's well-being, although it seems such strategies will be of limited relevance to the overall incidence of births outside marriage which occur predominantly in much older age groups.

From a situation in 1994 where about one in five births were outside marriage, such births have been increasing much more rapidly than births overall which has resulted in a situation in 2002 where nearly one in three births are outside marriage. It is concluded here that births outside marriage in Ireland can no longer be erroneously equated with teenage pregnancy or lone parenthood or framed as a 'social problem'; instead they are generating new social policy and family law responses which are extending social citizenship rights in the direction of families with children outside marriage.

Social policy and the International Social Survey Project (ISSP) data

International Social Survey Project (ISSP) data allow us to discuss the extent to which changing attitudes reflect changing family arrangements. The ISSP is a multi-country omnibus attitude survey that is repeated at five-year intervals. It is widely recognised that social science observations based on attitude survey data suffer from a number of shortcomings, although, in the absence of other convenient ways of accessing what people 'actually think', their usefulness is readily acknowledged by social scientists. The results from different studies in different national contexts over time show consistent patterns rather than random fluctuations. Findings from attitudinal studies have led to the specific conclusion that when analysing ISSP data it is 'reasonable to assume that something which has a relationship to social values is being measured' (Taylor-Gooby, 2001: 138; Evans, 1996: 202). The next section draws heavily upon findings presented from longitudinal (ISSP) data from surveys carried out in 1988, 1994 and 2002 (Rush, 2005b). Attitudes towards marriage, lone parenthood, cohabitation and raising children are discussed as well as findings in relation to the gender division of unpaid household labour.

Attitudes towards marriage, happiness and children

The ISSP revealed a decline in the percentage of male and female respondents who agreed with the statement that 'married people are happier'. The decline was greater among female respondents where a higher percentage disagreed that married people were happier. There was also a decline in the percentage of respondents who agreed with the statement that 'marriage is better if children are wanted'. Here the decline was less pronounced among the male respondents, where a clear majority still agreed with the statement, in contrast to the female respondents where attitudes were more evenly divided. Strong attitudes among respondents in relation to marriage being better for children were very uncommon.

Attitudes towards lone parents and children

In 1988 a higher percentage of respondents disagreed with the statement that 'one parent can raise children as well as two parents'. In 2002 a higher percentage of respondents agreed that one parent could raise children as well as two. Responsibility for this u-turn in attitudes rests largely with female respondents who since 1988 agreed with the statement in increasing numbers, although the data signal a slight hardening of attitudes towards lone parents among male respondents who agreed in decreasing numbers with the statement.

Occupation and attitudes towards families

Changes in the family in Ireland are matched by changes in the labour market where women, including married women, are increasingly active, giving occupational status a new significance to Irish attitudes (Richardson, 2003). From cross-tabulations of the data it was possible to classify attitudes by occupation in relation to two statements: the first statement was 'marriage is better if children are wanted' and the second statement was that 'one parent can bring up a child as well as two parents'. Farmers emerged as the only occupational group where a substantial majority percentage disagreed that one parent could raise a child as well as two parents. They were followed by agricultural and forestry workers (48.1 per cent) and professionals (47.9 per cent). In contrast the majority of people in most occupations agreed that one parent could a raise a child as well as two, including workers in textiles (71.4 per cent), engineering (63.1 per cent), construction (58.4 per cent) clerical (53.4 per cent) food and drink (50 per cent) and managerial (44.3 per cent). In relation to the statement 'marriage is better if children are wanted' farmers again emerged as far and away the most conservative group in favour of the marriage benefit, followed by agricultural and forestry workers.

These results in relation to farmers' conservative attitudes are notable because the welfare system in Ireland, including family policy, is increasingly influenced by Social Partnership negotiations where the four pillars of representation are Farmers, Trade Unionists, Employers and Voluntary and Community Groups (O'Donnell and Thomas, 1998; Peillon, 2001, Rush, 2004). According to the 2002 Census the number of people working in farming fishing and forestry has declined from 140,625 to 96,279 since 1996, and of these the vast majority (78,492) are farm owners or managers, and an even greater majority are male. The industry employs very few people directly. Farm owners and agricultural and fishery workers represented just over five per cent of the labour force in the 2002 which in total stands at 1,800,933 people.

Although the numbers employed in farming is haemorrhaging the continuing social status and influence of farmers are reflected in the centrality of the Farming Pillar to Social Partnership and to the construction of Irish social policy. The Farming Pillar were represented on the Parental Leave Review Group in 1998, where along with the Irish employers and the Department of Finance they were able to derail the primary recommendation of the Group that parental leave in Ireland should attract payment. Furthermore farming organisations as well as the employers were the only representatives on the Parental Leave Review Group who failed to support a recommendation to introduce statutory paid paternity leave. Farmers in Ireland continuously demand social solidarity from Irish society and the European community yet paradoxically fail to support the further extension of social citizenship rights to other working Irish parents. Such a position seems more paradoxical when male farmers themselves would be largely unaffected as an industry made up largely of self-employed sole traders, unless of course where farming-wives worked off-farm which would actually be beneficial to farming families.

Overall the ISSP findings showed that an overall majority of respondents supported the marriage benefit for children. A gender divergence of attitudes can be identified where male respondents held positive attitudes towards the marriage benefit in greater numbers and where female respondents hold positive attitudes to one-parent families in greater numbers. Attitudes are changing across a range of occupations, with the exception of the farming and agricultural and fisheries sector which remains a more conservative and predominantly male sector of the economy. Overall a diminishing minority of respondents held strong attitudes in favour of the 'marriage benefit'.

Attitudes towards cohabitation, and cohabitation as a transition to marriage

Favourable attitudes towards cohabitation increased to such an extent that by 2002 nearly two thirds of ISSP respondents agreed with the statement that 'it is all right to live together without intending to get married'. Similarly, the percentage of respondents who regarded cohabitation favourably as a transition to marriage also increased to the extent that by 2002 nearly two thirds of respondents agreed with the statement that it is acceptable to cohabit before marriage.

Overall findings from attitudinal data on cohabitation revealed a substantial majority of respondents were favourably predisposed to cohabitation both as a transition to marriage and as long-term family choice. An even more dramatic change of attitudes had taken place in relation to divorce where there was a complete u-turn in attitudes. Paradoxically, in 1988, several years prior to the introduction of the Family Law (Divorce) Act, 1996, a substantial majority of respondents agreed that divorce was too easy and that people did not take marriage seriously. By 2002, a sizeable majority agreed that divorce was the best solution when a couple could not solve their marital problems. Male respondents were slightly more predisposed than female respondents to regard divorce favourably

Overall the ISSP data showed an increase in positive attitudes to non-marital families whether in one-parent households or in cohabiting families and, paradoxically, in a situation where fathers outside marriage have very limited rights in relation to paternal registration and guardianship, the data show males to be slightly more predisposed to divorce and cohabitation than females but nonetheless see marriage as of benefit to children.

Children's rights to paternal identity outside marriage

Cohabiting families are ushering in changes to Irish family policy. However, in considering Irish family law in the context of the European Court of Human Rights, the Law Reform Commission highlights the fact that the concept of the *de facto* family remains unknown to the Irish constitution but concedes that the Supreme Court recognises that members of the *de facto* family 'might possess certain rights in the context of guardianship applications'. Such limited rights would not apply to fathers who had not lived in 'marriage like' relationships. Within such a legal and constitutional context non-resident and cohabiting fathers remain in a complex guardianship limbo leading to increasing criticisms from an otherwise burgeoning conservative fathers' movement in Ireland that the Constitution and the courts do not recognise the increasing diversity of modern families. In Britain the Children's Act, 1989 establishes that parental information is an essential factor in children's development. In Ireland a child born outside marriage has no automatic right to have their paternity established and there is no requirement to have a father's name on a birth certificate Adopted children have no rights to see their original birth certificate (Richardson, 2001b: 26; Rush, 2004). The Children's Rights Alliance and the Constitutional Review Group have both recommended a child's right to identity requires constitutional recognition (Richardson, 2001b: 26); however, family law debates in Ireland continue to frame the issue from the perspective of fathers' guardianship rights rather than a child's right to information.

The National Federation of Services for Unmarried Parents and their Children (Treoir) sought the establishment of a Central Register for joint guardian agreements following the introduction of the Joint Guardianship by Agreement (S.I. no. 5, 1998). Treoir are critical of the fact that such a register was not established under the recent Civil Registration Act. The requirement to register fathers of children born out of wedlock and to register guardianship agreements is not only an issue of socio-genetic connectedness and child well-being (Rush, 2004; Owusu-Bempah and Howitt, 1997) but also of significance to the longitudinal measurement of child well-being for social policy. This observation has emerged from researchers in the USA investigating cohabitation and family instability who have argued that social science research into family instability and children's well-being has been preoccupied with the impact of transitions into and out of marriage to the extent that a substantial amount of instability is being missed (Kelly-Raley and Wildsmith, 2004: 218).

Cohabitation 'qualified' for social citizenship rights

The *Consultation Paper on the Rights and Duties of Cohabitees* (Law Reform Commission, 2004) defines 'qualified cohabitees' as persons who live together in a 'marriage like' relationship for a continuous period of three years or, where there is a child, for two years. This includes same-sex or opposite-sex couples, where neither is married to each other or to another person. The Law

Reform Commission argument for excluding any person who is already married is that Article 41 of the 1937 Constitution necessitates such exclusion. A leading communitarian advocate of the marriage benefit in the USA describes cohabitation for the purposes of scientific investigation as a situation where 'two people live together for their own strictly private reasons, and carry their own, strictly private bargain about the relationship, without any legal or social pressures, we call that relationship, not marriage but "cohabitation"' (Waite, 2004: 1).

Ireland is moving away from treating cohabitation as a strictly privatised arrangement towards a Scandinavian approach in which cohabiting couples and their children are treated as full welfare subjects within the tax and welfare systems. The Scandinavian approach differs within each Nordic welfare system and there are instances of disparities and inconsistencies in each country. For example, although Swedish family law is based upon a declared neutrality between different family forms, only couples with shared biological offspring are entitled to a survivor's pension. The situation is similar in Norway. A Danish anomaly means cohabiting couples are treated more favourably for pensions purposes. In the Netherlands the household rather than the family is the basic social unit where 'sharing a household' is the important factor and where married and cohabiting couples are treated equally.

In Germany, a good example of a Continental European welfare model, the problem of cohabitation has been strongly contested between the left and the right with Christian Democrats wishing to maintain strong links between the constitutional definition of the family and marriage (Hatland, 2001: 130–2; Agell, 1980). Although Ireland is moving closer to a Scandinavian approach in relation to treating cohabiting couples as full welfare subjects, it is retaining a Continental European and Christian Democratic approach to marriage and the Constitution. The main disparity emerging from this approach is that cohabiting couples in Ireland who are already married will fall outside the entitlements of 'qualified cohabitation' and attendant social citizenship entitlements.

Social policy and attitudes towards raising children

The next section discusses attitudes towards raising children. The ISSP data revealed a modest decline in the percentage of respondents who regarded raising children positively, although the overwhelming majority of respondents still agreed with the statement that watching children growing was one of life's greatest joys. In addition the decline in favourable attitudes to raising children was accompanied by a shift toward ambivalence which was more pronounced among male respondents, where nearly one in six males failed to register a positive response. Such findings might lend support to the 'flight from fatherhood' hypothesis which contends that the escalating private ec‹ costs of families is driving men away from choosing household fath‹ (Rush, 2004; Jensen, 1994).

Egalitarian attitudes towards children have been traditionally depicted within policy discourse since the 1916 Proclamation of the Republic of Ireland declared that the pursuit of happiness and prosperity would involve 'cherishing the children of the nation equally'. In the past, however, these depictions of children as highly and equally valued by Irish society have not been translated into public policies. On the contrary, in keeping with an Anglo-Saxon model of welfare Ireland has traditionally subscribed to the 'maximum private responsibility' model of childcare as described by the OECD review of childcare policies as where the state intervenes only to provide a safety net of minimal childcare support for the poor or children at risk (Kiely, 1998: 98; Richardson 2003). Elsewhere, welfare states within the European union differ in their emphasis between public or private responsibility, although within an overall EU policy goal of gender equality it is becoming increasingly difficult for countries to maintain the 'maximum private responsibility' approach to children (Kiely, 1998: 99).

In contrast to the maximum private responsibility model, European social policy supports 'reproductive work' through a threefold package of services and social transfers which include: marriage or household taxation subsidies, universal child benefits and subsidised childcare services (Montanari, 2000). The concept of reproductive work is most clearly articulated in Scandinavian states where the 'maximum public responsibility' model is more highly developed. Within Scandinavian social policy it is argued that the equalising effects of complementing parental child care with non-parental childcare in the public sphere are superior in comparison with family or market solutions (Montanari, 2000: 328; Bjornberg, 2002: 36). Childcare has emerged within Irish social policy both as social inclusion measure and as a central mechanism in the gender division of paid employment and unpaid labour (Rush, 2003a).

The gender division of paid and unpaid labour

The radical changes in female attitudes to marriage, cohabitation, and lone parenthood, which are evident in findings from the ISSP surveys, can be placed against a background of a huge shift in the gender division of paid work in the Irish labour market. One of the more major changes that have taken place in Irish society has been the increase in the labour market participation rate of married women (Richardson, 2003: 3). In 1971, the participation rate, for married women in paid employment, was 7.5 per cent, which rose to 48.8 per cent in 2004. The labour market participation rate of married women in 2004 is not dissimilar to the participation rate of women overall which stands at 49.5 per cent (NQHS, 1st quarter 2004).

Overall the participation rates of women with children, whether in couples or autonomous lone parent households, are not dissimilar. However, recent reports from the Irish Congress of Trade Unions (2002: 10–13) and the Equality Authority both serve to show that parental childcare responsibilities are a major contributory factor to women's lower working hours and lower hourly rates (Richardson, 2003). Despite this situation, the highest participation rate of married women in the workforce (75.5 per cent) is between the ages of 25 and 34 'coinciding with the age when women are most likely to have young children' (Richardson, 2003). Recent estimates of non-parental childcare practices in Ireland show that 73,000 or 42.5 per cent of all families with pre-school children regularly rely on non-parental childcare arrangements (NQHS, childcare module 2002). Usage of non-parental childcare is less common for families with primary-school-going children, which may signal that it is at this juncture that the freedom for mothers to remain in the labour force comes under pressure, particularly in the absence of paid or unpaid out-of-school childminding supports.

The beginning of a proactive approach on the part of the state to childcare emerged from Social Partnership negotiations when trade unionists and other social partners, including women's organisations, highlighted the necessity for developing concrete measures to bring about a greater provision of childcare facilities. Subsequently an Expert Working Group on Childcare was established which culminated its work with the publication of *National Childcare Strategy* (Department of Justice, 1999). The strategy has provided the basis for the state to embark on developing a national childcare infrastructure by establishing city and county childcare committees throughout the country for the co-ordination of childcare delivery (Richardson, 2003; Rush, 2003b). Childcare is defined in the strategy as:

> day care facilities and services for pre-school children and school going children out of school hours. It includes services offering care, education and socialisation opportunities for children to the benefit of children, parents, employers and the wider community (Department of Justice, 1999)

The model of childcare being pursued in rural areas of Ireland where there is a marked absence of a market-based supply is being described as 'combination care'. The model seeks to combine parental care in the home with centre-based care, out-of-school services and child-minding A social inclusion perspective on childcare is developing in Ireland, which seeks to offer complementary care to parents, whether or not they are in paid employment (Rush, 2003a).

Individualisation, women in the home and shared household incomes

A social preference for home-based childcare, which is strongly depicted in *Strengthening Families for Life* (Commission on the Family, 1988; Rush, 2004; Fanning, 2003), can be to some extent evidenced from the Quarterly National Household Survey (QNHS, First Quarter 2004) which shows 557,800 people with a principal economic status of home duties, of which 553,400 or 99.21 per cent were women. Women in the home constitute a sizeable number of Irish parents with very little attention paid to them by researchers or policy makers and they receive minimal reward and status for their work (Richardson, 2003; O'Connor 1998).

Stay-at-home parents groups in Ireland, including Women in the Home (WITH), constitute a sizeable social force which was last spurred into opposition when the government announced 'individualisation' taxation proposals. The Budget 2000 was presented to the public as an attempt to bring Ireland further down the path of individualisation by giving dual earner families a lower tax liability than single breadwinner families to encourage more married women into the workforce. The change was maintained, but only after intense public debate and lobbying from stay-at-home parents resulted in the parallel introduction of a tax-free allowance for carers of children, the disabled or the elderly. The allowance was welcomed as a partial recognition of both the value of unpaid labour carried out in the home by stay-at-home parents, and of the social protection from the labour market for mothers, which is guaranteed under Article 41 of the Irish constitution.

Within theoretical welfare debates there are strongly contested frameworks of 'individualisation'. For advocates of a Scandinavian labour market equality approach it concerns women's liberation from income dependency on male-breadwinners In contrast with an Anglo-Saxon *laissez-faire* approach, where individualisation refers to 'a set of beliefs that puts paramount importance on the rights and freedoms of individuals and the power of free-market mechanisms' (Kiely, 2004).

Individualisation approaches are highly developed in Denmark, Finland and the Netherlands and to a lesser extent in Sweden and Norway, where in the latter case family related benefits are of much greater importance. A central anomaly, however, within the Nordic individualised systems is that family status is quite simply replaced by shared household status, particularly in relation to means-tested social assistance schemes. Another huge anomaly within these individualised social security systems, where family status is supposed to be meaningless, is that a prerequisite of shared biological parenting is a condition for entitlement to the major benefit of a survivor's pension; this is particularly the case in Sweden and Norway (Hatland, 2001).

It seems the shared family household, including the one parent household, remains a central unit of social solidarity and social policy, even within highly individualised welfare system, and one that is critical for children, who for obvious reasons cannot live alone. The shared household family unit remains of critical relevance to social policy particularly in relation to incomes policy and social assistance. The ISSP survey asked respondents to choose a category which best described their approach to the organisation of household income and the findings revealed that overall the stable 'mode' or pattern was towards couples pooling all or some of their income. Thus households where one partner managed the family income were a declining minority. The rise in individualisation where people did not pool their incomes at all rose from 3.0 per cent 1998 to 7.9 per cent in 2002 but it remained the exception rather than the rule which is reflected in the Irish welfare system where individual-isation maintains a virtually peripheral status. (Kiely, 2004).

The gender division of household tasks

Any findings which reveal a trend towards pooling financial resources fail to illustrate the actual gender division of organising household finances and in general very little research evidence is available in Ireland on unpaid work or household tasks. The Eurobarometer study (Malpas and Lambert, 1993) showed that in Ireland as many as 84 per cent of men said they did not have primary responsibility for even one of a selection of household tasks. A study of Irish urban families found that apart from household repairs, mothers carried most responsibility for household tasks and child care duties. In addition mothers emerged as the managers of the internal affairs of the family and this was in spite of over 80 per cent of the mothers expressing the view that husbands should share housework equally (Richardson, 2003; Kiely 1995).

The Eurobarometer study (Malpas and Lambert, 1993) showed that Ireland was similar to other European countries in the tasks undertaken by fathers and mothers. *Strengthening Families for Life* (Commission on the Family, 1998) argued that fathers in Irish society are reinforced in their traditional roles of household inactivity by the existing system of work patterns where men work longer hours than women, and by prevailing patriarchal social attitudes that view care work as women's work (Richardson, 2003; McKeown et al., 1998).

The depiction of care work as women's work is common to British welfare debates that recast work in the home within community care critiques to argue that caring reinforces the economic dependence of women (Johnson, 1999; Graham, 1997), whereas Scandinavian debates combine care and house-work under the banner of 'reproductive work' and publicly valorise it through advertising campaigns which encourage men and fathers to do their fair share (Bergman and Hobson, 2002). Similar efforts to valorise reproductive work and to highlight the social and economic value of unpaid labour have been made within the Irish policy discourse (Lynch and McLoughlin, 1995; Fahey, 1991; Kiely, 1995; 1998).

More recently theories of social capital have been used as frameworks in studies to investigate whether social policies influence the actual behaviour of men and women especially in relation to the gender division of paid work, childcare and unpaid household work (Richardson, 2003; Willemson and Finking, 1995; Rush, 2004). Research findings from one of these studies in Ireland has led to the conclusion that public policies were influencing the gender division of paid work through increased female participation without any significant impact on the gender division of unpaid work (Richardson, 2003) The findings from the ISSP Survey data support these previous findings and show that despite the overall emphasis on gender equality and making men into fathers (Hobson, 2002; Rush, 2004) within social policy discourses, female survey respondents are reporting an increase in their share of unpaid work rather than a decrease. In 2002 female respondents who answered positively to 'usually' or 'always' doing the laundry had risen to 90.1 per cent. From comparative analysis it was revealed that the Anglo-Saxon countries reported the least uneven distribution of unpaid domestic labour; however ISSP survey findings supported the conclusion that social policies across the different regime types have little impact on the gender division of unpaid domestic labour.

Similarly of those 'always' or 'usually' caring for the sick, the percentage of female respondents who responded positively rose from 55 per cent in 1994 to 63.8 per cent in 2002. The percentage of respondents who agreed that men and women shared the care of sick family members equally actually declined between 1994 and 2002. Overall the ISSP data seem to suggest that stability rather than change characterises the gender division of unpaid labour where female respondents are suggesting their share of the unpaid labour is increasing rather than decreasing. Similar findings were evident across a range of household tasks including grocery shopping, preparing the dinner, and cleaning. Stability rather than change is reflected in the responses to small repairs around the house where, in 2002, 80.4 per cent of men replied that they always or usually carried out small home repairs compared with 76.8 per cent in 1994.

Table 9.3 locates Ireland as being slightly right of centre in an ideological continuum of care, where on the left of the continuum the Nordic countries report the relatively high incidences of care-work for the sick being 'equally shared' while on the right, the Continental European countries report the lowest rate of gender egalitarianism in relation to the division of care-work. These findings suggest importantly that there maybe significant differences in

Table 9.3 **Care for sick family members, 2002**

Female Respon- dents	Norway	Sweden	Nether lands	USA	Great Britain	Ireland	Aus- tralia	Germany (West)	Northern Ireland	Aus- tria
Me	49.6	47.7	54.6	59.8	62.4	63.8	65.6	67.6	71.0	77.0
Equal	49.6	50.0	43.6	38.3	36.3	34.7	33.1	30.2	26.9	21.6
Partner	0.8	2.3	1.8	1.9	1.3	1.5	1.3	2.1	2.0	1.4
Total	100	100	100	100	100	100	100	100	100	100

Source: Rush (2005) from ISSP data.

the gender division of unpaid work across welfare states and that furthermore; national social policies can influence the gender division of unpaid care work as well as the gender division of paid work (Rush, 2005).

Social justice in the home

Despite the fact that the ISSP data suggest that men do very little in the home, over half of the male respondents were under the impression that household tasks were fairly evenly divided compared to about one third of female respondents. In total 61.2 per cent of female respondents answered that they did more household tasks than their male partners. A majority (76.9 per cent) of female respondents answered that they never or rarely had disagreements about the division of household tasks, which tallied well with the male responses (73.5 per cent). Over 90 per cent of male and female respondents expressed happiness in relation to their family lives.

Conclusion

O'Connor (2003, 398) has argued that liberalism stemming from a British colonial heritage may be gaining greater salience within the Irish policy discourse as the influence of the Catholic Church declines (see pp. 13–14 above). This chapter has shown that the influence of the Continental European values of Christian Democracy and social justice can still contest any shift toward economic liberalism because in Ireland the unconditional constitutional (but not financial) right for a mother to raise her children in the home contrasts strongly with the conditional right to labour market participation. Evidence of this is clear from the emerging policy discussions on the social citizenship rights of lone parents and cohabiting families.

Further indications of the strength of European Christian democratic values of social justice within Irish society can be gained from the relatively uncontested debate in relation to extending social citizenship rights to cohabiting families in comparison with the vociferous defence of the privileged status of marriage within the Constitution.

The ongoing debate into children's rights in relation to biological and genetic identity, and fathers' rights and the policies in relation to the work–life balance seems to be having no impact on the unfair distribution of unpaid reproductive work in the home. The ISSP survey merely reveals more of the same in Ireland – or even a bit more again of the same – in the case of unpaid work for women.

The emergence of a 'fertility gap', where women are reporting that they have fewer children than they would like to have, may be partly a result of the lack of social justice in relation to men not sharing unpaid reproductive work and the prohibitive costs of market-based childcare. This situation may also partly explain the rise in one-parent households. The value of reproductive work in the home provides a rhetoric of opposition in Ireland to Anglo-Saxon models of employment-dependent social citizenship.

Irish social policy is committed through taxation policies to increasing female employment. It is also still committed to retaining social protection and social citizenship for people outside the labour market. The statutory recommendation of a shift towards a more employment-focused 'participation income' (NESC, 2005), however, threatens to re-shape social citizenship in Ireland. Meanwhile, Ireland retains a commitment to marriage in the Constitution similar to the position under the German Basic Law, although despite this conservative stance, it is developing a nascent commitment to childcare provision outside the home. In comparative terms Ireland scores high on social citizenship and high on labour market participation, falling somewhere between Continental Europe and the Nordic models.

The limited constitutional 'right' to raise children in the home independent of labour market participation and, more recently, the extension of the social inclusion agenda into the provision of childcare indicates commonalities with elements of both Continental European and Scandinavian welfare goals. If Scandinavian and Continental European approaches are to be borrowed from it would require a shift away from an emphasis on employment-based welfare (the developmental welfare state approach advocated by NESC) towards one on the social (as well as economic) well-being of children. This would mean adopting goals of improving welfare outcomes for all adults independently of their labour market status.

Recommended reading

Department of Social, Community and Family Affairs (2000) *Review of One Parent Family Allowance Payment.* Dublin: Stationery Office.

Kiely, G. (2004) 'Individualisation, pp. 62–77 in Fanning, B. et al. (eds,), *Theorising Irish Social Policy.* Dublin: UCD Press.

Richardson, V. (2001) 'Legal and constitutional rights of children in Ireland', pp. 21–44 in Cleary, A. et al. (eds) *Understanding Children Volume 1: State, Education and Economy.* Cork: Oak Tree.

Rush, M. (2004) 'Fathers, identity and well-being', pp. 95–111 in Fanning, B. et al. (eds), *Theorising Irish Social Policy.* Dublin: UCD Press.

Chapter 10

The childcare question

Nóirín Hayes
Siobhán Bradley

Introduction

When major policy initiatives are undertaken, they are usually in response to new changes, needs and developments in the wider social fabric (NESF, 2005b). Irish society has undergone rapid transformation since the mid-1990s, both in terms of its economic development and its changing social and demographic structures. The impact of these changes on lifestyle choices has led to a unprecedented debate on the role the state should play in caring for families and supporting them in meeting their childcare responsibilities.

The changing demographic, social and economic context of Ireland, and the subsequent increased demands for childcare services as female labour force participation grew, highlighted many inadequacies in the provision of quality, affordable childcare places and the reconciliation of work and family life. This was complemented by a growth in recognition and acceptance of the developmental benefits of quality education and care in the formative years, and the positive effects such experiences could have on social cohesion and economic prosperity. The combination of these developments moved childcare to the fore of the political agenda, improving government intervention, support and funding in a policy area which had previously developed in an *ad hoc* and inconsistent manner, largely dependent on the support and commitment of voluntary, community and private organisations and individuals.

Any discussion of childcare requires a clear understanding of what exactly is being considered. In the main childcare refers to two different service types: (1) for younger children childcare has come to mean early childhood education and care (OECD, 2000; 2004) and refers to a wide variety of settings in which the raising of children is shared with the family including childminding and various forms of centre-based provision (OECD, 2004; NESF, 2005b) and (2) for older children, generally up to about the age of 12 years, childcare refers to the variety of afterschool arrangements that exist to meet differing needs at different times. The early childhood sector of childcare has generated far more discussion and policy action than the afterschool sector – which remains relatively unsupported and unregulated. With the exception of the recently published document on afterschool care *School Age Childcare in Ireland: Report of the National Childcare Co-ordinating Committee* (Department of Justice, Equality and Law Reform, 2005) there has been very little published on this aspect of childcare. In light of the fact that the policy emphasis to date has largely focused on early childhood education and care, this area of childcare will form the central component for analysis and discussion hereafter.

Demography

The 2002 population of 3.92 million was the highest recorded since the Census of 1871 (CSO, 2003a). Children aged under 14 accounted for more than a fifth of the total population (21.1 per cent) and children aged under six accounted for almost half of this group (46.5 per cent). The number of births has been increasing consistently since 1995 reaching a total of 61,517 in 2003, an increase of 2.1 births per 1,000 between 1994 and 2003 (NESF, 2005b). Much of this increase was attributed to the increase in the number of women of prime childbearing age (i.e. those aged 20–39 years), rather than increases in average family size; while some further increase in the number of births is predicted it is unlikely that the current number of births will be maintained beyond the next few years (CSO, 2004a).

Table 10.1 **Children under six years in Ireland, 2002**

	No.	% of total (0–14 years)
Under 1 year	54,499	6.6
1–2 years	111,709	13.5
3–4 years	111,422	13.5
5–6 years	107,082	12.9
7–14 years	442,716	53.5
Total (0–14 years)	827,428	100.0
Total population	3,917,203	21.1

Source: CSO, National Census of Population 2002, vol. 1, table 1

Recent years have witnessed a significant reversal of trends. Since 1996, there has been a downward trend in the number of emigrants together with a strong rise in the number of immigrants. Net immigration reached a peak of 41,000 in 2002 but fell back to 32,000 in 2004, yet even with this recent decline, CSO projections estimate immigration figures of between 250,000 and 300,000 for the period from 2002 to 2011 (CSO, 2004a). Immigration has led to the creation of a more multicultural society with an increasing proportion of immigrants originating from beyond European and US borders; almost 30 per cent in 2004 were nationals from outside the EU or USA.

In tandem with the overall demographic growth, there has been a growth in diversity of household types owing to increases in lone parenthood resulting from separation, divorce, widowhood, and births outside marriage. The number of divorces granted more than trebled from 9,800 to 35,100 between 1996 and 2002, reflecting the impact of the divorce legislation introduced in 1997. The number of separated (including divorced) persons increased by two thirds between 1996 and 2002 (from 87,800 to 133,800). Of the 61,517 births in 2003, almost one third or 19,313 occurred outside marriage, compared to 12,797, or just over a quarter in 1996 (CSO, 2004c).

Naturally, the increasing and diverse population and the growth in different household types have major implications for childcare policies as the level and type of need amongst households with children continue to diversify.

Economic growth and employment

Perhaps the most pertinent change, and that which has had greatest impact on childcare need in Ireland in recent years, is that of Ireland's unprecedented economic growth and its subsequent impact on labour market behaviour. Between 1994 and 2002, Ireland's GDP increased by 9.0 per cent annually, the highest rate of GDP growth of any OECD country in this time (Haughton, 2005). In 2003, Ireland had the second highest GDP per capita within the enlarged EU, which was almost one-third higher than the EU 25 average (CSO, 2005a). A decade earlier, Ireland was one of the poorest members of the EU, perceived at home and abroad as something of an economic laggard. The country has since reversed this image, moving to a position of virtually full employment with an active recruitment policy for migrant workers (NESF, 2005b).

Between 1993 and 2003, the total number in employment grew from 1.2 million to 1.8 million – an increase of over 51 per cent (CSO, 2005a). Increases in labour demand have been met by falling unemployment levels, increases in female labour market participation and labour immigration. It is the increase in female labour force participation in particular that has brought childcare to the fore of the political agenda in recent years. The number of women at work outside the home rose from 483,000 in 1995 to 771,000 in 2004, an increase of 60 per cent. The participation rates for younger women, in the 25–34 age group is now well over 60 per cent (NESF, 2005). Such increases are primarily due to the increased participation rate of married women and it is predicted that these increases will continue for the next decade. By 2006, it is expected that over 65 per cent of all married women aged between 30 and 50 years will be in the labour force, a figure that will be up from under 30 per cent less than 20 years ago (O'Hagan and McIndoe, 2005). Fifty-four per cent of women with a child under five years of age are now in employment. This major and ongoing change in the make-up of the workforce has profound implications for traditional child-rearing practices (NESF, 2005b).

As demand for childcare places intensified, the consequences of the *laissez-faire* approach to childcare adopted by successive governments became evident with many families experiencing substantial difficulties in balancing their work and family responsibilities. The historical position of women as carers within the home and the traditional approach adopted by successive governments, where care for children was viewed as a private matter, has shifted as the incidence of both parents earning becomes a regular pattern of family life. The long-standing neglect of childcare services has meant that families have limited and costly choices and children are subject to services of variable quality with little guarantee of appropriate developmental care, education and support. The increasing pressure on the state to address and respond to childcare shortages coincided with a more powerful ideological movement towards the value of children in their own right. Consequently all services accessed by children should place the needs and rights of children at their core and any such services should acknowledge children as individual citizens.

Tracking childcare policy

Internationally, during the latter part of the twentieth century, increased policy and legislative attention to the constituency of childhood, children and children's rights became evident. Notably, this included the UN Convention on the Rights of the Child (UN, 1989), which Ireland ratified in 1992. When Ireland became a state party to the Convention, it made a formal commitment to safeguard the rights of children and the Convention influenced the development of the National Children's Strategy (Department of Health and Children, 2000a).

The growing interest in the needs and rights of children, who traditionally have been 'conceived of in terms of their status within families, rather than as individuals in their own right' (CPA, 2005) has led to an enhanced commitment to ensure that policies and provisions directed at children are inclusive, comprehensive and appropriate to the needs of children in changing societies. Article 18 of the Convention endows children with a right to childcare:

> States Parties shall . . . render appropriate assistance to parents and legal guardians in the performance of their child-rearing responsibilities and shall ensure the development of institutions, facilities and services for the care of children . . . take all appropriate measures to ensure that children of working parents have the right to benefit from child care services and facilities for which they are eligible'. (UN, 1989, Article 18.2; 18.3)

The need for policy reform in the area of childcare in Ireland became evident well in advance of the ratification of the Convention. A series of different influencing factors, international and national, came together to give a critical momentum to the childcare debate. Internationally pressure came from Europe when, in the 1970s, Ireland was required to respond to directives on employment equality. The requirement that EU countries treat men and women equally with respect to pay and opportunities led to changes in employment policy and legislation which, along with other factors, contributed to a gradual increase in the number of Irish women working outside the home. Initially the childcare requirements of this group were met informally through family or neighbourhood childminding but gradually, as numbers increased, the call for state support of childcare became a political issue.

In addition to the influence of EU directives, increased funding was made available for the development of childcare services and associated training and research. Although children as a group do not come within the legal competence of the EU, childcare was one of the sectors eligible for European funding under a number of different programmes. Such funding led to the establishment of a number of pilot childcare projects at local level in Ireland. These initiatives coincided with the work of the European Childcare Network which highlighted, among other things, the very low level of state support for childcare in Ireland when compared to all other European countries (European Commission, 1996).

Nationally, the most influential factor has been the increased participation of women in the workforce, which has been actively encouraged in recent years because of the buoyant economy and associated labour shortages. A growing demand for action on childcare preceded any policy attention and gave rise to a flurry of committees and reports during the 1980s and 1990s, among them the *Report of a Working Party on Child Care Facilities for Working Parents* (Department of Labour, 1983) and the *Report on Minimum Legal Requirements and Standards for Daycare Services* (Department of Health, 1985). Because of the relatively limited response to these reports a second report on the childcare needs of working parents was published in 1994.

By this time the Childcare Act, 1991 had been published and it was the first piece of legislation to contain a section outlining a mechanism for the regulation of preschool services. Despite this there was a very limited response at a political or practical level and childcare services in Ireland remained unregulated until January 1997 when the relevant section of the 1991 Act was enabled. In the absence of policy and support there was an *ad hoc* growth in service provision, which gave rise to varied quality, distribution and costs.

Growing economic prosperity and a shortage of workers led to employer organisations and unions adding their voice to demands for childcare, an identified barrier to the full participation of women in the labour force.

Recognition by parents and professionals of the broad educational value of quality childcare experiences for children themselves led to increased private provision and to calls for a co-ordinated and integrated childcare strategy for all children (Hayes, 1995). The indirect role quality childcare services play in wider society has also been demonstrated by research showing the positive impact of quality early childhood services on disadvantaged children and their families. Furthermore, studies have linked the long-term economic benefits that derive from reduced costs in education, health and criminal justice to the provision of supportive childcare to families of 'at risk' children from a young age (Heckman and Cunha, 2005; Schweinhart, 2005). The combination of EU funding, increased national demand and a growing awareness of the positive short and long-term benefits of childcare on children and society began to yield a more concerted approach by interest groups in Ireland for policy action.

The Commission on the Family was set up in 1995 and published its report, *Strengthening Families for Life*, in 1998, which included a comprehensive set of recommendations relating to childcare and the family. At the same time as the Commission was considering the needs of families to additional support in the care of their children an Expert Working Group on Childcare was set up under Partnership 2000. This was a widely representative working group, which included childcare providers as well as employers, unions and statutory representatives and considered the wide range of childcare services for children from birth to 12 years of age. It was this group that brought the sector of after-school, as well as pre-school childcare into the policy arena for the first time. Meeting under the direction of the Department of Justice, Equality and Law Reform the group produced a national strategy for childcare in 1999.

In contrast to the nature of recommendations in the report of the Commission on the Family, where childcare was considered within a child and family context, a critical feature of the Expert Working Group was the restrictive nature of its terms of reference, which limited the group to considering the childcare needs of working parents alone. While there may have been expedient budgetary explanations for this focus, it laid the foundation for a fragmented policy response to childcare and failed to recognise the wider issue of childcare as a resource for all children, their families and society.

The report of the National Childcare Strategy led to the establishment of the Equal Opportunities Childcare Programme (EOCP), under the National Development Plan (2000–6). The programme operates under the Department of Justice, Equality and Law Reform to facilitate parents and especially mothers engaging in the workforce and in training/education. A budget of €499 million was made available under the Programme 2000–6 (Department of Justice, Equality and Law Reform, 2005). To manage the impact of the

EOCP, city and county childcare committees were established to develop locally focused county childcare strategies and to support delivery of services at local level.

While the Department of Education and Science supported a number of early childhood pilot initiatives such as the Early Start (Ryan et al., 1998) and support for Traveller preschools (Hayes, 1995) it took no policy position on the topic (Hayes, 2002). By the mid-1990s, however, the Department had also turned its attention to early childhood education and care.

In 1998 a Forum on Early Childhood Education was convened. The Forum was hosted at a period when: 'many social, economic and technological developments, internationally and in Ireland, have emphasised the significance of quality education for all within a lifelong educational framework. Many international agencies have highlighted the importance of early education in this context.' (Department of Education and Science, 1998b: 1)

Following the Forum, the Department produced a White Paper on Early Childhood Education, *Ready to Learn*. It was published in December 1999 and focused on the early educational needs of children from birth to six years, the compulsory school age in Ireland. The recommendations of White Paper covered the whole spectrum of early childcare services from: 'the development of very young children in the home, supports to parents concerning how best to help their children learn, a wide range of supports for private providers and voluntary/community groups and a strategy to enhance the quality of infant education in primary schools.' (Department of Education and Science, 1999: vii)

To commence implementation of these recommendations the Department supported a partnership initiative managed by the Dublin Institute of Technology and St Patrick's College, Drumcondra, which led to the establishment in 2001 of the Centre for Early Childhood Development and Education (CECDE). This represented an important co-ordinating initiative linking the wider care and education elements involved in working with young children up to the age of six. The primary tasks of the CECDE were to draft, in consultation, a quality framework for the early years sector; to develop initiatives for children with special needs and those at risk of educational disadvantage; to support research in the early education field and to prepare the groundwork for the establishment of the Early Childhood Education Agency as proposed in the White Paper. The CECDE also works closely with the National Council for Curriculum and Assessment (NCCA) which, under the Education Act, 1998, has responsibility for the development of an early years curriculum for all practitioners providing early childhood care and education. To this end, the NCCA have engaged in wide ranging discussion across the sector and published a discussion document *Towards a Framework for Early Learning* (NCCA, 2004).

In addition to the White Paper and the establishment of the CECDE, the Department also commissioned the OECD to carry out a thematic review of early childhood education and care in Ireland. The report was published in 2004 and provides a clear set of recommendations and a useful framework from which to move forward. In particular the OECD critiqued the fragmented and dispersed responsibility across the early childhood sector:

> No one Department or Agency has been given clear responsibility to lead integrated policy or to provide coherence across the various childhood bodies and services. Part of the reason for this lack of coherency is attributed to the fact that traditionally early childhood policy has been subsumed under larger issues, such as family policy, primary schooling and general health policy, rather than a defined age group with its own specific health, developmental and cognitive traits. (OECD, 2004: 23–4).

The recommendations call for clarity in departmental responsibility and integrated support of all early childhood services, including the early years of the primary school.

Taken together the investment in childcare through the EOCP, the establishment of the CECDE and the report of the OECD create a rich policy climate within which to improve the quality, accessibility and affordability of childcare in Ireland. Conscious of the extensive and varied recommendations in this policy area the National Economic and Social Forum chose Early Childhood Care and Education as a theme for its work in 2004/2005. They established a Project Team to consider the national situation in an international context and published their report *Early Childhood Care and Education* in September 2005.

Another body considering childcare is the National Children's Office (NCO), established to implement the National Children's Strategy (2000). It plays a key role in drawing together different departments on complex crosscutting issues towards developing and implementing integrated policy. Under Objective A the Strategy states that 'Children's early education and developmental needs will be met through quality childcare services and family-friendly employment measures' (Department of Health and Children, 2000a: 50). The NCO is due to report to government on childcare before the end of 2005 and, as has been noted elsewhere, the ability of the office to address this challenging policy issue will be a barometer of its success (Hayes, 2002).

Ireland's dilatory approach to the issue of childcare is not unique. International literature on childcare policy suggests that there is no society or country in which the basic direction for childcare has not been driven by economic factors, and childcare policy developments have generally mirrored expectations that mothers should work (OECD, 2001). In addition to the beneficial impact of affordable, accessible childcare on the labour market, there has been a simultaneous acceptance of the crucial role childcare services can play in addressing socio-economic disadvantage and assisting children in a more cost-efficient and effective manner (Walsh, 2003). To date Irish childcare policy has been driven by the two main agendas of equality and educational disadvantage. The fact that policy is being driven by different agendas under the direction of different government departments has hindered the development of an integrated policy for the support of high quality early childhood services for all young children.

The combination of all of these factors has led to the accelerated and intense series of developments within childcare policy and practice discussed earlier. Yet, despite advances, the strategy of the EOCP to increase provision in response to these changing societal structures has proved insufficient, and the lack of affordable, quality childcare remains a central and as yet unre-solved policy issue. To date, in excess of €500 million has been made available under the programme resulting in an additional 24,600 new childcare places. A further funding commitment has been made for an additional 12,000 places. Investing in childcare spaces, to the exclusion of concurrent investment in training and supports for quality, is insufficient to meet obligations and demand. Ireland is a party to the EU Barcelona Objectives (2002), which committed countries to provide childcare by 2010 to at least 90 per cent of children between three and the mandatory school age and at least 33 per cent of children under three years of age. If such targets are to be reached, in a manner that contributes positively to the development of children, it is more than timely to initiate serious action.

One of the most overlooked requirements of the EOCP Programme and one of the most pertinent issues in supporting equal opportunities is the Programme's failure to address the issue of affordability. As it stands, the Programme can only attempt to reduce costs indirectly, through increasing supply, a strategy which so far has failed as childcare costs continue to expand beyond the means of an increasing number of households (Hayes et al., 2005). The OECD Employment Outlook Study (OECD, 2002) showed that Ireland had a particularly high female drop out rate after the birth of a first and second children. Typically, a second earner in a couple family, with two young children in childcare, with earnings at two thirds of average salary has no net return after childcare costs (OECD, 2004). Such high costs have negative implications for equality amongst children, as very often children from the most vulnerable households, who ironically have been proven to benefit most from early quality early education and care, are excluded. Childcare costs are now amongst the highest in Europe and parents receive the lowest level of supports in meeting these costs.

Investing in childcare

Given the slow pace of childcare developments in the Irish context, an assessment of international childcare policies and practice can provide a lens through which to view our own country. It can also provide guidance on the effective delivery of quality accessible services, and the costs and benefits of such policy initiatives.

The level of state support and intervention in childcare, as in all social policies, varies across countries according to its public policy ethos: in other words, differences in childcare provision and policies can only be understood in light of the social, economic and political contexts in which they arise (OECD, 2004).

In considering state approaches to funding childcare, Bennett (2005) proposes a model, which groups countries according to the level of public investment in childcare (table 10.2). The model mirrors Esping-Andersen's common, if somewhat controversial, classifications of welfare state regimes into social democratic, conservative and liberal welfare states (Neyer, 2003).

Table 10.2 **Typology of early childhood systems**

High Investment Public Provision Model: *Found essentially in the Nordic countries*

Children's rights to society's resources are widely recognised. Investment is over one per cent of GDP. Programmes are designed to support the developmental potential of young children and the needs of working parents. Little difference is made between care and education and services and investment patterns across the age group obe to six years are continuous and integrated.

Low to Mid-Investment Pre-Primary Model: *Found in most European countries* (outside Nordic group)

Government provides large-scale educational services from three or four years to compulsory school age. Political discourse focuses on learning and laying the foundation for literacy and numeracy. Public investment is 0.4 to 1 per cent of GDP.

Low Public Investment, Mixed Market Model: *Found in Ireland, Australia, Canada, Korea and the US*

High value is placed on individual family responsibility for young children. National early childhood policies have traditionally been weak. Several departments share responsibility for policies affecting young children. The childcare sector is weakly regulated and conceived of as a service for working mothers. Public investment is less that 0.5 per cent of GDP.

Source: Bennett, 2005.

Within Bennett's model, Ireland remains in the 'liberal welfare state' classification of 'low public investment, mixed market model'. Given the diversity in public spend in the area of childcare across countries, it is useful to assess briefly the outcomes of such investment for children and families and, even more importantly, to review the consequences of low levels of investment for children and families.

The Nordic child and family policy model has historically focused on child well-being, female labour force participation and gender equality. *Social democratic* countries generally conform to a model of universalistic public services supported by high level investment. These countries offer attractive maternity and parental leave provisions with generous subsidisation policies thereafter to ensure access to good quality care and education services for children and to facilitate work/life balance for parents.

While there has been diversity in investment and provision across the *conservative countries*, there is now an increasing movement amongst all towards more generous leave periods for parents and universal provision for children aged three to six (e.g. Italy, Portugal, Belgium, France, the Netherlands). Quality is emphasised as integral to effective service provision and services have at their core the integration of care and education for young children in preparation for the commencement of primary schooling.

The basic tenet of child and family policy in *liberal welfare states* is the free market, where public investment tends to be low and the aim is to keep the social aspect of the state contained, needs-based and selective. In practice, this has meant that care of children has largely been viewed as a private responsibility and family policy benefits have been targeted only to poor families and to children at risk. Policies in the 'maximum private responsibility' model have three main aims:

1   To provide a 'safety net' of childcare services for the poorest families, as well as children at risk of physical abuse or neglect
2   To encourage the use of private or voluntary services
3   To guarantee minimum levels of quality for childcare. (OECD, 1990)

Lack of state intervention has meant that the vast majority of families in liberal welfare state regimes finance high childcare costs from their own private means, so that the bulk of day care is arranged unofficially, mainly through social and family networks. This situation has led to much concern about accessibility, quality and impact, as households with restricted incomes are often forced into low quality care, which may increase child or family-related developmental risks (Leseman, 2002).

Liberal welfare states also steer clear of direct investment/subsidisation of childcare, instead employing a universal childcare benefit, which they argue can be used by parents to subsidise childcare costs if they so desire. In Ireland, child benefit payments increased substantially between 2000 and 2005 (from €53.96 to €141.60 per child for first and second child and from €71.11 to €171.30 per child for third and subsequent children). The Government set a minimum Child Benefit target of €149.90 and €185.40 by 2003. These targets remain unrealised (CPA, 2005). While increases in fiscal provision appear to have formed the core of government's strategy in tackling both childcare and child poverty, increases have not contributed to the development of accessible, affordable, quality early childhood education, nor have they adequately assisted parents in meeting the additional costs of caring for their children, despite the opportunities access to such services provide to parents (facilitating parents in taking up labour market, education and training opportunities) and children (developmental and learning supports).

Policy review supports the contention that childcare services require direct investment in their own right if the guarantee of quality, affordable childcare is to be realised. Notwithstanding the historical differences in policy approaches adopted by different countries, recent years have witnessed a near-universal recasting of childcare policies in developed countries, which traditionally viewed childcare as a private concern. This enhanced commitment to the development of childcare policies is largely as a result of the widespread acceptance of the pivotal role such services play in facilitating equity of access to the labour market, subsequent reductions in child poverty and also because of the increased acknowledgement of both short and long term benefits of such services on children's development and lifetime opportunities. High quality childcare that is affordable, accessible and stable has a beneficial social and psychological impact on young children and a direct positive economic impact on society. Investing in childcare makes good economic sense (Hayes, 2002; Heckman and Cunha, 2005).

An example of the increased statutory commitment to childcare is evidenced through a brief review of the UK. Since Labour's return to power in 1997, the UK has embarked on an ambitious programme to tackle long-standing inequities in access to childcare. UK provision, which began from a very low base, is now benefiting from significant public investment and a radical reform of policy, co-ordination and planning. The government has significantly increased public expenditure in the area to a total budget of over £6 billion per annum for 2004–5 (including childcare tax and statutory maternity pay) with further increases planned for 2007–8. In practice, it is likely that government funding will continue to give priority to more disadvantaged areas but, in general, the long-term aims represent a clear move towards a more universal system of early years education and care (Daycare Trust, 2004). Furthermore, associated with the policy shift on childcare there is evidence that the rate of child poverty in the UK fell by over three per cent during the

1990s, the greatest decline of any OECD country. Despite Ireland experiencing the highest rate of economic growth of any OECD country in the same timeframe, child poverty increased by two per cent (UNICEF, 2005).

Through proactive supportive family and childcare policies, the UK has accomplished a great deal in a relatively short period of time. Bradshaw and Finch's *Study of Child Benefit Packages in 22 countries* (2002), found that the UK had moved from its traditionally liberal regime policy up the scale to a more generous and supportive position in the league table, a change he directly attributed to the effort the government has made since 1997 to improve family policy and benefits. This same study also found that of the 22 countries, only Ireland, Israel and Spain offered no help towards the cost of preschool childcare. In fact, Ireland has been persistently rated at the lower end of the spectrum in terms of provision and financial supports to assist parents in meeting their childcare responsibilities (Bradshaw and Finch, 2002).

The experience in Nordic countries and, more recently, that of the UK highlights the multiplicity of benefits accruable to society from statutory investment and support in childcare. Moreover, the lack of statutory intervention and the subsequent and continuing inequities for parents and children highlight the potential and actual cost a minimal interventionist role has had in countries such as Ireland. The best evidence available strongly suggests that good childcare is beneficial for children's development, both for the cognitive, language, academic skills of children and for the social behaviour of children in the family and classroom (Cleveland and Krashinsky, 1998). There is abundant research which shows that supporting children's development in their early years can help to prevent the emergence of the social and educational inequalities that will become evident as children progress through school and into work. There is also a potential link, backed up by many empirical studies, between cognitive and non-cognitive skills development in the early years and earning potential in adulthood (Daycare Trust, 2003).

Policy makers have recognised that equitable access to quality childcare can strengthen the foundations of lifelong learning for all children and support the broad educational and social needs of families (OECD, 2001). Assessments of quality early childhood programmes have found they make an important contribution to the preschool development of social, cognitive and language skills, provide disadvantaged children with a head start in primary school when formal instruction starts, reduce grade retention, reduce the need for special education and other remedial coursework, lower dropout rates, and raise high school graduation rates and levels of schooling (Heckman and Cunha, 2005; Lynch, 2004, Leseman, 2002; Schweinhart, 2005).

In *The Competitiveness Challenge*, the National Competitiveness Council noted that 'Pre-Primary development is a key determinant of performance at all levels of education' (NCC, 2004: 16), and highlights research findings which stress its great importance for cognitive and social development. It concluded that

> it is of concern, therefore, that Ireland's level of investment in pre-primary interventions and early childhood development is lower than nearly every other country benchmarked in the Annual Competitiveness Report . . . greater investment now in pre-primary interventions will, over time, result in savings in other programmes designed to address educational disadvantage and participation in later years. (2004: 18)

It is clear from even a very brief review of policies in a sample of European countries, that developments within Ireland remain insufficient to address adequately the increasing and diverse needs of an evolving Irish society. Childcare has a critical role to play in the creation of an egalitarian society for parents and children. In light of increased international investment in the provision and subsidisation of childcare, coupled with Ireland's exceptionally strong economic growth, it is clear that significant policy challenges remain for the state to support the needs of families with children effectively. The design of a comprehensive and appropriate policy to achieve this is one of the key challenges facing us in Ireland.

An emerging policy framework

As we have seen there has been a slow and fragmented response to the development of childcare policy. Childcare policy commitments seem to be compounded by the persistent separation of early education support from childcare support and an unaddressed conflict between the traditional ideology of the family in Ireland and the economic necessity to attract women into the workforce (Hayes, 2001). This conflict between state and family responsibility for children may also account for the fact that there appears to be resistance by government to take account of policy impact on children, even when the policy issue has a direct impact on them.

However, a review of recent policy documents reveals a shift in attention away from considering childcare policy from either the equality perspective (emphasising the care of children whose parents are working) or the education perspective (supporting provision of early education intervention services to children at risk of school failure). Both the OECD report (2004) and the NESF report (2005b) present comprehensive and nuanced arguments encouraging government towards the development of a co-ordinated and integrated policy response to childcare which recognises the value of investing in quality childcare services where there is excellence in both care and education for all children. In addition, both reports identify the need for implementation to be under the direction of one lead department. This more comprehensive consideration of childcare is also evident in a recent report from the National Women's Council of Ireland, *An Accessible Childcare Model* (2005)

While recent reports and policy advice seem to have moved on to this new dimension, reflecting the position of most of our European neighbours, the public discourse on the 'childcare debate' remains at a more basic level. Recent media articles and discussion have characterised consideration of the childcare issue as evidence of failing state support for families and increased support for the institutional care of children. The debate quickly shifts from a focus on children and their needs and rights to good quality early childhood experiences, irrespective of where that might occur, to a debate about how best to raise children. It is a debate which takes momentum from setting one set of childcare arrangements, those where one family member remains at home to care for the children, against another set where, for a variety of reasons and to varying extents, shared childcare is part of the child-rearing approach. This situation has been exacerbated by the current policy approach, which has seen investment in childcare driven by a policy to support families in the work/life balance and to attract more women into the workforce. These debates centre on wider issues of family and gender and extend far beyond childcare. The points raised are important, but they relate to separate policy issues. Though they deserve careful policy analysis they are not directly germane to the development, co-ordination and support of quality childcare services. The emergence of these policy topics in the debates about childcare actually confuses and clouds the issue and hinders effective policy development.

There is no doubt that resolving the childcare dilemma continues to challenge policy makers. A review of international approaches to support and subsidisation of childcare highlights considerable advancements, particularly among previously low provision countries in the past decade. Increasingly countries employ a variety of measures to finance childcare costs including extended maternity and parental leave, flexible working environments, direct subsidisation of childcare settings, a reduction or a rebate of charges for childcare according to family type, income, number and/or age of children, and off-setting some or all of the costs against taxable income. What is clear from reviewing the international response is that, while different countries have adopted different approaches, there has been a near-uniform policy of improving access for all children, and the provision of free services for all children of preschool age. Internationally childcare and early education services now form an integral part of government policies and are recognised as an essential component of improving gender equity, female labour market participation and educational and social opportunities for all children.

The economic, demographic and social changes in Ireland over the last decade have crystallised the urgency for policy action on childcare. The current policy of investing in the creation of childcare places for children of working parents has proved both divisive and insufficient. This policy approach has not led to the resolution of problems of accessibility and affordability; it has not contributed to the development of a sustainable, high-quality childcare sector nor the growth of a trained workforce to provide and maintain quality. There is now a rich knowledge base, national and inter-national, to inform a refocusing of policy attention towards an integrated, co-ordinated and mixed policy response so that the challenges presented by the diverse constituency of young children in contemporary Ireland can be met to the benefit of the children, their families and society as a whole.

Recommended reading

CPA (2005) *Ending Child Poverty: Combat Poverty Agency Policy Statement.* Dublin: CPA.
Department of Justice, Equality and Law Reform (2005) *School Age Childcare in Ireland: Report of the National Childcare Co-ordinating Committee.* Dublin: Stationery Office
NESF (2005b) *Early Childhood Care and Education*, Report no. 30. Dublin: Stationery Office.
OECD (2004) *Thematic Review of Early Childhood Education and Care Policy in Ireland.* Dublin: Stationery Office.

Chapter 11

Disability, children and social care

Suzanne Quin

Introduction

This chapter examines the theory and practice of supporting parents who are caring for a child with severe disability. It considers the challenges facing parents in providing such care and the role of professional service providers in the context of a partnership model of care provision. The provision of care for those who have needs in relation to the activities of daily living is an ongoing challenge in any society. Responses to needs are potentially as diverse as needs themselves. There are many assumptions resting behind the seemingly innocuous and virtuous term of 'social care'. The fact that the provision of personal social services in the Republic of Ireland is subsumed under the broad title of 'health' has implications for its resourcing, visibility and the extent to which it is prioritised in the context of the competing demands of other aspects of health services. The implications of an uneven geographical spread of such services and of varied levels of provision on offer to different diagnostic groups are examined. Whilst national policy on child welfare is to support families to care for children at home, the experience for a family caring for a child with a disability can be of inadequate information on the availability of services and inadequate support.

Social care in context

In their chapter on social care and disability, Finnerty and Collins (2005: 286) define social care as 'care for those who cannot care for themselves by virtue of their circumstances and/or condition'. In the same volume on applied social care, Share and McElwee (2005: 5) comment that the provision of social care is 'a rapidly changing and developing field, in Ireland as elsewhere'. In the UK, social care is a major public services area in its own right with an estimated 1.5 million service users at any given time relying on the provision of care services (Department of Health UK, 2005). It is further estimated that, in the UK, almost six million individuals provide care for the vast majority of disabled, ill or frail elderly relatives and friends living in private households. Not only is the population of carers a large one, it is also one that is in a constant state of flux in terms of its turnover, with an estimated third of the total either beginning or ceasing to provide care each year (Hutton and Hirst, 2001). While the majority will be providing care for older people, parents of children with chronic conditions constitute the second largest subgroup of family carers (Marks, 1996).

Most people will find themselves having to care for a family member in the course of their lives (Baldock, 1997). Bytheway and Johnson (1998: 242) refer to 'the multiplicity and reciprocal nature of many caring relationships'. Rather than distinguishing between the carers and those cared for, these authors (1998: 251) suggest that 'research and practice might be more effective if it were based on the assumption that all people are involved in a multiplicity of activities relating to care'.

The development of the mixed economy of welfare in the UK has resulted in the creation of care packages drawing on providers from the statutory, voluntary and private sectors to meet assessed needs. Twigg (2000: 111) notes that 'within the discourse of community care . . . carers still occupy a central place . . . Maximising the input of carers through the judicious use of formal support has been seen as a highly cost-effective strategy, and one in tune with New Managerialist thinking'. Regarding the success of the mixed economy of welfare in practice, Lewis and Glennerster (1996: 202) comment that 'the attempt to create and manage a social care market has proved both difficult and time consuming . . . It has proved difficult to stimulate the independent provision of domiciliary care'. Overall, Twigg (2000: 113) comments that 'the reality of social care is one of strictly limited resources in which there is little scope for the expression of preferences and where even basic needs are not always met'.

The public/private partnership model is the central feature of Irish service provision in this area. A marked difference between the UK and Ireland is the position of the voluntary sector in terms of its size and centrality. In Ireland, the voluntary sector has a long history as a major service provider for children with disabilities and their families. Some of the major providers are large, sometimes nationally based voluntary organisations offering a wide range of services for such children in partnership with the statutory sector. Examples of such organisations are the Central Remedial Clinic and Enable Ireland for children with primarily physical disabilities, and St Michael's House and the Brothers of Charity services for children with primarily learning disabilities.

Social care for children with disabilities: the Ir

There is a long tradition of formally acknowledg
dating back to the provisions of the Brehon L/
services for those with care needs has largely reliec
primarily family care, supported by voluntary involvemenc
and limited statutory provision. In policy terms, the importance oɪ ˎ
the provision of care has been acknowledged and the need to develop supᵣ
for the informal care system accepted, in theory if not always in practice.
Regarding the involvement of the wider community, the White Paper on
voluntary activity (Department of Community, Rural and Gaeltacht Affairs,
2000) draws attention to the fact that this has a long and valued tradition of
meeting social needs in Ireland. It puts forward recommendations for the
further development of the voluntary sector in tandem with state provision,
using a partnership model with a focus on the respective rights and responsibilities of the statutory/voluntary mix.

The involvement of the community is also seen as a key aspect in the
development of primary care to meet most of the overall health care needs of
a local population. The future of primary care is outlined in *Primary Care: A
New Direction* (Department of Health and Children, 2001a) that envisages a
general practitioner-led, multidisciplinary team providing most of the health
care and personal social services needs of a geographically defined population.
This development is seen as 'central to the planning and delivery of health
and personal social services for the future' (Department of Health and
Children, 2001a: 21)

An acknowledged impediment to the development of multidisciplinary
primary care has been the inadequate supply of qualified professionals such as
public health nurses, physiotherapists, occupational therapists, speech and
language therapists, social workers and care workers. Attempts to increase
numbers of available professionals by recruiting from abroad have had limited
success (NSQB, 2002) and the importance of increasing intake into courses
provided within the state has been acted upon to an extent. The Action
Progress Report on Quality and Fairness (Department of Health and Children,
2004) points to the additional training places created since the Strategy's
inception in 2001.

The Action Progress Report (Department of Health and Children, 2004)
also refers to developments in the partnership arrangements between voluntary and statutory service providers. It further sees the extension of the 'key
worker' approach, already in use in child welfare and protection, to older
people and to children with disabilities, an approach in keeping with the
National Children's Strategy (Department of Health and Children, 2000a:
139). The plan to create chronic disease management protocols is also of note.

n regard to services for children overall, the National Children's Strategy
s provided an integrated framework as well as the broader policy context
or all new initiatives for children (Department of Health and Children,
2001b). The Strategy's approach

- Recognises children as active participants in shaping their own health and
  well-being
- Supports families and their central role in protecting and promoting
  children's health and well-being
- Seeks to strengthen the effectiveness of the supports and services provided
  by the health services to children. (Department of Health and Children,
  2001b: 136)

All children have basic needs in common including the need for the support of their family and community (Department of Health and Children,
2000a: 46). It is acknowledged in the National Children's Strategy (2000a:
136) that some (such as those with disabilities) will also have additional needs,
and that the system 'must be flexible enough to the able to respond to more
complex needs'. Regarding the health care needs of children in general, the
co-ordinated approach to partnership with parents and health professionals is
endorsed in the National Children' Strategy (Department of Health and
Children, 2000a: 138). This is regarded as in keeping with the overall approach
to health care set out in the Health Strategy (Department of Health and
Children, 2001b).

Another dimension of health services for children that requires specific
attention is the fact that 'Ireland is now moving towards a more
multiethnic/multicultural society. In health, as in other areas of public policy,
this brings the need to plan for diversity with a wider range of needs to be
addressed – affecting both the health workforce and the patient/client group'
(Department of Health and Children, 2001b: 54). In regard to disability, as
Pierce (2003: 121) points out, 'in Ireland, policy makers tend to consider
ethnicity and disability in isolation from each other'. She (2003: 124) argues
for the importance of recognising multiple identities (such as those from
ethnic minorities who also have a disability) and ensuring that they are given
'due recognition and respect'. Such recognition and respect would include
health and personal social services that are appropriate in regard to their dual
identity. The complexities of providing ethnically sensitive health care is
demonstrated in studies from other countries such as the UK. In relation to
families of children with disabilities, for example, Fazil et al. (2002: 238) cite
research evidence that such families 'face widespread disadvantage and discrimination, particularly if they are members of minority ethnic groups'. In
their own study of families of Pakistani and Bangladeshi origin with a severely

disabled child, they found that language difficulties and misconceptions of service providers about extended family support and attitudes to respite care were significant barriers to appropriate service provision. The findings led Fazil et al. (2002: 239–10) to conclude that 'while all ethnic minority parents of disabled children face significant additional disadvantage compared to the white majority . . . there are deep differences between different ethnic minority groups'.

The special needs of children with disabilities

In line with the overall decline in the birth rate, there are now fewer children with disabilities in Ireland than in past decades. At the same time, the proportion of those with severe levels of disability has increased (Department of Health and Children, 2000a). This is attributed to improved survival rates for children born with severe disabilities as well as those children who develop such disabilities arising from accidents or illness. According to Murphy (2001a: 14), 'advances in both medical technology and health care have improved the outcome for many children with congenital abnormalities, chronic illness and injury related conditions'. Definitive figures for the numbers of children in Ireland who have disabilities are not available. Some indication of the numbers of families whose children have additional needs arising from disabilities can be gleaned from statistics in regard to the Domiciliary Care Allowance Scheme. This allowance is payable to the carer of a child with a severe disability who lives at home. A severe disability is defined as needing constant care and supervision, substantially more than a child without a disability at the same age would need. In 2003 there were over 14,000 carers in receipt of this allowance (Department of Health and Children, 2003). Most families of children with a disability have just one child with special needs. However, some families have two or more children with the same or even differing disabilities. Some genetic conditions, such as muscular dystrophy for example, only become evident during childhood and may present in another male child born subsequently to the first child's diagnosis. Data from the UK in the late 1990s (Lawton, 1998) indicates that around 17,000 families in the UK have more than one disabled child. About 6,500 families are caring for two or more severely disabled children. This represents well over 10,000 severely disabled children living in a family where there is another severely disabled child (Keegan Wells et al., 2002). The burden of care for parents in such circumstances can be enormous. So too, can the care of one child with severe disabilities as illustrated in Redmond and Richardson's (2003) study of mothers of babies and young children with severe/profound and life-threatening intellectual disability.

Having a child with special needs arising from disabilities poses a number of challenges for parents and other family members. To quote the Chief Medical Officer (Department of Health and Children, 2001c: 82) 'the occurrence of a disability in a child is a source of great anxiety and distress in families'. Issues of particular significance include:

- uncertainty about the prognosis
- the long-term implications of the disability for the quality of life of the child
- the availability of appropriate diagnostic and treatment facilities
- psychological and practical support for the families in caring for the child
- many other doubts and uncertainties

As well as the ordinary demands of parenting, Miles et al. (1993: 203) identify three specific roles required of the parents of a child with disability. First of all, they must acquire advocacy skills to ensure that their child's special needs are met. Secondly, they must develop specific protecting skills about the child's health to prevent treatment complications, and thirdly, they must provide special nurturing for a child coping with extraordinary demands. The physical as well as the psychosocial resources required to care for a child with serious disabilities can result in what Cummins describes as a 'chronic burden of care' (2002: 125) on other family members, especially parents. The cumulative wear and tear of parenting in such circumstances over a period of time can be considerable.

Apart from the challenges of providing care, parents of a child with a disability may be doing so in less than optimal circumstances. The very fact of having such a child may significantly limit their earning capacity while, at the same time, they may extra costs arising from the disability. Childcare may not be easily available and can be substantially more expensive than for children without a disability. Dobson and Middleton (1998) estimated the average cost of rearing a child with a disability to be at least three times more than the amount required to bring up a child without a disability. Moreover, the additional costs could be sudden, unpredictable and ongoing. Dobson and Middleton's (1998) study quoted one respondent who remarked 'You think it gets easier as they get older but it doesn't, the money still isn't there, and the debts are bigger. I don't worry about the bills now, that's the difference. What are they going to do to me, put me in prison? Great, a room to myself and a night's sleep. That would be the first in nearly 15 years.'

Accessing support services in caring for a child with a disability can be inherently stressful. Parents report constant battles with the range of service providers who are there to support them (Murphy, 2001a). Moreover, the pressures and challenges of trying to cope with the immediate needs of a child with severe disability may leave little time and energy to 'do battle' on the child's behalf for the technical and practical help that can be so evidently needed. Hence, parents can find themselves actively seek help in the context of depleted personal, emotional and physical resources. As Twigg (2000: 114) describes it, 'most people come into the orbit of social care at a time of considerable personal difficulty and distress in which they are in no position to be active, assertive consumers'.

It is considered good childcare practice that children with special needs should be cared for within the family home. The Child Care Act, 1991 is based on the principle that it is generally in the best interests of the child to be brought up in his or her own family. The Commission on the Family (1998: 51) endorsed this principle and argued for a strengths-based approach to support parents in their role of primary caregivers. At the same time, care in relation to health needs has increasingly shifted from hospital-based settings to home-based care where possible. Keegan Wells et al. (2002: 201) point out the 'extraordinary shift in health care delivery over the last decade such that patients are now expected to receive much of their illness-related care at home . . . parents caring for children with chronic conditions now constitute the second largest subgroup of family carers'. This includes children who are dependent on technology for survival. Murphy (2001a: 14) comments on the fact that 'there is a growing number of children dependent on the very technology that has ensured their survival . . . improvements in the portability of medical equipment have enabled these children to be cared for in the home environment'.

Partnership with parents and quality care: rhetoric and reality

It is acknowledged in the Annual Report of the Chief Medical Officer (Department of Health and Children, 2001c: 85) that disabled children and their families 'require appropriate, accessible and affordable health services at primary, secondary and tertiary level'. In line with good childcare practice, it is further acknowledged that services should be designed to ensure that, if at all possible, the most desirable location of care is within the family home. Working in partnership with parents to optimise the child's quality of life is the goal. However, optimising quality of life for the child and their family can prove difficult to achieve in practice. In spite of the rhetoric of policy planning, services on the ground to support families are limited and are often determined by factors other than need, such as geographical location, age and diagnostic category (Quin and Clarke, 2004; Department of Health and Children, 2005a; O'Reilly, 2005). This is by no means unique to Ireland: evidence from the UK indicates that a key service – respite care both within and outside the home – is a particular issue for families caring for a child with severe disability (Murphy, 2001b; Miller, 2002). According to Murphy (2001b: 25) 'there is no consistency in the amount and type of provision [of respite care]. It appears to bear no relationship to the extent of technology dependence and varies across the country.'

Especially for families caring for more than one child with a disability, the burden of care may be such that they must depend on some level of additional help on an ongoing basis or at least in times of crisis. Yet, adequate help is not always available to them. In the UK, a national survey of over 1,000 families found that one fifth of parents with two disabled children said they had no one to look after their disabled children if they were unable to care for their child owing to an illness (Lawton, 1998). In a recent, much publicised case in the UK, parents of two children with severe cerebral palsy left their children in a local children's hospice. They stated that they did so to highlight their circumstances and to protest that the local authority would provide them with no more than four hours a day respite for children who both required round the clock care and attention.

Rummery (2002: 181) comments that 'the role of professionals within the welfare state as it is presently constituted within the context of the UK (and most other similar welfare states) is to ration access to scarce resources'. Professionals working with families in such circumstances can feel a sense of disempowerment when they must act as a gatekeeper to scarce resources or represent the human face of a service that is not adequately meeting the needs of their clients. Stainton (1998: 137–8) uses the concept of 'structural paternalism' whereby no one person determines what is 'in one's best interest but rather it is the structure which inherently makes this determination'. Hallstedt and Högström (2005: 26–7), writing on social care and disability, refer to the work of Foucault in pointing out that the most effective form of dominance is that which does not appear as dominance. 'If we conceive of something as taken for granted and 'normal' we will not have the sense of being dominated at all . . . [the worker] will act individually within the domain of the discourses, but may even against their own will, be the conduit for dominating norms in society.'

Sometimes professional service providers may lack awareness of the impact of social conditions on the family's ability to cope. For example Oldman and Beresford (1998) comment on the low level of awareness among professionals of the ways in which housing can make life very difficult for children with disabilities and their parents. On the other hand, professionals in the field can be only too aware of the individual family's struggles and experience a sense of helplessness from overwork and under-resourcing. This is graphically described by a social worker in relation to a family carer (Brotchie, 1988: 14). She states 'I know the carer is under pressure, but I dare not ask her if she is all right because I haven't the time to listen . . . and I'm not sure I can cope with the answer'. Thus professionals providing care for families of children with severe disability can, from their perspective, feel frustrated in their desire to work in full partnership with parents because of their own limited power and control over much needed, over-stretched resources. As Share and McElwee (2005: 14) comment in relation to the social care in general 'there can be a large gulf between desires, expectations and reality'.

Improving services for children with disabilities and their families

'In recent years, the increasing challenge posed by disability in childhood has been recognised' (Department of Health and Children, 2001c: 86). The Disability Act, 2005 establishes that service provision will be based on a full assessment of an individual's needs. It is hoped that this will mark a shift away from the current position in which the availability of support services such as home care and respite are dependent on such arbitrary criteria as age, diagnosis and geographical location. What is of crucial importance is that the needs identified are matched by the provision of adequate resources. As mentioned at the beginning of this chapter, the fact that personal social services are subsumed under health makes them vulnerable to under-resourcing and cutbacks in relation to the many aspects of health care – particularly acute care – with which they must essentially compete for funding.

As well as the most important issue of resources, other factors can impact on the development of quality care for children with severe disabilities and their families. Co-ordination of services on offer by different agencies should obviously be addressed. The National Children's Strategy (Department of Health and Children, 2000a) has recognised the need for increased inter-sectoral collaboration in relation to children's health and welfare.

The Health Service Executive has been created to ensure that health services are planned and provided on a national basis. The development of partnerships between statutory and voluntary service providers is designed to maximise and rationalise service provision and to minimise overlap, dupli-cation and gaps in what is on offer from the many agencies involved. That there are many voluntary organisations, a few of which are large scale and many which are local or focused on one diagnostic category, is evident from the list of non-governmental agencies listed under disability in the Directory of National Voluntary Organisations (Comhairle, 2004).

Just as co-ordination of care is required at the macro level so also must it be a core feature of service provision at the micro (i.e. individual case) level. The use of the key worker approach mentioned above, already a feature of working with children who have been abused and/or neglected, has been extended to children with special needs (Department of Health and Children,

2003). The key worker, as well as providing direct services to the child and family, acts as a service co-ordinator and advocate on behalf of the family. This system of key worker for children with disability has been operation-alised in the UK for some time with apparent success (ACT, 2003).

What is important to service users is to feel that their needs are acknow-ledged and responded to appropriately. Having to rely on others for help within the privacy of one's own home can be stressful it itself. In their study of home based services, Francis and Netten (2004) found that the qualities that families most valued were reliability, flexibility, continuity, communica-tion, trustworthiness, attitudes, skills and knowledge.

It is now an accepted principle in Irish health policy to engage service users in policy planning (Department of Health and Children, 2001b). Another accepted principle is the importance of a child centred approach in services for children and their families: 'a child-centred approach to disability would require a more central role for disabled people in the planning, develop-ment, implementation and monitoring of rehabilitation services' (Department of Health and Children, 2001c: 85). Social care, Baldock (1997) argues, is a highly complex form of social exchange, it is interactive and how it is provided is as important to what is provided. Professionals offering social care services can find themselves at the interface between the family and the agency they represent. How then, in the context of limited resources, can they provide the best quality service? Stainton (1998: 144) suggests that 'the committed worker can seek to redress the imbalance of power through a true commitment to consumer rights'. In practice, this requires a fourfold approach to working with clients: first of all, to actively advocate and seek support for services to meet their clients' needs while ensuring that such clients understand the process and its limitations; second, to maximise the individualisation of need through the creative use of resources and accessing resources on offer from a wide variety of sources; third to advocate within their own system for the development of appropriate and adequate resources to meet needs; fourth, to be honest 'about their abilities, their limitations and their conflicts' with themselves and with their clients. This multiple-level intervention strategy offers a model to enable professionals to reconcile their difficulties of pro-viding a service to families when service provision is inadequate. What is certain is that there are challenges for social care in the field of disability and, in particular, in the support of children with severe disabilities and their families. Hirst (2004: 31) argues that 'caregiving should be recognised as a public health issue' in order to release more resources and ensure policies that contribute to the well-being of the carer and for the person for whom the care is provided. This has particular relevance for Ireland where personal social services are subsumed under health. Defining caregiving as a public health issue may help to ensure that it is identified as a priority for resources.

Recommended reading

Department of Health and Children (2001c) *Annual Report of the Chief Medical Officer 2000: The Health of Our Children.* Dublin: Stationery Office.

Finnerty, K. and Collins, B. (2005) 'Social care and disability', pp. 271–87 in Share, P. and McElwee, N. (eds), *Applied Social Care: An Introduction for Irish Students.* Dublin: Gill & Macmillan.

Hudson, B. (ed.) (2000) *The Changing Role of Social Care.* London: Jessica Kingsley.

Quin, S. and Redmond, B. (eds) (2003) *Disability and Social Policy in Ireland.* Dublin: UCD Press.

Chapter 12

Older people and social care

Maria Pierce

Introduction

In Ireland, the basic social services, commonly identified as income maintenance, health, housing and education, are provided to meet the welfare
needs common to all citizens of Irish society (Curry, 2003). The term 'social
care services' can be used to refer to a wide range of services that are provided
for specific user groups such as older people, children and families, and
people with disabilities (Curry, 2003). Social care includes personal care such
as bathing, toileting and dressing, practical assistance including help with
housework and preparation of meals, as well as opportunities for social and
leisure activities (Blackman, 2001). This chapter examines social care services
and older people as a specific user group of such services in Ireland.

A distinction, although not always helpful, is usually made between social
care and health care services (Blackman, 2001; Victor, 2005). Whereas health
care services are designed to cater for those with health problems and in need
of medical or nursing care, social care services are designed to cater for those
who have non-health problems such as needs for personal care or housework.
Compared with health care, social care tends to have a relatively low status
(Munday, 1996a). Garavan et al. (2001) and O'Hanlon et al. (2005), in their
studies of the use of health and social services by older people in Ireland, have
attempted to make the distinction between the more 'medical' services and
those with a more 'social' emphasis. For example, day hospital and day care
centres, places where people may receive services such as physiotherapy,
chiropody, or blood pressure checks, would fall into the former category,
whereas day centres or day clubs offering a range of social activities such a
meal or a bath would be classified in the latter category. In Ireland, unlike the
UK, social care services are organised and funded from within the same
administrative department (Convery, 2001; Munday, 1996a), that is, the
Department of Health and Children, so that the boundary between the two
tends to be blurred.

Social care settings

Older people receive social care in many settings. Higgins (1989) has devised a model of care that distinguishes between three main care settings: *in* 'a home', *at* home and *from* home. The first where care is given *in* 'a home' refers to care in an institutional setting such as a hospital or nursing home. Figures relating to long-stay care indicate that less than five per cent of the population of older people are in institutional care in Ireland. The degree to which care *in* a home offers social care vis-à-vis health care is difficult to assess. In a hospital setting, for example, social care may be subsidiary to medical treatment (Baldock and Ely, 1996). For the vast majority of older people needing social care, care is provided to them in their own homes. Higgins (1989) refers to this setting as care *at* home. Social care services that are home-based include home help services, meals on wheels and personal care attendants. In addition to social care, home-based or domiciliary care may also include medical or nursing care. Social care can also be given *from* home. In this instance, the person resides in their own home and travels to a social care setting in the community. Examples of such community-based social care services would be meals services, day centres and clubs, and respite care.

Since the 1960s successive governments in Ireland have stated a commitment to pursuing policies with the intended effect of enabling as many older people who can do so to continue living *at* home (Inter-Departmental Committee on the Care of the Aged, 1968; Working Group on Services for the Elderly, 1988). The *Care of the Aged Report* was one of the first official documents to clearly articulate the policy preference for domiciliary and community-based care (Timonen and McMenamin, 2002). It stated that 'it is better, and probably cheaper, to help the aged to live in the community rather than to provide for them in hospitals or other institutions' (Inter-Departmental Committee on the Care of the Aged, 1968: 49). This represented in principle a radical shift in Irish policy towards the care of older people *at* and *from* home, as prevailing policies of care were based on institutionalisation (Blackwell et al., 1992). In practice, policy has favoured the growth of institutional-based as opposed to community-based or home-based responses to care needs (NESF, 2005a).

In recent years policy issues relating to care *in* a home have tended to dominate policy debates about the social care of older people, so that the issue of poorly resourced community and home-based social care services has tended to be overshadowed. However, home-based social care is receiving renewed attention as policy makers seek to avoid the need for older people to have to move into an institutional setting when they come to need care. Proposals for a new social insurance scheme for home care as well as other forms of long-term care have been the subject of a report on the future financing of long-term care commissioned by the Department of Social, Community and Family Affairs (2002). The NESF Project Team on Care for Older People has focused on the changes that are required in policy and practice to ensure that older people, if they so wish, can live for longer as independently as possible in their own homes and communities. This includes a focus on the legal dimension of community care (NESF, 2005a).

The mixed economy of social care

Social care services for older people in each setting – *in a* home, *at* home, and *from* home – are provided by the state as well as other sectors of society. The 'mixed economy of social care' (also referred to as social care pluralism) is a term that can be used to describe the balance of social care provision within a society between the formal, informal, voluntary and private sectors (Fanning, 1999). Formal social care is care that is publicly provided or financed or managed. Care given by extended family members, neighbours or friends is referred to as informal social care. The voluntary sector is a not-for-profit sector, which includes religious organisations and charitable bodies. Although separate from the state, it is difficult to clearly distinguish voluntary sector provision from public sector provision, as the voluntary sector is financed mainly through the state (Convery, 2001). An alternative sector engaged in the provision of commercial social care services for older people is the private (or for-profit) sector (Fanning, 1999). Social care of older people in Ireland, which has developed in a piecemeal manner, has always been characterised by a mixed economy of social care although the balance of this mix has changed over time.

Long-term residential care for older people in Ireland is characterised by a mixed provision. With the historically strong role of the Catholic Church in the provision of services in Ireland, accommodation in voluntary nursing homes has also been an important element in the long-term residential care of older people. The public provision of long-term care for older people was traditionally based on institutionalisation in hospitals and welfare homes. However, there is an under-provision of public residential care places to cater for all those older people who need them. This has given rise to an increasing plurality of social care provision. Of particular note is the increasing use in recent decades of private residential and nursing home care. This move towards increasing long-term social care plurality is influenced partly by financial concerns and partly for ideological reasons. With respect to social care, the emphasis in many Western states is on reducing the level of state provision, emphasising informal and extending private and voluntary sector provision to reduce reliance and pressure on the public sector. However, as governments withdraw from their role of providing social care services, a major concern is that both the quality and quantity of social care services will deteriorate (Munday, 1996b; Bartlett and Blackman, 2001).

There is general agreement that the current system of regulating, inspecting and enforcing standards in nursing homes needs to be developed. There is no inspection system for the public nursing home sector and the inspection system for the private sector is not an independent inspectorate. Regulation of the private nursing home sector rests with the statutory sector under the auspices of the Health Service Executive (HSE), which is obliged to inspect and monitor private nursing homes to ensure that they meet and maintain certain standards. The inspection system is considered to be unsatisfactory. A major problem with the current system is that the HSE is generally reluctant to instigate sanctions against nursing homes that fail to maintain standards, for when it does it is left with the onerous task of providing alternative accommodation for residents affected. Other matters raised by the existing division between the public and private provision of long-stay residential care for older people include concern about the large increase in spending by the Department of Health and Children on private nursing home care (O'Loughlin, 2005). Controversial issues surrounding the nursing home subvention scheme and the pocket money issue have also surfaced in recent years (O'Loughlin, 2005).

The vast majority of older people, however, live in their own homes. Together with a longstanding preference in Irish policy for domiciliary and community-based care, research testifies to the importance of social care services in helping older people to continue living at home (McGee et al., 2005). Yet there remains a very low provision and usage of publicly funded and provided home-based and community-based social care services in Ireland (Baldock and Ely, 1996; Garavan et al., 2001; O'Hanlon et al., 2005). The reality is that many older people have little formal support available to them to manage at home. The low level of such formal social care services for older people in Ireland coincides with a long tradition in Ireland of state inactivity in the field of social policy and the provision of social services on a residual and selectivist basis. Other factors contributing to the underdevelopment of public social care services in Ireland include the low priority given to social care services in a system dominated by the medical and hospital sector, and the lack of legislation to underpin the provision of social care services to enable older people to remain at home (Convery, 2001; NESF, 2005).

The public provision of domiciliary social care services in Ireland is very low by international standards (O'Hanlon et al., 2005a). Ireland lies in sharp contrast to Denmark and Sweden, where generous levels of domiciliary social care services amount to near universal provision as well as to Britain and the Netherlands, both of which are countries with abundant publicly provided domiciliary social care services for older people (Anttonen and Sipilä, 1996; Baldock and Ely, 1996). A recent study comparing take-up rates within the Island of Ireland shows that the usage of home helps, meals-on-wheels and personal care attendants is much lower in the Republic than in Northern Ireland (McGee et al., 2005).

Little is known at present about the mixed provision of home-based social care services in Ireland. However, a study of home-based social care services for older people in Dublin offered by the statutory sector, non-profit organisations and private agencies is currently under way. The study, which is being conducted by the Ageing and Social Policy Research Programme in Trinity College, Dublin, is also examining employment practices relating to home help and personal care assistants in each of these sectors.

Traditionally, formal care services that existed in Ireland were almost entirely directed to the very poorest without families. 'In the past, services for the aged, other than those provided from their own resources or with the help of relatives and friends, were confined almost entirely to the destitute.' (Interdepartmental Committee on Care of the Aged, 1968: 48) Formal social care services in Ireland were thus provided not only on a residual basis but also in accordance with the principle of subsidiarity (Kiely, 1999). Although not explicitly stated, the limited provision of formal social care services for older people in Ireland has traditionally been based on the assumption that much of the care required would be provided informally by the family (Fahey, 1997).

In the Irish welfare system as elsewhere (Johnson, 1999), families have been and continue to be a major source of social care for older relatives (Convery, 2001). The family not the state is regarded as and expected to be the first line of support for older relatives (Blackman, 2001; Convery, 2001). While the *Care of the Aged Report* depicted the state as the most significant provider of social care services, *The Years Ahead Report* heralded a shift in policy thinking away from a particular focus on state-provided services by highlighting the major role of the family in the social care of older people. It stated that not only is the family a major partner in the care of older people, alongside the statutory and voluntary sectors, but that 'families make by far the largest contribution' (Working Group on Services for the Elderly, 1988).

Research studies too point to a strong caring commitment of families in Ireland towards older relatives. O'Connor et al. (1988) first made an attempt in the mid-1980s to quantify the extent and nature of family care of older relatives within an Irish context. The gap in knowledge about those, the 'forgotten army', who care for 'dependent elderly people' in the community, provided the impetus for the study. The study found that co-resident family members cared for approximately 77 per cent of those over 65 resident at home and requiring some degree of care. Persons, mainly relatives, living in separate households cared for the remaining 23 per cent of 'dependent elderly people' (O'Connor et al., 1988: 33–4). However, the study found that non-relatives also played a significant role in cross-household care of older people (O'Connor et al., 1988).

In a later study, Fahey and Murray (1994) point to a similar pattern of care giving, although there was some movement away from co-resident care towards care by family members across separate households. The Census of Population 2002 provides information on the number of people in Ireland who give regular unpaid personal help to a friend or family members with a long-term, health problem or disability (CSO, 2004b). The Census data indicates that there are 148,754 such carers in Ireland. This figure includes family members who provide personal help for relatives of all ages with a long-term illness, health problem or disability. However, it is not possible to select out the numbers of family members who are providing regular unpaid personal help to older relatives.

The voluntary sector is considered to play a residual role in the provision of social care services for older people in Ireland in comparison with the family (Convery, 2001). Nevertheless, Ireland has a large number of local and national voluntary sector organisations involved in the provision of social care both *at* home and *from* home. With some funding from the HSE and other sources, these organisations have played a key and longstanding role in supplementing state services for older people. In some areas the voluntary sector has been the sole provider of social care services for older people (Department of Social Welfare, 1997). The emergence of the private sector as a provider of social care services *at* and *from* home is a relatively recent development in Ireland, as illustrated by the fact that *The Years Ahead Report* (Working Group on Services for the Elderly, 1988) makes no mention of the private sector.

Although Ireland is characterised by a mixed economy of social care, the existing model of social care for older people places the family firmly at the centre of social care provision. This model is supported and reinforced by ageing-related policy reports and documents as well as reports in a range of related policy areas such as health and social welfare. The National Council on Ageing and Older People, which has referred to the family as the 'back-bone of community care' (Finucane et al., 1994: 13), supports the model of informal care for older people at home, albeit with the support of a range of social services.

There are disadvantages associated with this policy approach. Debates about the role of the state vis-à-vis the family in the provision of social care are sidelined (Yeates, 1997). The availability of public social care services (residential, community-based and domiciliary) for older people is a significant factor influencing the social care given to older relatives by family members. In countries with well-developed social care provision, older people are less likely to depend on family for social care and assistance. Denmark is the country with the most developed domiciliary care provision for older people, and older people living there are less likely to receive family care than other EU member states. In others, where state support is in short supply, family care is often the only option (McGlone and Cronin, 1994).

Without adequate public social care services, the problem remains of how to care for older people with significant social care needs that cannot be adequately met within the family (Blackman, 2001). Furthermore, a consequence of placing the family at the centre of the social care model is that consideration is not given to alternatives models of care provision for older people such as moving to a universal system of care, introducing long-term care insurance, expanding entitlement to institutional care or expanding the state's responsibility for care provision (Timonen and McMenamin, 2002).

Payments for social care and paying for social care

The financing of social care is as complex and varied as the mix of social care provision (Baldock and Ely, 1996). Social care is likely to be financed using a combination of financial subsidy and cash benefits from the state, private income and assets, financial support from family, friends and charities as well as unpaid voluntary assistance from family, friends, neighbours and volunteers.

Although a feature of social care services is that they are predominantly non-cash services (Munday, 1996a), in Ireland it is usual for older people to make a personal payment for home-based and community-based social care services they receive from the HSE as well as those provided by voluntary organisations (Convery, 2001, O'Hanlon et al., 2005). Indeed, there has been a trend from the year 2000 to 2004 of increasing numbers of older people paying for home-based and community-based social care services (O'Hanlon et al., 2005). For older people with the ability to pay, care may be purchased from the private sector. In addition, older people may be paying for social care provided informally by family, friends and neighbours (Garavan et al., 2001). As Garavan et al. (2001) point out, making a contribution towards social care services is important for feelings of autonomy for some older people. However, the cost of paying for social care services, particularly for those on a low income, is considered to present a barrier to utilisation and can raise significant concerns for older people if social care services are needed on a long-term or intensive basis. The NESF (2005a: 52) points out that 'the policy of promoting care at home requires that the supports available are on a par with those available for institutional care. This is not the case at present'. To address this imbalance, the NESF (2005a) recommends the development of community-based subventions to contribute towards the care needs of older people in community settings.

As non-cash services, it is usual to distinguish social care services from the means tested or insurance-based cash benefit systems of a country. However, this distinction is not altogether clear as the cash benefit system of a country can play a role in encouraging families to provide social care for older people. The Irish cash benefit system has been classified as a social security model, where allowances (and more recently benefits) are paid directly to the family carer through the national social security system (Glendinning et al., 1997). One of the main forms of financial support provided by the state for carers is the Carer's Allowance, a social assistance payment to carers of older people (as well as carers of other groups of people). Its primary aim is to partially replace income foregone through lost employment opportunities, which is seen as a cost of social caring. However, these payments tend to be very low and in reality do not fully compensate the caregiver for loss of earnings. The Carer's Allowance can be seen as a means of compensating carers in a limited way as well as acting as a financial incentive to carers to provide such services (Cousins, 1994). Although take up remains extremely low, Carer's Benefit, a social insurance benefit to enable family carers to interrupt work in order to provide social care for older relatives is another form of financial support aimed at encouraging the provision of informal social care for older people.

There are advantages associated with the social security model. It recognises the independent rights of family caregivers to their own income; family caregivers are not dependent on the care recipients for their income, and it affords caregivers a degree of financial independence. In addition, entitlement does not depend on medical assessments of care needs of the older relatives, and, as payments are not intended as substitutes for social care services, family caregivers or older people are not precluded from receiving such services (Glendinning et al., 1997). Nevertheless, the social security model is consistent with the familist principle of Irish social care policy, which is predicated on the assumption that the family and not the state will be the principal source of social care in the community (Yeates, 1997). Furthermore, making payments directly to the caregiver can be considered to undermine the purchasing power of older relatives receiving care (Glendinning et al., 1997).

Gender dimension to social care

While many carers of older people are men, in Ireland as elsewhere social care is generally constructed as women's work and the majority of carers tend to be women. Research which has drawn attention to the gendered nature of family care of older relatives has consistently shown that women in all countries are the primary carers for older relatives (Hantrais, 1997). In Ireland O'Connor et al. (1988: 34) found that close to 80 per cent of 'dependent elderly people' are cared for by women, a finding confirmed by later studies (Blackwell et al., 1992). This concurs with studies in other countries, which show that the majority of carers of older people are women (McGlone, 1992; McGlone and Cronin, 1995).

Feminists have drawn attention to the extent that community care policies, including those for older people, rely on the unpaid work of women within the domestic sphere (Finch and Groves, 1980; Graham, 1997). Social care provided by family members including that for older relatives is, for the most part, unpaid work (Kiely, 1998). Finch and Groves (1980: 494) argue that the reality of community care can be expressed in a double equation: 'in practice community care equals care by the family, and in practice care by the family equals care by women'. In Ireland social security schemes such as the Carer's Allowance are 'strongly associated with strengthening the constitutional role of women as homemakers and caregivers' (Yeates, 1997: 33), while the low level of public care services further reinforces the role of women in caring for older relatives (Yeates, 1997).

Graham (1997) notes although care is usually conceptualised as women's unpaid work in the private domain of the family, this concept of care ignores women who provide social care on a paid basis to older people who are non-relatives in their own homes as well as in other social care settings. The gendered nature of informal social care giving is echoed in the public workplace. Reflecting the widespread assumption that the skills required to care for older people come naturally to women, those working in the social care sector where jobs tend to be poorly paid with low levels of training and little prospect of promotion, are predominantly women (Kiely, 1998; O'Donovan, 1997).

Additionally, the majority of older people who are receiving social care or using social care services are women. This is partly explained by greater longevity of women. However, when this is taken into account, the rate of disability after the age of 75 is consistently higher among women than men. As McGlone (1992: 12) puts it: 'although women generally outlive men, they do so in poorer health'.

Combining social care and work

With changes in family structures and an increase in women's participation in the labour market, a recurring theme in the social policy literature is that the model of informal social care is under pressure since carers, particularly women carers, will no longer be available or willing to provide social care for older relatives (Blackman, 2001; Comhairle, 2002; Timonen and McMenamin,

2002). Social care policy in Ireland relies on the continued availability of informal carers to carry out the vast bulk of care and support in the community (Cullen et al., 2004). Women and older people (generally where one spouse is caring for another) are key providers of social care for older relatives (Johnson, 1999). Yet both groups have been identified as a source of potential workers for the Irish labour market and targeted in return to work initiatives (NESF, 2000a). Thus, an incompatibility exists between labour market policy and social care policy (Cullen et al., 2004).

Policy initiatives aimed at enabling both women and older carers – particularly older women who care for older relatives, to combine work and caring responsibilities include: greater support from employers; more flexible and care-friendly work arrangements; and the provision of financial incentives such as adequate income support during absence from paid work to care (NESF, 2003a). To a certain extent, the Carer's Leave Act, 2001, allows a greater degree of flexibility in work and time off. However, Carer's Leave is unpaid, and, as for other forms of unpaid leave such as parental leave in Ireland, it is more likely to be taken up by those who are in a financially secure position to do so. Furthermore, unpaid leave does little to address the gender division of care provision (Timonen and McMenamin, 2002).

While such policy initiatives and improvements may go some way to facilitating family members to combine work and caring responsibilities, additional policy initiatives are needed if carers are to be offered a genuine choice between caring, employment or the combination of caring and working (Comhairle, 2002; Cullen et al., 2004). The provision of publicly funded accessible social care services could provide an alternative to or substitute for family care (Cullen et al., 2004). However, as Comhairle (2002) points out, if Ireland is to continue to rely on a model of family care, there is a need for payments to carers and the conditions attached to these payments to be reformed. In particular, Comhairle (2002: 32) argues that 'social insurance credits must be awarded to all people undertaking caring duties', that is, both long-term carers and people who combine paid employment with care work should have an unbroken record of social insurance contributions that entitle them to social insurance benefits.

The perspective and preferences of older people

In Ireland the social policy literature relating to the social care of older people has tended to emphasise the providers of care (Boyle, 1997). An examination of informal social care of older people serves to illustrate this. It is crucial to recognise the support needs of family caregivers. However, a consequence of focusing on family carers is that it 'shifts attention away from older people themselves' (Boyle, 1997: 47). As a result, the perspective of older people is often missing from the picture.

The disability movement has developed an important critique of informal care that can usefully be applied to social care of older people. Morris (1997), adopting a disability rights perspective, takes issue with the way in which family care has been identified as a women's issue. She is especially critical of the ways in which feminist literature in the 1970s and 1980s marginalised women with disabilities and older women by focusing on 'the burden of care' imposed on women carers within the family (Morris, 1995: 71). Arguing that the feminist agenda excluded the subjective experiences of people with disabilities and older people, Morris (1991) calls for the incorporation of the subjective experiences of the recipients of care. While most feminist analysis has emphasised the needs of carers (Graham, 1997), some feminists such as Arber and Ginn (1991: 130) agree that focusing exclusively on carers leads to 'a one-sided account' of care, and stress the importance of recognising that there are two sides to the care relationship – the 'care-giver' and the 'care-recipient'.

In the UK, studies have argued for a greater emphasis on the perspective of those receiving care (Graham, 1997). In the Irish context, Fahey (1997) points out that little is known about the strains and trauma that becoming care dependent places on older people themselves, a situation that may in some ways be worsened if the older person has to rely heavily on family members. The Commission on the Family considers that, in supporting the care of older people, a priority issue in public policy is 'to be sensitive to both the needs of family carers and the needs of the dependent older people' (Commission on the Family, 1998: 314). However, the needs of older people receiving social care are not necessarily prioritised. A study reporting on the thematic issues that arose during a year-long nationwide public consultation on how the government could best support the family reported that, in discussions of family care, the needs of carers rather than those requiring care dominated the discussion (Daly and O'Leary, 2004). Boyle (1997) contends that by focusing predominantly on responses aimed at carers in recommendations for policy and policy itself, policies that may be the preferred options of older people are not given adequate consideration. Many questions remain unanswered such as: What is it that older people want? Who do they want to provide them with assistance with daily living? Do they want their relatives to give them this assistance or would they prefer that paid workers take on the responsibility? (Boyle, 1997: 48)

The *Health and Social Service for Older People* (HeSSOP I) study, which consulted older people living in the community in two regions in Ireland about their views on health and social services, sheds some light on the expectations of older people for social care, and their preferences regarding family or professional care (Garavan et al., 2001). When asked about their preferences for who would care for them if they continued to live in their current home, just over half of the respondents reported that they would prefer family or friends for either housekeeping or personal care, and slightly over a quarter of respondents reported that they did not have a preference and that family or friends or professionals were acceptable for both of these types of social care. A higher proportion of respondents expressed a preference for professionals as a source of personal care (23 per cent) compared to housekeeping care (19 per cent) (Garavan et al., 2001).

The reasons for older people's preference for home-based informal care are unclear (Garavan et al., 2001). The HeSSOP I report (Garavan et al., 2001) suggests that older people have little choice either because alternatives to home-based family care are so unsatisfactory, or not actually available to them for a variety of reasons including lack of transportation to community-based services, lack of information about services, lack of know-how, financial reasons, geographical considerations, short supply and waiting lists. In some countries (and this tends to be countries with low levels of public provision) a stigma is often attached to receiving public social care services. This deters older people and their families from seeking help and reinforces a reliance on the family (McGlone and Cronin, 1994). In Germany, for instance, family carers may be reluctant to seek public help because of its association with social assistance. The public in Ireland have traditionally had a dislike for public care solutions (Timonen and McMenamin, 2000). Garavan et al., (2001) found that there is stigma attached to certain public social care services by a small but significant proportion of older people. Stigma or embarrass-ment appears to act as a significant barrier preventing some older people from using home help services and personal care attendants (Garavan et al., 2001). It would appear, however, that older people are feeling less stigmatised over time about using social care services (O'Hanlon et al., 2005).

The HeSSOP I study in 2000 revealed that despite concerns among some older people about the possible need for long-term care, the vast majority had not discussed their preferences for care with their family and a small proportion indicated that they were either not sure or believed that their preferences would not be honoured (Garavan et al., 2001). This did not change over four years (O'Hanlon et al., 2005). Other studies have shown that the views of older people and their relatives may not always coincide, the interests of older people are not necessarily the same as their relatives and that serious conflict between the two parties may arise (Boyle, 1997). Such factors can serve to limit the choice of older people and led Garavan et al. (2001: 210) to conclude that in reality, older people in need of assistance 'may have a lack of real choice'.

Demographic considerations

There is widespread concern that Ireland's ageing population will give rise to serious challenges for the social care of older people (as well as placing a greater strain on state pensions and health services). The population of older people in Ireland has grown at a steady pace since 1926, the first year in which a Census took place. At the time of the 1926 Census the population of people aged 65 and over stood at 271,680. In 2002, there were 436,005 people aged 65 or over (CSO, 2003a). Population projections suggest that the population of older people is expected to grow slightly to 2011 and to increase thereafter at a somewhat faster rate to approximately 850,000. The population of older people is therefore predicted to almost double between 2002 and 2031.

Projections suggesting that the population of people over 65 years of age is predicted to increase substantially raises concern about the increased need for social care services in the future. An increase in the numbers of older people is likely to cause an increased demand for social care services. However, population ageing is a highly emotive subject and can lead to an inflated sense of crisis about the growing social care 'burden' of older people (Vincent, 2003). Too often, the influence of demographic changes on the future demand for social care and other social services is given a significance that is not warranted. The role of other and often more significant factors is ignored. Similarly to health services (Fahey, 1998), it is likely that social care services are only partially influenced by changes in the demographic structure. Factors other than demographic trends tend to be more influential. These include economic factors such as the rising cost of care, changes in the structure of social care services, changes in the purchasing power of service users, rising expectations of social care users as well as political willingness and political ideology.

As Fahey and FitzGerald (1997) point out, demographic projections rest on uncertain foundations. It is an uncertain exercise and does not allow for major demographic shifts that might occur in the future. Moreover, the use of emotive words such as 'demographic timebomb' and 'growing burden' of older people implies that this group of people are less eligible or even blameworthy to a degree (Baldock and Ely, 1996) and 'serves to undermine the individuality and agency of older people' (Shakespeare, 2000: 54). Despite the rhetoric of dependency, many older people are not in need of personal care. They live independent lives in their own homes and even after withdrawing from the labour market, older people contribute in many ways including caring for grandchildren while parents go out to work, providing care for family members and participating in the community and voluntary sector.

Migration and social care

Since the early 1990s asylum seekers and refugees have arrived in Ireland, accompanied by an increasing number of migrant workers from all parts of the world, with Central and Eastern Europeans strongly represented (Immigrant Council of Ireland, 2003). The vast majority of these older people come from other Western EU countries, America, Australia and New Zealand, with a small minority coming from Central and Eastern European Countries, Asia and Africa (CSO, 2003b). Compared with Ireland as a whole in which people aged 65 years and over represent 11.1 per cent of the population, Census figures indicate that slightly over five per cent of people from outside Ireland are aged 65 years and over (CSO, 2003b). Ageing in migrant communities is, therefore, less pronounced, than in the wider population. As such, most migrants and their families in Ireland would have few older relatives living in Ireland. Though this group of older people is currently small, with a growing number of asylum seekers, refugees and migrant workers coming to live in Ireland, the social care needs of older people within these communities is likely to emerge as a policy issue in the future.

Little is known in Ireland about the situation or the social care needs of the current cohort of older people in immigrant and newly emerging minority ethnic communities. The under-use of social care services by minority ethnic communities is well documented in Britain (Drake, 1999). Studies there have found that, although there are noticeable differences between minority ethnic communities (and within the majority population), older people in minority ethnic community tend to have substantially lower pensions than older people in the wider population (Blakemore, 2002). Thus, some older people in minority ethnic communities, like some older people in the wider population, may not be in a position to meet their social care needs from their own resources (Blakemore, 2002).

Evidence from studies in Britain suggests that, like access to health services, older people in black and minority ethnic communities and their carers face structural barriers in accessing social care services, both formal and informal (Graham, 1997; Blakemore, 1998). With respect to informal social care, there is no statutory right for migrants to family reunification in Ireland (Immigrant Council of Ireland, 2003), which means that older migrants may have no close relatives in Ireland to assist them with tasks they find difficult to perform alone. Others may be reliant on a rather narrow base of family support (Blakemore, 2002). This presents a problem as in Ireland the family has been defined in policy as central to the social care of older people.

The issues facing migrant workers working in the field of social care are another aspect of migration. There has been limited debate about the employment of migrant workers as social care workers in public and private residential, community-based or domiciliary services. Employment in the social care sector is not well rewarded in money or status. It is in low-skilled sectors such as the care work sector that migrant workers tend to be concentrated (Immigrant Council of Ireland). Migrant workers doing social care work are likely to be working through employment agencies as well as working in the private, live-in sector, where the work provides accommodation as well as pay.

One aspect of migration is the return of older Irish migrants, who have been living outside Ireland since the wave of emigration that lasted from the 1930s to the 1960s (Winston, 2002). Winston (2002: 40) argues that, given the considerable remittances sent by older emigrants to their family members in Ireland over the years, 'there is a strong social justice case for supporting the relocation of those emigrants who wish to return to Ireland but cannot afford to do so'. The Safe-Home programme and organisations including Mayo Migrant Liaison Committee and the Kerry Emigrant Support Groups are facilitating the return from Britain of some older Irish migrants who have experienced disadvantage in terms of income, housing and health (Winston, 2002). These programmes have highlighted the need for a range of easily accessible personal care services as an important issue for returning older Irish migrants (Winston, 2002). Winston (2002: 40) stresses that if the social care needs of returning older Irish migrants are to be met considerable investment will be required to expand on and improve the very limited social care services that currently exist. This holds true for older asylum seekers, refugees and migrant workers, and, indeed, for all older people in Ireland.

Conclusion

Enabling as many older people as possible to remain in their own homes, if they so wish, has been widely adopted as a desirable outcome of social policy in Ireland. Indeed, the vast majority of older people in need of social care in Ireland manage to remain in their own homes. This is despite the low level of public community-based and domiciliary social care services. A large volume of social care *at* home is provided on an informal basis by family, friends and neighbours. The model of informal social care for older people at home that currently exists reflects the historical pattern of social care provision in Ireland. It is based on a principle of subsidiarity, placing responsibility for the social care of older relatives on the family, particularly women who are constructed as carers within the family. Financial support for informal care in the form of social security payments 'confirm and formalise without question' private, informal arrangements of social care (Glendinning et al., 1997: 129). The increasing participation of carers, particularly women, but also older people, in the labour market has given rise to concern about the care potential of families especially in view of the growing number of older people in Ireland. This has prompted interest in the development of policy initiatives to encourage and support carers in combining work and caring responsibilities.

The public sector plays a relatively modest role in the provision of social care services for older people in Ireland. Despite recent controversy, the trend towards involving the private sector in the residential care of older people is likely to continue. The Minister of Health, Mary Harney announced that she was examining measures to increase support for older people *at* home, including plans to make community based and domiciliary social care services available on a more comprehensive basis. The details of this plan are still unclear and questions of balance between nursing and social care services, eligibility to such services and who will pay and provide these services have yet to be answered. The inclusion of the perspective of older people and their families using such measures would benefit the plan.

Besides demographic considerations, a range of factors influence the development of social care policies for older people. Much attention has been drawn to the impact of an ageing population, but while immigration has in some instances been suggested as a possible response to the problem of Ireland's ageing population, much less attention has been paid to the social care needs of older immigrants or the role of migrant workers in providing social care to older people. These issues are likely to emerge in the future.

Recommended reading

McGee, H. M., O'Hanlon, A., Barker, M. Stout, R., O'Neill, D., Conroy, R., Hickey, A., Shelley. E. and Layte, R. (2005) *One Island – Two Systems: A Comparison of Health Status and Health and Social Service Use by Community-Dwelling Older People in the Republic of Ireland and Northern Ireland.* Dublin: IPHI.

NESF (2003a) *Labour Market Issues for Older Workers.* Forum Report no. 26. Dublin: NESF.

NESF (2005a) *Care for Older People,* Report no. 32. Dublin: NESF.

Chapter 13

Social policy and the Irish diaspora

Nessa Winston

Introduction

This chapter examines the context within which the Irish state has begun to extend statutory funding towards welfare organisations in Britain aimed at addressing some welfare needs of Irish citizen emigrants. It traces the development of policy, assessing the role of both statutory and non-statutory agencies. In addition, it examines the main issues arising subsequent to the *Report of the Task Force on Emigration* (Task Force on Policy Regarding Emigrants, 2002). It is estimated that the Irish diaspora consists of approximately 3 million people living outside Ireland, 1.2 million of whom were born in Ireland (Walter et al., 2002: 22). Britain has been the main destination for emigrants since 1922, but they have not always been welcome and there is evidence that they have experienced some difficulties integrating (Connolly, 2000; Delaney, 2000; Douglas, 2002; Jackson, 1963; Task Force, 2002). Numerous studies reveal their relative disadvantage in employment, housing and health. However, the needs of the Irish in Britain are often invisible to mainstream services owing to inadequate monitoring in census and other ethnic monitoring systems. In addition, there is evidence that some health and welfare professionals discriminate against the Irish, employing negative stereotypes of them. The stereotype of the Irish person commonly found in English culture includes 'drunks', 'violent', 'stupid' and/or 'fraudsters' (Hickman and Walter, 1997: 110–11). For these reasons, this chapter focuses on social policy and the Irish in Britain.

A sizeable Irish Catholic voluntary sector operates in England and Wales, which provides a range of culturally sensitive social services for this community. Until very recently, the Irish state has played almost no role in the provision of welfare for emigrants, despite frequent demands for action from a range of pressure groups. While the Irish government now provides some funding towards the cost of running these voluntary services, there is a significant shortfall in the resources required to meet needs. It can be argued that the traditional policy of the Irish state has been to facilitate emigration and deny responsibility for the care of emigrants. It did not produce a policy regarding emigrants until 2002 and progress on implementing this policy has been disappointing.

The needs of the Irish in Britain

The Irish are the largest migrant community in Britain. The last census revealed that there were approximately 494,147 Irish-born people living there (National Statistics, 2005). Part of the explanation for the large Irish population is the 'special' position, which Ireland occupies in relation to Britain. Following independence in 1922, the Irish Free State became a dominion in the Commonwealth and Irish citizens remained free to take up residence in Britain. When Ireland withdrew from the Commonwealth in 1948, the Irish were neither British subjects nor Commonwealth citizens. Because of the value of Irish labour and the situation in Northern Ireland, among other reasons, the 1948 British Nationality Act made special provision for the Irish so that any law that applied to British subjects would also apply to Irish citizens. The Ireland Act, 1949 confirmed this special status by allowing Irish citizens to enter and settle in Britain without restriction. As a result, Irish citizen emigrants are treated as British citizens. They have the same entitlements as their British counterparts in relation to education, employment, housing, social security, health and personal social services.

Despite having the same entitlements as British citizens, there is evidence that Irish people have problems accessing certain benefits and services. Numerous studies show problems for Irish people in accessing affordable, good quality housing and that they are overrepresented among the homeless and rough sleepers (Cope, 2002; Hickman and Walter, 1997; Owen, 1995). Irish welfare agencies report that some Irish people are deterred from applying for social housing by 'gate-keeping' staff in the reception area (Hickman and Walter, 1997: 116). Similarly, newly arrived migrants may be told that they have made themselves 'intentionally homeless' by leaving Ireland and are therefore not a priority for housing allocations (Hickman and Walter, 1997: 115).

There are serious concerns about the physical and psychological health of the Irish in Britain (Balarajan, 1995; Bracken et al., 1998; Harding and Balarajan, 1996; Kelleher and Hillier, 1996; Kelleher and Cahill, 2004; Leavey, 1999; Owen, 1995; Tilki, 1996). A study for the Commission for Racial Equality concluded that 'Irish needs were even more marginalised within the health service than elsewhere' (Hickman and Walter, 1997: 101). In general, this ill health is higher than would be expected given the demographic and socio-economic characteristics of the Irish community (Harding and Balarajan, 1996). However, negative stereotyping by health care professionals and a reluctance to make demands on the health care system may also be important (Kelleher and Hillier, 1996: 121).

While the Irish are entitled to claim social security on the same basis as British citizens, research has shown that not all social services staff take this into account when dealing with Irish claimants (Hickman and Walter, 1997: 115). For example, the habitual residence clause does not apply to Irish people, yet some claimants are told that it does. The use of exclusionary practices by staff because of their stereotyping of Irish people as fraudsters results in delays in processing claims, long waiting times for receipt of benefits, excessive requests for identification and refusal of claims. Gordon and Newnham (1985) noted that white people were rarely asked to produce passports when applying for social security. However, research has shown that Irish people are asked to produce passports and birth certificates and that staff frequently question the authenticity of these documents (Hickman and Walter, 1997: 112–13). These demands contravene the 1948 British Nationality Act and a 1987 government directive on the issue (Hickman and Walter, 1997: 112–13).

There is evidence that some people do not claim the health and social welfare benefits to which they are entitled (Hickman and Walter, 1997: 181). People who were denied mainstream services in the past may never apply again, despite entitlements. In particular, this issue arises for older people who, on reaching pension age, become entitled to a range of benefits and services but are reluctant to claim them. These older emigrants arrived in Britain during a time when anti-Irish discrimination was quite blatant. In addition, Irish paramilitary bombing campaigns in Britain and the Prevention of Terrorism Act arguably contributed to their feeling that they had to 'keep their heads down' about being Irish and in part explains their reluctance to access certain services (Hillyard, 1993). In some cases, they do not approach mainstream agencies because of a history of negative encounters with British services providers. Other older people are determined to be 'independent' and avoid the stigma of social welfare, problems which have been identified among older people in Ireland (Garavan et al., 2001: 19–22). For these reasons, many older Irish people living in Britain do not receive the social care they require.

Many of the problems faced by older Irish people have been recognised by the Irish voluntary sector in Britain for some time (Tilki, 1998; Williams and Mac an Ghaill, 1998; Winston, 2000). For example, as early as the late 1970s, the Hammersmith Irish Welfare Centre turned its attention to 'aged Irish people living in isolation', including single homeless men who had been employed in the construction industry (O'Shea, 1985: 59). The appalling social situation of some older Irish people in Britain has been highlighted in a number of studies (Tilki, 1998; Winston, 2000; 2002). The picture revealed is one of people living in very poor housing, existing on minimal financial resources, in poor health, isolated from services and social networks.

Most Irish agencies have responded by establishing specialist services to meet the needs of older Irish people in their areas, creating 'elders outreach' posts as well as a network of volunteer 'befrienders'. This work involves visiting people in their homes as well as founding drop-in centres for older people, luncheon clubs and other special events for this group. Irish welfare agencies play an important role informing people of their welfare entitlements and assisting them with the applications. However, even Irish service providers consider the older Irish to be extremely 'independent', referring to them as 'service refusers' (Tilki, 1998). In recent years, there has been considerable interest in assisting the return to Ireland of some of these older migrants which is now an issue of concern to policy makers. A number of voluntary organisations in Britain and Ireland have been facilitating their return on a small scale (for example the Aisling project; Arlington House, Camden; Kerry Resettlement; Mayo Emigrant Liaison Committee). Extending this work, the Safe-Home Programme assists the return of older people who lack the finance and/or ability to return without assistance.

Despite the available evidence of significant needs, there is an assumption that the Irish 'unproblematically assimilate into the "white" population within a fairly short space of time' (Walter et al., 2002: 38). Irish people tend to be included in a 'white' majority category for official purposes, including resource distribution along ethnic lines. They have been excluded from policies and programmes to address discrimination (Fanning and Pierce, 2004: 8). The Commission for Racial Equality only accepted the principle of Irish ethnicity in 1997, following pressure from the Irish Research Advisory Group, and it advocated successfully for the inclusion of an Irish category in the 2001 census of England and Wales (Fanning and Pierce, 2004: 8). However, it is likely that that the Census underestimated the Irish population as there are numerous problems with the question, including the location of the Irish category under 'white' ethnic groups, and the lack of hyphenated British identities (Howard, 2004; Walter, 2004). The Irish are still excluded from some ethnic monitoring systems, including a British study of housing and ethnic communities (Office of the Deputy Prime Minister, 2003). As a result, many of their specific needs remain invisible to mainstream service providers (Hickman, 1998; Garrett, 2004; Parekh, 2000). Not only does this limit Irish access to mainstream services, it also has important implications for service provision by Irish welfare agencies. These agencies have encountered a long-standing 'battle to be heard' by British funding sources as they have difficulty gaining recognition for the special needs of the Irish population (Walter et al., 2002: 48).

The response of the Irish statutory and voluntary sectors

The first record of Irish statutory 'involvement' in the welfare of Irish emigrants was the establishment of an Interdepartmental Committee on Seasonal Emigration in 1938. This was a response to the death of ten Irish migrant workers from a fire in their sleeping quarters in Scotland (Walter et al., 2002: 21). However, that committee concluded that the Irish state should not become involved in the welfare of emigrants, a statement repeated on a number of occasions over the following decade. In 1948, the new coalition government established a Commission on Emigration. It made a number of important recommendations, which were largely ignored owing to changes in government and general apathy (Ferriter, 2004: 480). It is not difficult to explain this apathy. Given the significant inequalities in Irish society, and the fact that it was predominantly the more disadvantaged who left, emigration provided an important 'safety valve against revolution' (Lee, 1989: 374). From a financial perspective, many Irish governments would have had a very difficult task funding unemployment payments and, as far back as 1942, the Department of Finance noted the importance of emigrant remittances as an 'inflow of ready money' to the near-subsistence economy (Lee, 1989: 227).

The development of the Irish voluntary sector in Britain can be traced back to early services provided by the Irish Catholic Church. Frustrated by government inaction, the Church began to establish its own services for emigrants in the 1940s (Acheson et al., 2004: 83–4). Its response was motivated primarily by a concern for the spiritual welfare of emigrants, including concerns that some were joining 'left-wing groups' (O'Shea, 1985: 15). However, even in the early stages, it provided a range of social welfare services, which were expanded over time. In 1942, Archbishop John Charles McQuaid established an emigrant section of the Catholic Social Welfare Bureau in Dublin to assist migrants before leaving Ireland with issues such as employment, accommodation, and religious practice. In 1953, this became the Irish Episcopal Commission for Emigrants (IECE), whose role was to respond in a more co-ordinated way to the needs of the Irish in Britain and, subsequently, in other countries (Acheson et al, 2004: 84). This entailed securing personnel for an emigrant chaplaincy scheme, providing advice on emigration, and establishing the Dublin Diocesan Emigrant Welfare Resource Centres (O'Shea, 1985: 66–7). Today, these chaplaincies are in Britain, continental Europe, the USA and Australia and they play a significant role in the provision of welfare services for the Irish diaspora (Harvey, 1999).

While the chaplaincy scheme responded to a range of needs, housing issues became a priority as many Irish emigrants had problems accessing affordable, adequate housing. In 1955, the Catholic Church founded the Irish Centre in Camden Square, London, to 'provide hostels with chapels, canteens, libraries, living rooms and residential accommodation in a Christian atmosphere for workers unable to find or afford suitable lodgings' (O'Shea, 1985: 14). This centre remains an important part of the Irish voluntary sector in London, offering a broad range of social services. In the 1960s, Fr Eamon Casey designed a number of innovative responses to these housing needs (O'Shea, 1985: 43–7). Subsequently, a number of Irish voluntary agencies in Britain established housing associations and hostels to meet the housing needs of the Irish population though people from other ethnic backgrounds are accommodated.

During the 1970s, the chaplaincy scheme opened a number of welfare centres to cater for the increasing number of 'problem cases' they encountered among Irish emigrants (O'Shea, 1985: 55). The Federation of Irish Societies was established in this period to act as an umbrella body for the Irish voluntary sector in Britain. It plays an important role co-ordinating the activities of these organisations, providing information on new policies and funding opportunities and informing Irish governments on relevant issues. Its members provide a wide range of services to the Irish Community. It is estimated that there were approximately 52 Irish welfare or social service agencies in Britain at the end of the twentieth century, with a further 16 in the United States, eight in continental Europe and four in Australia (Acheson et al., 2004: 137). These emigrant organisations have been lauded for their professionalism:

> These services set standards for social provision far ahead of their time, employing social workers from an early stage and setting standards for documentation and accountability. They provided a joined up set of services in the area of accommodation, work, integration into the host community and advice and recreation, long before such approaches were formally articulated as good practice (Acheson et al., 2004: 86).

When emigration rose significantly in the 1980s, the Irish government established the Interdepartmental Committee on Emigration (ICE) to co-ordinate the work of government departments and statutory bodies in relation to emigration. However, this committee was ineffectual both in co-ordinating and in improving services (Harvey, 1999: 28–9). The establishment of the Dion Committee in 1984 represented the first serious attempt to provide Irish statutory funding for the welfare of emigrants in Britain. Earlier attempts to obtain statutory funding for these services were opposed as being 'unsound from the point of view of state finance' or because they represented a shift from voluntary to statutory provision (Delaney, 2000: 259). Dion stemmed from the Committee on Welfare Services Abroad, established in the Department of Labour in the early 1970s to assist young emigrants with

limited financial resources or information. Little is known about this committee, which raises questions about its effectiveness. Following on Dion
recommendations, the government provides financial support to some
voluntary agencies working with the Irish in Britain. However, Dion funding
has always fallen far short of what was required and most of the voluntary
agencies cannot meet the demand for their services because of inadequate
funding (Task Force, 2002: 47).

After a sustained period of emigration in the 1980s, there were a number
of important developments in the 1990s. First, the Mary Robinson Presidency
(1990–7) 'was marked by a symbolism which acknowledged the Irishness of
emigrants and their descendants' (Fanning, 2002: 3). In her inaugural speech
in 1990, President Robinson stated that she would be 'proud to represent' the
diaspora. In 1995, she addressed the Irish parliament on 'a matter of public
importance' in a speech entitled 'Cherishing the Irish diaspora'. In it, she
highlighted many of the policy issues and praised the agencies working with
emigrants abroad. The responses by parliamentarians were lukewarm, hostile
or indifferent (O'Leary and Burke, 1998: 196–204).

The following year saw the publication of a NESC report on emigration,
which highlighted many of the difficulties faced by the Irish in Britain.
Furthermore, it concluded that between 15 and 17 per cent of emigrants arrived
ill prepared to access housing and employment in the new country. The 1996
White Paper on Foreign Policy reiterated these points, and stated the inten-
tion of the Irish government to provide assistance to organisations catering
for emigrants in 'particular need' (White Paper, 1996: 289–90). The report of
the Commission on the Family (1998), which dedicated a chapter to the Irish
diaspora, echoed these concerns for vulnerable young migrants. It also
emphasised the need for more advice to be given to those likely to emigrate,
and recommended funding for this purpose. Following its publication, the
Department of Social, Community and Family Affairs initiated a funding
scheme to provide this information.

Coinciding with a decline in emigration figures from about 1996, emigration slipped down the policy agenda again. It did not feature in the National
Anti-Poverty Strategy or the Green and White Papers on the Voluntary
Sector (Government of Ireland, 1997b; 1997a; 2000c). However, following
the Good Friday Agreement in 1998, Article 2 of the Constitution of Ireland
was amended to state that it is the entitlement of people born on the 'island
of Ireland' to be 'part of the Irish Nation'. While the text was written with a
view to solving some constitutional issues for the Northern Irish, it may be
argued that this redefinition of the Irish nation expanded the scope for
developing policy and services for the Irish abroad. There have been no legal
challenges by emigrants and there is no clear interpretation of their entitlements derived from the change, but it could be interpreted as a movement in

the direction of a rights-based approach. At the very least, it might involve the Irish government working with host countries to address the special needs of the most vulnerable Irish. The issue of extending voting rights to emigrants has been dismissed on number of occasions, most recently in 2002 (All Party Oireachtas Committee on the Constitution, 2002). Similarly, calls for free travel for emigrants aged 66 years and over when visiting Ireland have also been dismissed.

In 2001, the government designated the Safe-Home project the 'National Repatriation Organisation of Ireland'. Later that year, the Irish Minister for Housing introduced a scheme to facilitate the provision of sheltered housing in the voluntary/co-operative sector to older returning migrants. Under the scheme, up to 25 per cent of new sheltered housing units may be allocated to older emigrants on the Safe-home waiting list. This was an important development as it enabled older people to apply for social housing from abroad, something which had previously not been possible. One survey of older emigrants in England suggested that a minority (27 per cent) would wish to return and thought it possible to do so (Winston, 2002). However, those most likely to wish to return are the most deprived, financially and socially (Malcolm, 1996; Winston, 2002). A number of studies have highlighted the inadequacies of the health, housing and social services for older people living in Ireland (Convery, 2001; Garavan et al., 2001; Ruddle et al., 2000). In particular, there are difficulties regarding housing, community care and access to health services. In light of these shortcomings, and given that the Irish population is an ageing one, considerable investment is required in order to both expand on and improve all of the services required by older people.

The IECE and its sister organisation the Irish Commission for Prisoners Overseas (ICPO) have played an important role as pressure groups criticising successive governments for their lack of policy on emigrants and failure to meet the needs of the most vulnerable. A 1999 evaluation of their services called for the establishment of a Task Force to develop policy in the area (Harvey, 1999). The cumulative effect of all of these events since the mid-1980s has been a change of mindset among some policy makers and government ministers, from a denial of responsibility for the social care of emigrants to one in which their care has become a policy issue. In 2000, the Irish government made a commitment in the *Programme for Prosperity and Fairness* to establish a Task Force on policy regarding emigrants (Government of Ireland, 2000a).

The Task Force on Policy Regarding Emigrants

The Task Force on Policy Regarding Emigrants was established in 2001. Its membership included representative of relevant government departments and the Irish voluntary sector. In its report, it argued that one of the objectives of policy should be to 'ensure as far as possible, that Irish people who emigrate do so voluntarily and on the basis of informed choice, and are properly prepared to live independently in different societies' (Task Force, 2002: 3). Stemming from this, it recommended the development of a comprehensive information package for those intending to emigrate and increased funding for voluntary agencies supplying this information. Emigrant Advice, part of Crosscare, the Dublin Diocesan Social Care Agency, provides an excellent information service with minimal resources (Harvey, 1999: 29). However, research shows that many emigrants do not access this advice prior to departure (Winston, 2000). A central issue is identifying ways to communicate this information to those who need it.

The Task Force argued that a key objective for policy was to 'protect and support the Irish Abroad, particularly those who emigrate involuntarily and those who find themselves marginalised or at risk of social exclusion' (Task Force, 2002: 3). It proposed the establishment of a new independent statutory agency (The Agency for the Irish Abroad) to facilitate and support co-operation between statutory and voluntary agencies and services in Ireland and destination countries. An important role of the Agency would be the allocation of funding for services following recommendations from the Dion Committee and similar committees in other countries. An inter-departmental working group established to consider the recommendations of the Task Force argued that this agency 'might not be practicable at the present time' (2003: 5). Instead of creating an independent statutory body, the government established a dedicated unit in Department of Foreign Affairs in 2004. The 'advisory' nature of this unit suggests that it will have limited powers to implement policy compared with those of a statutory body.

The Task Force recommended a substantial increase in funding for voluntary agencies providing welfare services to marginalised Irish people living abroad. Specifically, it argued that these services required €18 million for 2003, rising to €34 million in 2005 (Task Force, 2002: 5). Dion funding was cut by five per cent between 2001 and 2003. A *Prime Time* television documentary in 2003, portraying the appalling conditions in which some older Irish people lived in Britain, evoked much public and political discussion on the topic and, arguably, triggered an increase in funding from government. However, as €7m was allocated in 2005 (a shortfall of €27m), the commitment of government to implement this recommendation seems relatively weak. The inter-departmental working group, established to consider the recommendations of the Task Force, argued that 'in the present budgetary circumstances, the level of resources recommended by the Task Force for emigrant services could not be provided' (2003: 2). Moreover, it noted that the provision of support for migrants at risk of poverty and social exclusion in the EU now came under the National Action Plans on Social Inclusion. The latest of these was being prepared at time of going to press.

Another objective of the Task Force was to 'facilitate the return to Ireland and reintegration into Irish society of emigrants who wish to do so, especially the vulnerable and the elderly' (Task Force, 2002: 3). It called on housing associations to allocate places for returning emigrants and for increased funding for the Safe Home programme. In addition, it highlighted the need for a new funding scheme dedicated to care and support services for older returning emigrants in supported housing schemes in Ireland. An announcement was due to be made by the minister in 2005 on this matter but this had not been done at time of going to press.

In recent years, there has been some collaboration among British and Irish government departments. The Task Force called for the establishment of a structure to facilitate contact between Irish statutory agencies providing services to emigrants, their British counterparts and Irish voluntary agencies in Britain (Task Force, 2002: 50). Another suggestion was that at the Inter-Governmental Conference, established under the Good Friday Agreement, both governments should support this type of collaboration and that ministers from both countries should have more frequent discussions of progress on issues relating to the Irish in Britain. To date these conferences have been preoccupied with the peace process, but there may now be space on the agenda for the social care of Irish emigrants.

Conclusion

This chapter has highlighted the significant needs of some members of the Irish population in Britain. While there has been a considerable response to these needs by the Irish voluntary sector, the Irish state adopted a laissez-faire approach until very recently. There has been some improvement since about the year 2000 owing to a combination of factors such as the publication of major reports highlighting needs, pressure from a variety of sources especially at high levels, and the improved Irish economy. The report of the Task Force represents the most significant change because it introduced a policy for the care of the Irish diaspora. Another important and welcome advance has been the increase in Irish government funding for the voluntary sector. However, this funding continues to fall significantly below what is required. The establishment of an advisory body rather than an independent, statutory body to implement the Task Force recommendations is also disappointing.

At the very least, article 2 of the constitution places an onus on the Irish government to ensure that the needs of the most marginalised Irish emigrants are met. This could happen in a number of ways. First, the government could work in partnership with the British and Irish statutory and voluntary sectors to address the issues. For example, the British and Irish Inter-Governmental conferences could resolve a number of important problems, such as the inadequacy of ethnic monitoring systems in Britain. Adequate ethnic monitoring would assist the Irish voluntary sector in their battle for the recognition of these needs and improve the capacity of both mainstream and voluntary organisations to meet the needs of the Irish population.

A second way in which the Irish government could meet the needs of marginalised emigrants would be by increasing funding for emigrant services to the level recommended by the Task Force. One could argue that the constitutional redefinition of the Irish nation places a new emphasis on Irish social policy to cater for the needs of emigrants. Enhancing services for older Irish emigrants is an urgent issue and would include assisting the return of those who wished to come back to Ireland. In doing so, the government would have to address another pressing policy issue, namely improving the health and social services for our older population generally.

Recommended reading

Hickman, M. and Walter, B. (1997) *Discrimination and the Irish Community in Britain.* London: Commission for Racial Equality.

NESC (1991) *The Economic and Social Implications of Emigration,* Report no. 90. Dublin: NESC.

Task Force on Policy Regarding Emigrants (2002) *Ireland and the Irish Abroad.* Dublin: Department of Foreign Affairs.

Winston, N. (2000) *Between Two Places: A Case Study of Irish-born People Living in England.* Dublin: Irish National Committee of the European Cultural Foundation.

Chapter 14

Community development and care

Mary Ellen McCann

Introduction

This chapter considers the rationale for a community approach to care using examples from community development work. The benefits and limitations of employing community development strategies in responding to care needs will be explored within a consideration of different interpretations of 'community'. The community and voluntary sector has a long and valued tradition of meeting social needs in Ireland. It now has a large presence in the development of social policy, especially in the roles of service providers, advocates and identifiers of new needs (Government of Ireland, 2000c: 68). Since the 1980s in Ireland, 'community' has been presented as a progressive approach to care for a range of groups in the population, and a positive alternative to residential care (NESC, 1987). For example, in the care of people with mental health issues (Government of Ireland, 1984), in treatment for those with drug related problems (McCann 1998: 151), in services for the elderly (O'Loughlin, 2005: 212), and in the approach to long-term unemployment (Government of Ireland, 1989: 75). Local communities were described as the 'primary movers' in strategies which would 'integrate the various existing initiatives' (Government of Ireland, 1989: 75). Area-based approaches to many issues have been adopted, leading to the growth of a plethora of local interventions (Duggan, 1998: 65).

This chapter examines the challenges involved in reconciling the dual focus upon individual interventions and upon collective actions aimed at promoting social change. It considers areas that are likely in the future to benefit from adopting community development approaches to care, such as responses to immigrant communities and ethnic minorities. The chapter identifies a number of organisational challenges and ambiguities that, it is argued, necessitate the reform of traditional hierarchical structures if these are to be resolved. The overall structure of a learning organisation, where people learn together at all levels in the organisation (Senge, 1990: 3), is suggested as an appropriate model.

A community approach to care

In the area of housing, tenant participation in management of local authority housing estates is part of a broader reform movement within local authorities aimed at providing a better, more responsive and efficient service to people (Conway, 2001: 3). In a parallel development, the expansion of Community Employment Schemes in the mid-1990s (Fitzgerald, 2005: 130), provided paid staff for many community and voluntary organisations. These schemes have been found to be a useful support in drug rehabilitation projects (Bruce, 2004: 86). Furthermore, participation and consultation are increasingly demanded by users of services, for example in the case of people with disabilities (Quin and Redmond, 2005: 138). This emphasis has carried into the Primary Care Strategy (Department of Health and Children 2001a). Primary care is the first point of contact that people have with the health and personal social services. In an effort to bring primary care more into the central focus of the health system, a team-based approach to service provision is outlined in the Strategy (Department of Health and Children, 2001a: 7). Community involvement is named among its actions (2001a: 9). However, how such aspirations actually look in practice can vary, depending on interpretation. 'Community' can mean a site for action; or it can be used to describe a resource to professional teams; or it can mean self help. But community work differs from community 'based' work such as service delivery, and community-based inter-sectoral partnerships, in that it is consciously, actively and specifically focussed on bringing about social change in favour of those most marginalised or excluded in society (CWC 2004: 15). Using this definition, the primary health care model calls for an approach in which individual stories and experiences can ultimately come together – in one voice – to call for essential structural and institutional change (Shapiro et al., 1994: 229).

The case for community development

The arguments for community development are succinctly outlined by the Combat Poverty Agency (CPA, 2000: 5). The first one is that it promotes greater social inclusion, that it is rooted in a broad understanding of citizenship, and that it is potentially a means by which people can achieve the right to influence and participate in decisions that affect them. Projects funded under the CDP (Community Development Programme) are concerned with the needs of women and children, those with disabilities, the homeless, lone parent families, the elderly, the unemployed, young people at risk, Travellers, and other disadvantaged groups. These groups are often those whose voices are not heard in policy making, who rarely have the chance to participate in the decisions that affect their lives. The second main argument is a pragmatic one. Programmes and services are more likely to be efficient and effective if those with direct experience of the problems, or those who live in communities affected by these problems, are involved in their design and implementation.

These benefits were recognised by The World Health Organisation in 1978, when it formally incorporated a community development dimension to primary health care in its *Declaration of Alma Ata* (WHO, 1978: iv). Community involvement was important where need for services was greater than could be provided by the state agencies, or where the problems being faced were particularly intransigent and difficult. The notion of community involvement in its own health care had grown significantly in the early 1970s through reports of what was happening in China. Returning visitors enthused about the 'barefoot doctor' system they had seen being used to great effect, providing health care and health education to the 500 million rural Chinese (Rifkin, 1978: 34).

Subsequently, a similar approach was adopted in health promotion, with the adoption of the Ottawa Charter in 1986, in which health promotion was described as 'the process of enabling people to increase control over, and to improve, their health' (WHO, 1986: 1). The focus was to achieve equity in health, through people taking control of the determinates of health, and through intersectoral collaboration (WHO, 1986: 1–2). In Ireland, where responsibility for social care rests with the Department of Health and Children and is subsumed under the global title of health, such an approach would seem to be particularly relevant (see chapter 11).

Access and availability

A major difficulty with service provision is access and availability for those who need it most. Service delivery is often varied, fragmented and diffuse. Some areas experience gaps in service provision, while others have multiple agencies addressing a similar issue from different perspectives without reference to each other (ADM, 2004: 2). An example of the difficulties faced by ethnic minority women clearly articulates the issues. The women identified that they were having difficulty accessing HIV services, were experiencing racism within the Irish hospital system and society, that they were having difficulty registering with GPs, and that they had poor accommodation or problems finding accommodation. Many were living in poverty (CWC, 2004a: 56). Women feared disclosure of their HIV status within their own communities because they had direct experience of a relative being isolated or rejected. In drugs research too, experience has been that it is difficult to access these 'new communities', and that services are slow to develop appropriate materials and approaches (Corr, 2004: 12). Rourke (2003: 17) considers community development strategies and policies to be particularly important for ethnic minorities who, in addition to experiencing racism, social exclusion and uncertainty about their own futures, are also experience high levels of poverty and socio-economic disadvantage. A strength of community development lies in its ability, through local networks, to reach those who are not benefiting.

Many new groups of people are coming to live in Ireland. These groups have various different cultural, political, and family experiences. Their central involvement is crucial in developing services to meet their needs, and in responding to the conditions which affect their levels of well being. State agencies need their participation, so that primary care can be 'readily available to all people regardless of who they are, where they live, or what health and social problems they may have' (Department of Health and Children, 2001a: 7). Otherwise, traditional individual interventions will be implemented and will be found inadequate.

Participation

The concept of community participation in primary health care was found to be particularly relevant in rural Ireland, where services struggled with social, economic and environmental conditions (Quirke et al., 1994: 170). The benefits included improving the design of services, increasing the effectiveness and efficiency of delivery systems, strengthening the monitoring and evaluation of services and care, improving the mobilisation of community resources, and the progressive assumption of responsibility for health care by the community, with technical and administrative assistance from the HSE. Similarly, in an urban setting, community involvement was recognised as critical to effectiveness in responding to problem drug use (Government of Ireland, 1996a: 12). A central, fundamental role was outlined for communities by WHO. In 1991, WHO clarified outlined the rationale for what it described as the 'essential ingredient of massive public involvement' as involving 'not just in the support and operation of health services, but more importantly in the determination of health priorities and the allocation of scarce health resources' (WHO, 1991: 3). This kind of participation is being called for by groups of service users, for example people with disabilities. Key players in advocating full participation and consultation rights have been people with disabilities themselves and families of those with disability, who have been the recipients of inadequate and/or inappropriate services (Quin and Redmond, 2005: 144).

Equity

The principle of 'equity' or fairness is an important issue in the delivery of scarce services. The idea of equity is linked with 'distributive justice': people are treated 'fairly' when they receive services or resources commensurate with their circumstances (Spicker, 1995: 146). The traditional medical model of health care in Ireland institutionalised inequality between service providers and service users. The professional giver was expected to play a dynamic role while acting 'in the best interests of the patient'. The recipient was expected to be a grateful and passive receiver of professional care (Murphy-Lawless and Quin, 2004: 131). The resulting system has led to a large degree of inequity. Some people benefit, and some do not. Those who benefit are those who can pay – those who are in a position to afford health care insurance. People who are dependent on the state medical service find themselves in long queues for treatment, and on trolleys in Accident & Emergency departments of large hospitals. Single-issue groups, such as people with disabilities, or local communities concerned about proposed hospital closures, are challenging this state of affairs, and attempting to ask searching questions about decision making on the allocation of health resources (Murphy-Lawless and Quin, 2004: 129).

Intersectoral collaboration

Community development models emphasise that no one sector or agency can solve problems on its own. Collaboration is a process through which people, groups and organisations work together to achieve desired results. Starting or sustaining a collaborative journey is exciting, sometimes stressful, and even new for many people, groups and organisations (IPH, 2001: 5). Moving from problem-solving solutions to vision-driven solutions offers greater potential for maximising resources, developing sustainable outcomes, greater community ownership and commitment to the course of action (IPH, 2001: 5). For example, central to the Irish approach to drugs currently is the bringing together of key agencies, in a planned and co-ordinated manner. This has been built on the Irish experience of social partnership, particularly area-based partnerships. Local drugs task forces (LDTFs) work at local level to prepare and implement plans appropriate for their communities. These task forces are supported at national level by a National Drug Strategy Team (NDST), also representative of various sectors, including the community and voluntary sectors. This model has been replicated throughout the country, through the establishment of Regional drugs task forces (RDTFs). It has been claimed that Ireland leads the way in Europe in involving the community and voluntary sectors and in allocating dedicated resources towards the development of local plans (NDST, 2002: 9).

Supporting voluntary activity

In 2000 the relationship between the state and the community and voluntary sector(s) was formally outlined. A White Paper on Supporting Voluntary Activity set out the framework for a relationship with the vision of promoting active citizenship, equality of opportunity, respect for individual freedom in the pursuit of social goals, and strengthening social dialogue (Government of Ireland, 2000c: 63–5). Through this, the government aimed to provide a more cohesive framework of support and encouragement for the sector and give formal recognition to the partnership ethos that informs much of the working relationship between the two sectors, while recognising the differences between them. However, there have been difficulties in the implementation. The lack of a representative national organization means that the community and voluntary sector is not in a strong position to engage effectively in the 'high' politics represented by the white paper and the highly contested political terrain around it (Harvey, 2004: 40). The relationship between the state and the community and voluntary sector, far from being improved in the years since the White Paper was published, has at the very least been fraught with conflict. The Community Platform, which provided an access route for a broad range of national anti-poverty, social inclusion and equality organisations to engage effectively in national social partnership, did not endorse the national agreement, Sustaining Progress, in 2003 claiming that the agreement committed no new resources to addressing poverty, social exclusion, or inequality (CWC, 2003: 6). The community pillar of national social partnership has since been restructured, and the Community Platform has been excluded. Efforts by the government to ensure coherence in local development planning have been strongly criticised for the role given to CDBs (City/County Development Boards) in 'endorsing' community sector plans. CDBs are seen as essentially local authority structures, and questions are asked about the right of such structures to have a say in setting priorities and actions (CWC, 2004b: 7).

A political issue

Duggan has found evidence that in at least some cases local interventions have been reasonably effective to very effective in reaching the specific target groups and that local agencies can act as catalysts of change at local level.

She emphasises the important of local partnerships as a forum for a local focus on problems such as unemployment (Duggan, 1999: 71). Ruddle et al. in their evaluation of Local Drugs Task Force projects found that the support of the community was a key factor in the success of these (2000: 95). Notwithstanding evidence of the value of 'bottom up' community participation, many community workers have reported negative experiences of 'top down' social partnership processes with those at the bottom (community actors) finding statutory bodies difficult to work with (Powell and Geoghegan, 2004: 237). No matter how much one claims to be 'apolitical', or even 'eclectic', the practice of community work is invariably bound up in questions about power, status and resources (Fraser, 2005: 298).

Approaches to community development

Fundamentally different relationships of power and control are embedded in, and therefore reproduced by, different approaches to community development. These issues are often put aside under the pressure of practical action (Beattie, 1986: 17). Four approaches were identified, which are useful here: *community outreach, community co-ordination, community empowerment,* and *community action* (Beattie 1986: 16).

Strategies to site methadone maintenance clinics in local communities in Dublin could be said to be an example of *community outreach*. Rather than people having to travel to central services, the services are brought closer by placing them in the locality. Services are staffed by traditionally trained professionals and often led by a medical practitioner. Another example is seen in local psychiatric clinics. The dominant theoretical frameworks guiding the actions come from individual interventions, often those of medicine and psychology. Local 'organic' knowledge is not normally valued. Questions of the relationship between service users, local people and structures are not normally addressed. Minority groups, for example drug users, while appreciating the convenience of local services, do not view themselves as achieving the same rights and entitlements as the general population (O'Reilly et al., 2005: 23).

Community Co-ordination is concerned with linking services to the people most in need by integration and co-ordination. This approach takes a more systems view, and attempts to ensure that there is proper statutory provision. The focus for the intervention is the individual. By working together, overlaps in services are minimised, and the strengths of each service is maximised. LDTFs are among several examples in Ireland of this interpretation. Drug problems are approached as a cross-cutting issue, being of concern to various government departments, and a variety of services. Bodies such as the

LDTFs have representatives of all the agencies who can bring expertise to bear on the problems, including the community and voluntary sector. LDTFs have been evaluated as being effective in responding to drug problems locally (NDST, 2002: 14). However, while it makes sense to make maximum use of all the resources, improving co-ordination is a challenging task. Structures, processes and cultures all need to be addressed (Boyle, 1999: 61). Community representatives can feel isolated and unsupported, unsure of their roles and what they could contribute, and lacking in confidence or skills they see in representatives of statutory agencies (Rourke, 2003: 23). Community agencies are limited to being involved as 'just another agency'. The presence of CityWide Drugs Crisis Campaign, funded through the Community Development Programme, has helped support these representatives in LDTFs. However, securing sustained, mainstreamed funding for projects and initiatives still saps energy (Rourke, 2003: 29). In addition, concerns are expressed that some key government departments, statutory agencies and voluntary organisations are absent from the table, and in the way in which the drugs crisis seems to have slipped off the political agenda (Rourke 2005: 32). A serious limitation can be the presumption that felt needs are easily agreed upon by community members (Rifkin et al., 2000: 22). Again in the drugs field, various different responses have been seen at community level, with some groups lobbying for drug treatment, and some protesting against any drug services. Serious divisions grew in some communities as a result.

Community Empowerment suggests the improvement of social relations in a community with minimum 'State' presence. It attempts to reduce alienation and apathy through self-help. Education becomes an important player. Education is obviously a major bridge in assisting people to move through the various levels of participation, from participating as a service user to participating in policy making and management. Individuals are encouraged to take part in programmes, and reduce problems through linking with other like-minded people. The state provides expertise, for example on drugs awareness. However, on its own, it can be criticised for failing to address the structural nature of marginalisation, and may merely cloak the existing long-term inequalities. The potential for capacity building through community education is evident in the experience of community drugs groups in Dublin (King et al., 2001: 64; An Cosán, 2002: 7). Yet training for people involved in the drugs structures has been minimal (Rourke, 2003: 30).

Community Action often involves protest. The focus is on organising communities to demand and obtain resources from the authorities (Rifkin et al., 2000: 20). Social problems are analysed as being embedded in political and economic systems. The focus of the intervention is on these political and economic systems. In the drugs issue, strong street protest was seen in Dublin, in the 1980s, and again in the 1990s.

Problem drug use in Dublin is analysed as being connected to social and economic difficulties in certain communities (Government of Ireland, 1996a: 23). This analysis led to the National Drug Strategy 2001–8 being firmly placed within a social inclusion framework. Targeted resources have gone in since 1997, and services have grown significantly. However, questions remain about what difference this analysis makes in practice in Ireland. Many of the drug services which have developed have been in treatment. The community lobby was successful in its demand for more resources. But the question remains – resources for whom? These services are, with a few exceptions, controlled by the health authorities. Communities who set up and pioneered many of them are relegated to support roles, often poorly paid or unpaid (King et al., 2001: 62). There are struggles with career structures and criteria for qualification.

A continuum of care

In reality, community groups are involved in all the approaches described above. They engage in individual interventions and social action (Duggan and Ronayne, 1991: 5). When seen as a spectrum of activity, difficulties in defining community approaches become evident. An example of such a continuum in Ireland is to be found in Traveller organisations where Community Health Workers (CHWs) have been trained to work within their own communities: 'They are not employed solely to deliver a service, their remit is much broader than that, it is as much about the ability to influence national policy development and the social determinants of their health status as it is about delivering health education messages locally.' (CWC 2004a: 70).

The capacity to deliver welfare services attracts state funding. The need for services is often immediate, as in the drugs situation in Dublin in the 1990s. Local involvement in service provision has its advantages. Services are often more appropriate, accessible, and hard-to-reach groups are catered for. In this regard, the potential of local groups to act as service providers or as the site for the delivery of provision to a client community is emphasised. The types of work done by Community Drug Workers is varied and diverse. Individual support, family support, education, networking and lobbying have been identified as the core types of work done. Models overlap; each has benefits. Which model is considered to be superior is guided by the values one holds (Fraser 2005: 296).

Ambiguities

Such a remit gives rise to various ambiguities in practice. A tension is created between extremes at either end of this continuum going from service provision to social action. For example, community involvement in care makes use of natural social and family networks. Much of the work appears informal. It is a culturally appropriate way of operating for groups in many of our more marginalised areas. It is effective in building contact and relationships. It is effective in engaging people in services, and in providing safe places for vulnerable populations. Community drugs workers like to work in this manner (McCann, 1999: 197). However, some formality is needed, to organise decisions and resources in an efficient manner, and to promote professional practice and set ethical standards. Community groups delivering drugs services may have to set up appointment systems, or regular times for some activities. Privacy and confidentiality need to be protected. Skill is required to ensure that the valued informal atmosphere is still experienced by service users, while standards are upheld and resources organised efficiently. Sensitive leadership is required, which values the interaction of informal networks. Hierarchical structures can be looked for in groups, particularly during periods of difficulty. This runs the risk of recreating traditional power relationships within community organisations.

The role of service provider is of primary importance to statutory funding agencies. However, if issues of equity are to be seriously addressed, the role of collective organising and analysing are also important. This led to the rejection of the tag of 'treatment centre' by Ballymun Youth Action Project in 1985. It claimed the approach was not only about delivering services, but was also to do with power and resources (McCann, 1999: 200). *Process* is fundamental to community development practice. How things are done and who does them define the work. It can be difficult to make service development congruent with community development as *process*. However, through the training of local people, traditional power relationships between 'professionals' and 'clients' may be challenged. For example, training provided by Community Health Workers for Travellers challenges racism and discrimination at both individual and institutional level (CWC, 2004a: 70). In addition, community development research suggests that people who have had 'little access to therapeutic resources see members of their community respected and trained in therapy' (Dulwich Centre, 1990: 33).

The promotion of training in individual helping skills, for example in drugs counselling or in health care, which can provide career paths for people who previously had no access to such training, obviously makes a valuable contribution to the development of an appropriate range of services. The success in recruiting and training people in the delivery of services to individuals in their own community, and in integrating internal and external skills, can avoid the 'cultural invasion' which communities often experience in service provision (Hunt, 1990: 180). Services are developed in a culturally appropriate way. However, as service needs continue to grow, the tendency is for staff involved in individual interventions to become more and more divorced from community work. For example, this challenge has been identified by the Community Health Workers in Traveller organisations. As noted in a report by the Community Workers Co-operative; 'There is a concern that as the number of projects expands, some are beginning to replicate the outcomes of the Project and not the process. The Community Work practice needs to be strengthened and supported.' (CWC, 2004b: 71).

Such ambiguity can cause tension and friction. It is at the local level that the lack of consensus, confusion and conflict become most apparent. At this level, if conflicts are not worked through, the ineffectiveness of the response produces yet more fragmentation and duplication. In the vacuum created by the lack of agreement, groups which have gained respect and credibility for innovation and participation can be co-opted into supporting a traditional top-down management paradigm, with the capacity for transformation diminished.

Resolving ambiguity

Leaders in community groups hold very powerful positions. The style of leadership is important. The role of the leaders is crucial in determining whether or not significant participation continues beyond the initial set-up stage, and whether ambiguities are resolved and used creatively, or cause conflict. Organisations are needed which place a premium on working collaboratively with diversity. This disturbs traditional hierarchical notions of leadership (Kirk and Shutte, 2004: 237). The 'learning organisation', with its focus on problem solving, offers an effective way for dealing with such complexity, and managing change in a creative manner (McCann, 1999: 235). Change is a fundamental feature of community development and care. It is necessary to develop systems that can learn and adapt, capable of bringing about their own continuing transformation (Schon, 1973: 28).

In considering the unique contribution of community development to care, perhaps the questions lie not so much in which model is best, but in what happens when they overlap. Do they collide, or do they complement one another, improving each other's contribution? The ability of community workers to cross boundaries, their facilitation and conflict resolution skills, together with experience of reflective practice, are very valuable resources for learning to understand, for questioning assumptions, for considering strengths and limitations of professional knowledge, and ultimately to influencing and managing the changes necessary to build new theories from practice. A process of reflective practice makes it possible to construct new understandings. Through such a process, the implicit knowledge and skills that underpin action becomes more explicit (Redmond, 2004: 37).

Conclusion

Community involvement in care, in areas such as addiction and social health, is now strongly embedded within Irish social policy. Here, the case for community participation has been strongly made (CWC, 2004a: 22). Primary care units are required to consult with the local community in relation to the piloting and development of the Primary Care Programme (CWC, 2004a: 13). Traveller health policies envisage Travellers and their representative organisations being involved in determining health priorities for their community (Government of Ireland 2002b). The policies outlined in the White Paper *Supporting Voluntary Activity* continue to shape government policy (Government of Ireland, 2000c). Community development, both as an idea and an area of work, is more vigorous now in Ireland than ever, but is also much more complex. Throughout the 1990s and into the new millennium, there has been rapid expansion in community development activity (Lee, 2003: 48). People are still willing to volunteer time to help others, as witnessed by the response to the Special Olympics in 2003. However, levels of funding to voluntary organisations to engage in reflective policy work or critical commentary is very small (Harvey, 2002: 99). Concerns from the community sector about the track record of local authorities in responding to local needs are justified. The ethos of the Irish state is essentially centralist, offering little support for citizen involvement and has long been hostile to devolved local government (Lee, 1989: 562). Such local government as exists has been criticised as continuing to reflect the perspectives of 'men with Victorian mindsets with little concern for the vulnerable' (Ferriter, 2001: 13).

The response in Ireland to health problems arising from poverty has been to treat the symptoms rather than the underlying causes (Barrington, cited in Murphy-Lawless and Quin, 2004: 142). Community development sets out to enable groups to 'address the social, political and economic causes of this marginalisation' (CWC, 2004a: 15). It is an essential ingredient of responses to social problems caused by inequality. Here the challenges are major ones encompassing health inequalities, the persistence of poverty in a now prosperous Ireland, huge educational inequalities on the basis of social class, inadequate social housing and a whole range of infrastructural shortcomings. The promotion of social care through civic action and community development has a crucial role to play in addressing these problems.

Recommended reading

Government of Ireland (2000d) *White Paper on Community and Voluntary Activity.* Dublin: Stationery Office.

Harvey, B. (2004) *Implementing the White Paper 'Supporting Voluntary Activity'*, The Wheel website, www.wheel.ie

Powell, F. and Geoghegan, M. (2004) *The Politics of Community Development.* Dublin: A. & A. Farmar.

Taylor, M. (2003) *Public Policy in the Community.* Basingstoke: Palgrave Macmillan.

References

Abrahamson, P. (1999) 'The Scandinavian model of welfare', pp. 31–60 in *Comparing Social Welfare Systems in Europe*, vol. 4. Paris: MIRE-DREES.

Acheson, N., Harvey, B., Kearney, J. and Williamson A. (2004) *Two Paths, One Purpose: Voluntary Action in Ireland North and South*. Dublin: IPA.

ACT (RCPCH) (2003) *A Guide to the Development of Children's Palliative Care Services*, 2nd edn. Bristol: Orchard Press.

ADM (2004) *Rapid in Focus Programme: Study of Service Integration in the RAPID Programme*. Dublin: ADM.

Agell, A. (1980) 'Cohabitation without marriage in Swedish law', pp. 245–57 ion Eeklar, J. M. and Katz, S. M. (eds), *Marriage and Cohabitation in Contemporary Societies: Areas of Legal Social and Ethical Change*. London: Butterworths.

All Party Oireachtas Committee on the Constitution (2002) *Seventh Progress Report of the All-Party Committee on the Constitution*. Dublin: Stationery Office.

Allen, K. (2000) *The Celtic Tiger: The Myth of Social Partnership in Ireland*. Manchester: Manchester University Press.

Amann, M., Bertok, I., Cofala, J., Gyarfas, F., Heyes, C., Kilmont, Z., Schopp, W. and Winiwarter, W. (2005) *Baseline Scenarios For The Clean Air For Europe (CAFE) Programme* http://europa. eu. int/comm/environment/air/cafe [Accessed 14 Oct. 2005].

Amarach (2004) *Quality of Life in Ireland 2004 Report: A Study for Diageo Ireland*. Dublin: Amarach.

An Cosán (2002) *Community Drugs Work: Past, Present and Future*. Tallaght: An Cosán.

An Taisce (2005) http://www. antaisce. org/projects/greenschools. html [Accessed 14 Oct. 2005].

Anttonen, A. and Sipilä, J. (1996) 'European social care services: is it possible to identify models?', *Journal of European Social Policy* 6 (2): 87–100.

Arber, S. and Ginn, J. (1991) *Gender and Later Life: A Sociological Analysis of Resources and Constraints*. London Sage.

Archer, P. (2001) 'Public spending on education, inequality and poverty', pp. 197–234 in Cantillon, S., Corrigan, C., Kirby, P. and O'Flynn, J. (eds) (2001) *Rich and Poor: Perspectives on Tackling Inequality in Ireland*. Dublin: Oak Tree.

Atkinson T. Cantillon B, Marlier E. and Nolan B. (2002) *Social Indicators: The EU and Social Inclusion*. Oxford: Oxford University Press.

Bairner, A. (2005) 'Introduction', pp. 1–4 in Bairner, A. (ed.), *Sport and the Irish: Histories, Identities, Issues*. Dublin: UCD Press.

Baker, G. (2002) *Civil Society and Democratic Theory: Alternative Voices*. London and New York: Routledge.

Balarajan, R. (1995) 'Ethnicity and variations in the nation's health', *Health Trends* 27 (4): 114–19.

Baldock, J. (1997) 'Social care in old age: more than a funding problem', *Social Policy and Administration* 31 (1): 73–89.

Baldock, J. and Ely, P. (1996) 'Social care of elderly people in Europe: the central problem of home care', pp. 196–225 in Munday, B. and Ely, P. (eds), *Social Care in Europe*. London: Prentice Hall.

Barber, B. (1984) *Strong Democracy: Participatory Politics for a New Age*. Berkeley: University of California Press.

Barnes, C. and Mercer, G. (1996) *Exploring the Divide: Illness and Disability*. Leeds: The Disability Press.

Barrington, R. (1987) *Health Medicine and Politics in Ireland*. Dublin: IPA.

Barry, J., Herity B. and Solan, S., *The Travellers Health Status Study* (Dublin: HRB, 1989).

Barry, M. (2001) *Report to the Secondary Schools Network*. Dublin: Dublin Inner-city.

Bartlett, M. and Blackman, T. (2001) 'Models of care', pp. 27–41 in Blackman, T., Brodhurst, S. and Convery, J. (eds), *Social Care and Social Exclusion: A Comparative Study of Older People's Care in Europe*. Houndmills: Palgrave.

Beattie, A. (1986) 'Community development for health: from practice to theory?', *Radical Health Promotion* 4 (Summer): 12–18.

Beere, T. (1975/2003) ' Commission on the Status of Women: Progress Report, pp. 240–57 in Fanning, B. and MacNamara, T. (eds), *Ireland Develops: Administration and Social Policy 1953–2003*, Dublin: IPA.

Begley, M., Condon, M., Gavaran, C., Kelly, I., Holland, K. and Staines, A. (1999) *Asylum in Ireland: A Public Health Perspective*. Dublin: UCD.

Bennett, J. (2005), *Where Does Ireland Stand?* Presentation to the NESF Project Team 24 February. Paris: OECD

Bergman, H. and Hobson, B. (2002) 'Compulsory fatherhood: the coding of fatherhood in the Swedish welfare state', pp. 92–124 in Hobson, B. (ed.), *Making Men into Fathers: Men Masculinities and the Social Politics of Fatherhood*. Cambridge: Cambridge University Press.

Bergman, S. (2002) 'Care values and the future of welfare', CAVA Paper, Bristol University.

Bhatti, M. and Dixon, A. (2003) *Special Focus: Housing, Environment and Sustainability Housing Studies Journal* 18 (4): 501–4.

Bjornberg, U. (2002) 'Ideology and choice between work and care: Swedish family policy for working parents', *Critical Social Policy* 22 (1): 33–52

Blackman, T. (2001) 'Social care in Europe', pp. 100–26 in Blackman, T., Brodhurst, S. and Convery, J. (eds), *Social Care and Social Exclusion: A Comparative Study of Older People's Care in Europe*. Houndmills: Palgrave.

Blackwell, J., O'Shea, E., Moane, G. and Murray, P. (1992) *Care Provision and Cost Measurement: Dependent Elderly People at Home and in Geriatric Hospitals*. Dublin: ESRI.

Blakemore, K. (2002) 'Problematizing social care needs in minority communities', pp. 121-9 in Bytheway, B. et al. (eds), *Understanding Care, Welfare and Community: A Reader*. London: Open University Press.

Bochel, H. et al. (2005) *Social Policy: Issues and Developments*. Harlow: Pearson/Prentice Hall.

Boggs, C. (1976) *Gramsci's Marxism*. London: Pluto.

Boyle, G. (1997) 'Community care for older people in Ireland: a conceptual critique of the literature', *Administration* 45 (2): 44–58. .

Boyle, R. (1999) *The Management of Cross-Cutting Issues*. Discussion Paper 8, Committee for Public Management Research. Dublin: IPA.

Bracalenti, R. (2002) 'The role of families in the integration process: new approaches', paper presented at the European Observatory on the Social Situation, Demography and Family seminar on Immigration and Family, Helsinki.

Bracken, P., Greenslade, L., Griffen, B. and Smythe, M. (1998) 'Mental health and ethnicity: an Irish dimension', *British Journal of Psychiatry* 172: 103–5.

Bradshaw, J. and Finch, N. (2002) *A Comparison of Child Benefit Packages in 22 Countries*. Department for Works and Pensions, Research Report no. 174. Leeds: Corporate Document Services.

Breen, R. (1984) *Education and the Labour Market: Work and Unemployment among Recent Cohorts of Irish School Leavers*. Research Series, no. 119. Dublin: ESRI.

Breen, R. (1991) *Education, Employment and Training in the Youth Labour Market*, General Research Series, no. 152. Dublin: ESRI.

Breen, R., Hannan, D. F., Rottman, D. B. and Whelan, C. T. (1990) *Understanding Contemporary Ireland: State, Class and Development in the Republic of Ireland*. Dublin: Gill & Macmillan.

Brotchie, J. (1988) 'Caring is not a commodity', *Community Care* 20 (15): 14–15.

Brown, T. (1985) *Ireland: A Social and Cultural History 1922–1985*. London: Fontana.

Bruce, A. (2004) *Drugs Task Force Project Activity for FÁS Community Employment Participants A Review*. Dublin: FÁS.

Bulmer, M. (1986) *Social Science and Social Policy*. Boston: Allen & Unwin.

Burke, H. (1999) 'Foundation stones of Irish social policy, 1831–1951', pp. 11–32 in Kiely, G. et al. (eds), *Irish Social Policy in Context*. Dublin: UCD Press.

Burley, J. (2004) 'Introduction', p. xxiii in Burley, J. (ed.), *Dworkin and His Critics: With Replies from Dworkin*. Oxford: Blackwell.

Bussemaker, J. and van Kersbergen, K. (1999) 'Contemporary social-capitalist welfare states and gender equality', pp. 15–44 in Sainsbury D. (ed.), *Gender and Welfare State Regimes*. Oxford: Oxford University Press.

Byrne, A. Canavan, J. and Millar, M. (2003) *Developing Inclusive Research Methodologies*. Galway: Western Health Board.

Bytheway, B. and Johnson, J. (1998) 'The social construction of 'carers', pp. 241–53 in Symonds. A. and Kelly, A. (eds), *The Social Construction of Community Care*. London: Macmillan.

Cabinet Office (2000) *Minority Ethnic Issues in Social Exclusion and Neighbourhood Renewal.* London: HMSO.

Camic, C. (1986) 'The matter of habit', *American Journal of Sociology* 91 (5): 1039–87.

Cantillon, S. et al (2001) *Rich and Poor: Perspectives on Tackling Inequality in Ireland*. Dublin: Oak Tree.

Castles S. and Davidson A. (2000) *Citizenship and Migration: Globalisation and the Politics of Belonging*. London: Routledge.

Charter 77 (1977) *Text of Charter 77 – Declaration*. Samizdat publication.

Christie, I. and Warburton, D. (2001) *From Here to Sustainability: Politics in the Real World*. London: Earthscan.

Chubb, B. (1997) *The Government and Politics of Ireland*. Harlow: Longman.

Clancy, L., Goodman, P., Sinclair H. and Dockery D. W. (2002) 'Effect of air-pollution control on death rates in Dublin, Ireland: an intervention study', *The Lancet* 360, 19 Oct.

Clancy, P. (2003) *Supporting Equity in Higher Education: A Report to the Minister for Education and Science*. Dublin: Department of Education and Science.

Clancy, P. (2005) 'Education policy', pp. 80–114 in Quin, S. et al. (eds), *Contemporary Irish Social Policy*, 2nd edn. Dublin: UCD Press.

Clann Housing Association (1999) *From Bosnia to Ireland's Private Rented Sector: A Study of Bosnian Housing Need in Ireland*. Dublin: Clann Housing Association.

Cleveland, G. and Krashinsky, M. (1998) *The Benefits and Costs of Good Childcare: The Economic Rationale for Investment in Young Children – A Policy Study*. Toronto: Childcare Resource and Research Unit.

Clinch, P., Convery, F. and Walsh, B. (2002) *After the Celtic Tiger: Challenges Ahead*. Dublin: O'Brien.

Coakley, A. (2004) 'Poverty and insecurity', pp. 112–27 in Fanning, B. et al. (eds), *Theorising Irish Social Policy*. Dublin: UCD Press.

Cohen, J. and Arato, A. (1992) *Civil Society and Political Theory*. Massachusetts, MIT Press.

Collins, T. (2002) 'Community development and state building: a shared project', *Community Development Journal* 37 (1): 91–100.

Comby, B. (2000) *Environmentalists for Nuclear Energy*. http: //www. comby. org/livres/ nupreen. htm [Accessed 14 Oct. 2005].

Comhairle (2002) *Supporting Carers: A Social Policy Report*. Dublin: Comhairle.

Comhairle (2004) *Directory of National Voluntary Organisations and Other Agencies*. Dublin: Comhairle

Comhlámh (2001) *Refugee Lives: The Failure of Direct Provision as a Social Response to the Needs of Asylum Seekers in Ireland*. Dublin: Comhlámh.

Commission on Emigration and other Population Problems (1955) *Reports 1948–1954*. Dublin: Stationery Office.

Commission on the Family (1998) *Strengthening Families for Life: Final Report to the Minister for Social, Community and Family Affairs, Executive Summary*. Dublin: Stationery Office.

Commission on the Family (2000) *Supporting Voluntary Activity. A White Paper on a Framework for Supporting Voluntary Activity and for Developing the Relationship Between the State and the Community and Voluntary Sector*. Dublin: Stationery Office.

Commission on the Status of People with Disabilities (1996) *A Strategy for Equality*. Dublin: Stationery Office.

Community and Voluntary Pillar (2001) *Towards an Equality and Rights Based Health Care System*. Submission to the NAPS Process on Health.

Connolly, L. (2002) *The Irish Women's Movement: From Revolution to Devolution*. Basingstoke: Palgrave.

Connolly, T. (2000) 'Emigration from Ireland to Britain during the Second World War', pp. 51–64 in Bielenberg, A. (ed.), *The Irish Diaspora*. Harlow and New York: Longman.

Conroy, P. (1994) *Progress Through Partnership*. Dublin: CPA.

Conroy, P. (1998) 'Lone mothers: the case of Ireland', pp. 76–95 in Lewis, J. (ed.), *Lone Mothers in European Welfare Regimes: Shifting Policy Logics*. London: Jessica Kingsley.

Conroy, P. (1999) 'From the fifties to the nineties', pp. 33–50 in Kiely, G. et al. (eds), *Irish Social Policy in Context* (Dublin: UCD Press).

Conroy, P. (2005) 'Mental health and the workplace', pp. 39–49 in Quin, S. and Redmond, B. (eds), *Mental Health and Social Policy in Ireland*. Dublin: UCD Press.

Conroy, P. and Carroll, A. (2002) *Migrant Workers and Their Experiences*. Dublin: Ralaheen.

Constitutional Review Group (1996) *Report of the Constitutional Review Group*. Dublin: Stationery Office.

Convery, J. (2001) 'Ireland', pp. 83–95 in Blackman, T., Brodhurst, S. and Convery, J. (eds) *Social Care and Social Exclusion: A Comparative Study of Older People's Care in Europe*. Houndmills: Palgrave.

Convery, J. (2001) 'Social inclusion of older people in the health and social services in Ireland', pp. 30–4 in *Towards a Society for All Ages: Conference Proceedings*, Dublin: National Council on Ageing and Older People.

Conway, B. (2001) 'Housing and social inclusion: democratising the local authority and the tenant community relationship', *Administration* 49 (3): 3–19.

Cope, H. (2002) *Still Beyond the Pale? The Response of Social Landlords to the Housing and Related Needs of London's Irish Community*. London: Irish Housing Forum.

Corman, D. (2002) 'Success at work and in family life hand in hand: patterns in the disruption risks of four immigrant groups in Sweden', paper presented at the European Observatory on the Social Situation, Demography and Family seminar on Immigration and Family, Stockholm.

Cornell, S. and Hartmann, P. (1998) *Ethnicity and Race: Making Identities in a Changing World*. Thousand Oaks, CA: Pine Forge Press.

Corr, C. (2004) *Drug Use Among New Communities in Ireland: An Exploratory Study*. Dublin: Merchants Quay.

Costello, D. (2005) 'Some remarks on the establishment of the Irish Naturalisation and Immigration Service', paper presented at the European Technical Seminar on Integration, Dublin 4 Oct.

Cotter, G. (2004) *A Guide to Published Research on Refugees, Asylum-Seekers and Immigrants in Ireland*. Dublin: Integrating Ireland.

Coughlin, A. (1984) 'Public affairs 1916–1966: the social scene', *Administration* 14 (3): 204–14.

Council of Europe, (1996) *European Social Charter* (revised). Strasbourg: Council of Europe.

Council of the EU (2004) 'Treaty establishing a constitution for Europe', *Official Journal of the European Union*, C series, no. 310, 16 Dec.

Cousins, M. (1994) 'Social security and informal care: an Irish perspective' *Administration* 42 (1) 25–46.

Cowley, U. (2001) *The Men who Built Britain: A History of the Irish Navvy*. Dublin: Wolfhound.

CPA (2000) *The Role of Community Development in Tackling Poverty*. Dublin: CPA.

CPA (2003) *Educational Disadvantage in Ireland*. Poverty Briefing no. 14. Dublin: CPA.

CPA (2005) *Ending Child Poverty: Combat Poverty Agency Policy Statement*. Dublin: CPA.

Cradden T. (1999) 'Social partnership in Ireland: against the trend', pp. 46–63 in Collins, N. (ed.), *Political Issues in Ireland Today*. Manchester: Manchester University Press.

Cradden, T. (2004) 'Social partnership: a rising tide lifts all boats?', pp. 79-100 in Collins, N. and Cradden, T. (eds), *Political Issues in Ireland Today*, 3rd edn. Manchester and New York: Manchester University Press.

Cremer-Schäfer, H., Pelikan, C., Pilgram, H., Steinert, I. and Vobruba, G. (2001) *Social Exclusion as a Multidimensional Process: Subcultural and Formally Assisted Strategies of Coping With and Avoiding Social Exclusion*. Brussels: European Commission. Targeted Socio-Economic Research (TSER) SOE1–CT98–2048).

Crickley, A. (2001) 'Women and racism', pp. 88–98 in Farrell, F. and Watt, P. (eds), *Responding to Racism in Ireland*. Dublin: Veritas.

Cross, M., Henke, R., Oberknezev, P., and Pouliasi, K. (2000) *Building Bridges: Towards Effective Means of Linking Scientific Research and Public Policy: Migrants in European Cities*. Utrecht: Netherlands School for Social and Economic Policy Research.

Crouch, C. (1982) *The Politics of Industrial Relations*. Glasgow: Fontana.

Crowley, N. (1996) 'Frameworks for partnership', pp. 155–70 in Conroy, P. et al. (eds), *Partnership in Action*. Galway: Community Workers Co-operative.

Crowley, N. (2005) 'Travellers and social policy', pp. 231–55 in Quin, S. et al. (eds), *Contemporary Irish Social Policy*, 2nd edn. Dublin: UCD Press.

CSO (2003a) *Census of Population of Ireland 2002*. Dublin: Stationery Office.

CSO (2003b) *Census 2002, Volume 2: Ages and Marital Status*. Dublin: Stationery Office.

CSO (2003c) *Census 2002, Principal Demographic Results*. Dublin: Stationery Office.

CSO (2004a) *Population and Labour Force Projections, 2006–2036*. Dublin: Stationery Office.

CSO (2004b) *Census of Population 2002, vol. 10, Disability and Carers*. Dublin: Stationery Office.

CSO (2004c) *Statistical Year Book of Ireland 2004*. Dublin: Stationery Office.

CSO (2005a) *Measuring Ireland's Progress*. Dublin: Stationery Office.

CSO (2005b) *Regional Population Projection 2005*. Dublin Stationery Office.

Cullen, E. (2004) 'Unprecedented growth: but for whose benefit?' in *Growth: The Celtic Cancer. Why the Global Economy Damages Our Health and Society, Feasta Review*, no. 2. Dublin: Feasta.

Cullen, K., Delaney, S. and Duff, P. (2004) *Caring, Working and Public Policy*. Dublin: Equality Authority.

Cummins, J. M. (2002) 'Exploring family systems nursing and the community children's nurse's role in caring for children with cystic fibrosis', *Journal of Child Health Care* 6 (2): 120–32.

Curry, J. (2003) *Irish Social Services*, 4th edn. Dublin: IPA.

Cuyvess, P. and Kiely, G. (2000) 'The family roller coaster ride' in *Family Observer*, no 2. Luxembourg: European Observatory on Family Matters.

CWC (2003) 'National social partnership where to from here?' *News & Views*. Galway: Community Workers Co-op.

CWC (2004a) *Community Work Approaches to Address Health Inequalities*. Galway: Community Workers Co-op.

CWC (2004b) *Endorsement of Community Development Project Plans by City and County Development Boards Consultation Report*. Galway: Community Workers Co-op.

D'Arcy, J. (1999) 'Citizenship and Irish social policy', pp. 195–209 in Kiely, G. et al. (eds), *Irish Social Policy in Context*. Dublin: UCD Press.

Daly, M. (2002) 'Care as a good for social policy', *Journal of Social Policy* 31 (2) 251–70.

Daly, M. and O'Leary, O. (2004) *Families and Family Life in Ireland: Challenges for the Future. Report of the Public Consultation Fora*. Dublin: Stationery Office.

Daly, M. and Yeates, N. (2003) 'Common origins, different paths: adaptation and change in social security in Britain and Ireland', *Policy and Politics* 31 (1) 85–97.

Daycare Trust (2003), *Universal Childcare Provision in the UK: Towards a Cost Benefit Analysis*. London: Price Waterhouse Coopers.

Daycare Trust (2004), *Universal Early Education and Care in 2020: Costs, Benefits and Funding Options*. London: Social Market Foundation and Price Waterhouse Coopers.

DeBoer-Ashworth, E. (2004) 'The "Celtic Tiger", pp. 1–14 in a global context', in Collins, N. and Cradden, T. (eds), *Political Issues in Ireland Today*, 3rd edn. Manchester and New York: Manchester University Press.

Delaney, T., and Fahey, T. (2005) *The Social and Economic Value of Sport in Ireland*. Dublin: ESRI.

Delaney, E. (2000) *Demography, State and Society: Irish Migration to Britain. 1921–1971*. Liverpool: Liverpool University Press.

Department of Arts, Sport and Tourism (2000) *The Irish Sports Council: A Code of Ethics and Good Practice for Children's Sport*. Dublin: Stationery Office.

Department of Arts, Sport and Tourism (2003) *The Irish Sports Council – Statement of Strategy*. Dublin: Stationery Office

Department of Community, Rural and Gaeltacht Affairs (2000) *Framework for Supporting Voluntary Activity and for Developing the Relationship between the State and the Community and Voluntary Sector*. Dublin: Stationery Office.

Department of Education (1977) *A Policy for Youth and Sport*. Dublin: Stationery Office.

Department of Education (1994) *The Economic Impact of Sport in Ireland*. Dublin: Stationery Office.

Department of Education and Science (1995) *Charting our Education Future*. White Paper on Education. Dublin: Stationery Office.

Department of Education (1997) *Targeting Sporting Change in Ireland: Sport in Ireland, 1997–2006 and Beyond*. Dublin: Stationery Office.

Department of Education and Science (1998a) *Education Act*. Dublin: Stationery Office.

Department of Education and Science (1998b) *Report of the National Forum on Early Childhood Education*. Dublin: Stationery Office.

Department of Education and Science (1999) *Ready to Learn: White Paper on Early Education*. Dublin: Stationery Office.

Department of Education and Science (2000) *Statistics*. Dublin: Stationery Office.

Department of Education and Science (2002) *Statement of Strategy 2003–2005*. Dublin: Stationery Office.

Department of Education and Science (2003/4) Key Statistics 2003/2004. www. education. ie/statistics/keystatistics

Department of Education and Science (2004) *Statistical Report 2002/2003*. Dublin: Stationery Office.

Department of Education and Science (2005) *Retention Rates of Pupils in Second-level Schools: 1996 Cohort*. Dublin: Department of Education and Science.

Department of the Environment and Local Government (1997) *Sustainable Development: A Strategy For Ireland* Dublin: Stationery Office.

Department of the Environment and Local Government (2002) *Making Ireland's Development Sustainable*. Dublin: Stationery Office.

Department of Equality and Law Reform (1994) *Working Group on Childcare Facilities for Working Parents*. Report to the Minister for Equality and Law Reform. Dublin: Stationery Office.

Department of Health (1985) *Minimum Legal Requirements and Standards for Daycare Services*. Unpublished report to the Minister for Health.

Department of Health (1994) *Shaping a Healthier Future: A Strategy for Effective Health in the 1990s*. Dublin: Stationery Office.

Department of Health and Children (2000a) *Our Children – Their Lives: National Children's Strategy*. Dublin: Stationery Office.

Department of Health and Children (2000b) *Annual Report*. Dublin: Stationery Office.

Department of Health and Children (2001a) *Primary Care: A New Direction*. Dublin: Stationery Office.

Department of Health and Children (2001b) *Quality and Fairness: A Health System for You. Health Strategy*. Dublin: Stationery Office.

Department of Health and Children (2001c) *Annual Report of the Chief Medical Officer 2000, The Health of Our Children*. Dublin: Stationery Office.

Department of Health and Chilren (2003) *Health Statistics*. Dublin: Stationery Office.

Department of Health and Children (2004) *Quality and Fairness: A Health System for You. Health Strategy. Action Plan Progress Report 2003*. Dublin: Stationery Office.

Department of Health and Children (2005a) *A Palliative Care Needs Assessment for Children*. Dublin: Stationery Office.

Department of Health and Children (2005b) *The Report of the National Taskforce on Obesity: Obesity the Policy Challenges*. Dublin: Stationery Office.

Department of Health, UK (2005) www.dh.uk/IPolicy and Guidance/Health and Social Care Topics/Social Care/fs/en 18.4.2005.

Department of Justice, Equality and Law Reform (1999) *National Childcare Strategy: Report of the Partnership 2000 Expert Working Group on Childcare*. Dublin: Stationery Office.

Department of Justice, Equality and Law Reform (2000) *First Progress Report of the Committee to Monitor and Co-ordinate the Implementation of the Recommendations of the Task Force on the Travelling Community*. Dublin: Stationery Office.

Department of Justice, Equality and Law Reform (2005) *School Age Childcare in Ireland: Report of the National Childcare Co-ordinating Committee*. Dublin: Stationery Office.

Department of Labour (1983) *Report of the Working Group on Childcare Facilities for Working Parents*. Dublin: Stationery Office.

Department of Social, Community and Family Affairs (2000) *Review of One Parent Family Allowance Payment*. Dublin: Stationery Office.

Department of Social, Community and Family Affairs (2001) *Ireland: National Action Plan against Poverty and Social Exclusion (NAPSincl) 2001–2003*. Dublin: Stationery Office.

Department of Social, Community and Family Affairs (2002) *Review of the National Anti-Poverty Strategy under the Programme for Prosperity and Fairness*. Dublin: Stationery Office.

Department of Social and Family Affairs (2002) *Study to Examine the Future Financing of Long-term Care in Ireland*. Dublin: Stationery Office.

Department of Social Welfare (1997) *Supporting Voluntary Activity: A Green Paper on the Community and Voluntary Sector and its Relationship with the State*. Dublin: Stationery Office.

Devine, D., Nic Ghiolla Phádraig, M. and Deegan, G. (2004) 'Time for children – time for change children's rights and welfare during a period of economic change', pp. 211–71 in Jensen, A. et al. (eds), *Children's Welfare in Ageing Europe*. Norwegian Centre for Child Research.

Dobson, B. and Middleton, S. (1998) *The Cost of Childhood Disability*. York: YPS for the Joseph Rowntree Foundation.

Douglas, R. (2002) 'Anglo-Saxons and the Attacoti: the racialisation of Irishness in Britain between the world wars', *Ethnic and Racial Studies* 25 (2): 40–63.

Drake, R. (1999) 'Minority ethnic communities and disability', pp. 148–62 in Drake, R. (ed.), *Understanding Disability Policies*. London: Macmillan.

Dublin Inner City Partnership (2001) *Strategic Action Plan 2001–2006: Achieving Equality, Overcoming Exclusion – Strategy to Secure Social and Economic Rights in the Inner City*. Dublin: DICP.

Duggan, C. (1998) 'Locally based interventions to combat poverty and exclusion: how effective can they be?', in McCashin, A. and O'Sullivan, E. (eds), *Irish Social Policy Review*. Dublin: IPA.

Duggan, C., and Ronayne, T., (1991) *Working Partners? The State and The Community Sector*. Dublin: Work Research Centre.

Dulwich Centre (1990) Newsletter No 1 *Social Justice and Family Therapy*. A discussion of the work of The Family Centre, Lower Hutt, New Zealand. Adelaide: Dulwich Centre Publications.

Dunning, E. and Rojek, C. (1992) 'Introduction: sociological approaches to the study of sport and leisure', pp. xi–xix in *Sport and Leisure in the Civilising ProcesS: Critique and Counter Critique* by Dunning, E. and Rojek, C. (eds), Toronto: University of Toronto Press.

Eardley, T. (1996) 'From Safety nets to springboards? Social assistance and work incentives in the OECD Countries', *Social Policy Review*, no. 8. London: Social Policy Association.

Elliot, J. A. (1994) *An Introduction to Sustainable Development*. London: Routledge.

Ellis, K. (2004) 'Dependency, justice and the ethic of care', pp. 29–48 in Dean, H. (ed.), *The Ethics of Welfare, Human Rights, Dependency and Responsibility*. Bristol: Policy Press.

ERC (2002) *Further Evaluation of Early Start: Progress Report*. Report to the Department of Education and Science. Dublin: ERC.

ERC (2003a) *The Evaluation of Breaking the Cycle: A Follow-up of the Achievement of 6th Class Pupils in Urban Schools 2003*. Report to the Department of Education and Science. Dublin: ERC.

ERC (2003b) *Review of the Home-School-Community Liaison Scheme*. Report to the Department of Education and Science. Dublin: ERC.

Esping-AndersEn, G. (1990) *The Three Worlds of Welfare Capitalis*m. Cambridge: Polity.

EU (2001) *European Governance. A White Paper*. Brussels, Commission of the European Communities (Com 2001, 248 final).

European Commission (1996) *A Review of Services for Young Children in the European Union 1990–1995*. Brussels: European Commission.

Eurostat (2000) *Review of One-Parent Family Payment*. Brussels: European Commission.

Eurostat (2002) *The Social Situation in the European Union*. Brussels: European Commission.

Evans, G. (1996) 'Cross-national differences in support for welfare and redistribution', pp. 158–208 in Taylor, B. and Thomson, K. (eds), *Understanding Change in Social Attitudes*. Aldershot: CREST.

Fahey, T. (1991) 'Measuring female labour supply: conceptual and procedural problems in the official statistics', *Economic and Social Review* 21 (2): 163–91.

Fahey, T. (1997) 'Report to the Joint Committee on the Family', pp. A. 1–A. 144 in Oireachtas Joint Committee on the Family, *Interim Report of the Joint Committee on the Family: The Elderly, the Family and the State in Ireland*. Dublin: Stationery Office.

Fahey, T. (1998) 'Population ageing, the elderly and health care', pp. 183–98 in Leahy, A. and Wiley, M. (1998), *The Irish Health System in the 21st Century.* Dublin: Oak Tree.

Fahey, T. and FitzGerald, J. (1997) *Welfare Implications of Demographic Trends.* Dublin: Oak Tree.

Fahey, T., Layte, R. and Gannon, B. (2004) *Sports Participation and Health Among Adults in Ireland.* Dublin: ESRI.

Fahey, T. and Murray, P. (1994) *Health and Autonomy Among the Over-65s in Ireland.* Dublin: National Council for the Elderly.

Fanning, B. (1999) 'The mixed economy of welfare', pp. 51–69 in Kiely, G. et al. (eds) *Irish Social Policy in Context.* Dublin: UCD Press.

Fanning, B. (2002) *Racism and Social Change in the Republic of Ireland.* Manchester: Manchester University Press.

Fanning, B. (2004a) 'Locating Irish social policy', pp. 6–22 in Fanning, B. et al. (eds), *Theorising Irish Social Policy.* Dublin: UCD Press.

Fanning, B. (2004b) 'Denizens and citizens', pp. 65–75 in M. Peillon and M. Corcoran (eds), *Place and Non-Place.* Dublin: IPA.

Fanning, B. (2004c) 'Communitarianism, social capital and subsidiarity', pp. 42–61 in Fanning, B. et al. (eds), *Theorising Irish Social Policy.* Dublin: UCD Press.

Fanning, B., Loyal, S. and Staunton, C. (2000) *Asylum Seekers and the Right to Work in Ireland.* Dublin: Irish Refugee Council.

Fanning, B. and Pierce, M. (2004) 'Ethnic data and social policy in Ireland', *Administration* 52 (3): 3–20.

Fanning, B. and Veale, A. (2004) ' Child poverty as public policy: direct provision and asylum seeker children in the Republic of Ireland', *Child Care in Practice* 10 (3): 241–51.

Fanning, B., Veale, A. and O'Connor, D. (2001) *Beyond the Pale: Asylum Seeker Children and Social Exclusion.* Dublin: Irish Refugee Council.

Fassmann, H. (2002) 'Immigration to the European Union: causes, patterns, future trends', paper presented at the European Observatory on the Social Situation, Demography and Family seminar on Immigration and Family, Helsinki.

Faughnan, P. and O'Donovan, A. (2002) *A Changing Voluntary Sector: Working with Minority Communities in 2001.* Dublin: Social Science Research Centre.

Faughnan, P. and O'Connor, A. (2002) *A Changing Voluntary Sector: Working with New Minority Communities in 2001.* Dublin: Social Science Research Centre, UCD.

Faughnan, P. and Woods, M. (2000) *Lives on Hold: Seeking Asylum in Ireland.* Dublin: Social Science Research Centre, UCD.

Fazil, Q., Bywaters, P., Ali, Z, Wallace, L. and Singh, G. (2002) 'Disadvantage and discrimination compounded: the experience of Pakistani and Bangladeshi parents of disabled children in the UK', *Disability and Society* 17 (3): 237–53.

Feldman, A. (2003) *Developing a Code of Practice for Research and Development Work with Minority Ethnic Communities: Report of a Workshop.* Dublin: Social Science Research Centre.

Feldman, A. (forthcoming 2006) 'Alterity and belonging in diaspora space: changing Irish identities and "race"-making in the "age of migration"', in Yuval-Davis, N. et al. (eds), *Situating Contemporary Politics of Belonging.* London: Sage.

Feldman, A., Frese, C. and Yousif, T. (2002) *Research, Development and Critical Interculturalism: A Study on the Participation of Refugees and Asylum Seekers in Research- and Development-Based Initiatives.* Dublin: Social Science Research Centre.

Feldman, A., Ndakengerwa, D. L., Nolan A., and Frese C. (2005) *Diversity, Civil Society and Social Change in Ireland: A North-South Comparison of the Role of Immigrant/'New' Minority Ethnic-Led Organisations.* Dublin: Migration and Citizenship Research Initiative, Geary Institute UCD.

Ferriter, D. (2001) *Lovers of Liberty? Local Government in 20th Century Ireland.* Dublin: National Archives of Ireland.

Ferriter, D. (2004) *The Transformation of Ireland 1900–2000.* London: Profile Books.

Finch, J. and Groves, D. (1980) 'Community care and the family: a case for equal opportunities?' *Journal of Social Policy* 9 (4): 487–511.

Finnerty, K. and Collins, B. (2005) 'Social care and disability' pp. 271–87 in Share, P. and McElwee, N. (eds), *Applied Social Care: An Introduction for Irish Students.* Dublin: Gill & Macmillan.

Finucane, P., Moane, G. and Tiernan, J. (1994) *Support Services of Elderly People Living at Home,* Report no. 40. Dublin: National Council for the Elderly.

Fitzgerald, E. (2005) 'Employment policy', pp. 115–37 in Quin, S. et al. (eds), *Contemporary Irish Social Policy,* 2nd edn. Dublin: UCD Press.

Fitzpatrick, T. and Cahill, M. (2002) *Environment and Welfare: Towards a Green Social Policy.* New York: Palgrave.

Florence, E. and Martiniello, M. (2005) 'The links between academic research and public policies in the field of migration and ethnic relations: selected national case studies – thematic introduction', *International Journal on Multicultural Societies* 7: 3–10.

Forum on the Workplace of the Future (2003) *Consultation Paper: Modernising Our Workplaces to Deliver Ireland's Competitive and Social Vision.* Dublin: National Centre for Partnership Performance.

Forum on the Workplace of the Future (2004) *National Workplace Strategy.* Dublin: National Centre for Partnership Performance.

Foster, R. F. (1989) *Modern Ireland, 1600–1972.* London: Penguin.

Fotakis, C. (2000) 'How social is Europe', *Family Observer,* no 2. Luxembourg: European Observatory on Family Matters.

Francis. J. and Netten, A. (2004) 'Raising the quality of home care: a study of service users' views'. *Social Policy and Administration* 38 (3): 290–305.

Fraser, H. (2005) 'Four different approaches to community participation', *Community Development Journal* 40 (3): 286–300.

Friends of the Earth (2005) http: //www. foe. ie/FOE%20/Campaigns/transport. html [Accessed 14 Oct. 2005].

Gaffney, M. (2001) 'Rebuilding social capital: restoring the ethic of care in Irish society', pp. 57–64 in Bohan, H. and Kennedy, G. (eds), *Redefining Roles and Relationships: Our Society in the New Millennium.* London: Veritas.

Gallagher, C. (2005) 'Social care work and the older person', pp. 258–301 in Share, P. and McElwee, N. (eds), *Applied Social Care: An Introduction for Irish Students.* Dublin: Gill & Macmillan.

Garavan, R., Winder, R. and McGee, H. M. (2001) *Health and Social Services for Older People (HeSSOP): Consulting Older People on Health and Social Services: A Survey of Service Use, Experiences and Needs.* Dublin: National Council on Ageing and Older People.

Garrett, P. M. (2004) *Social Work and Irish People in Britain: Historical and Contemporary Responses to Irish Children and Families.* Bristol: Policy Press.

Garvin, T. (2004) *Preventing the Future: Why Ireland Was So Poor For So Long.* Dublin: Gill & Macmillan.

George, V. and Wilding, P. (1994) *Welfare and Ideology.* Hemel Hempstead: Prentice Hall/Harvester Wheatsheaf.

Giddens, A. (1998) *The Third Way: The Renewal of Social Democracy.* Cambridge: Polity.

Gillespie, P. (2005) 'Halting the erosion of social capital', *The Irish Times,* 10 Sept.

Gilligan, C. (1982) *In a Different Voice.* Cambridge MA: Harvard University Press.

Glendinning, C., Schunk, M. and McLaughlin, E. (1997) 'Paying for long-term domiciliary care: a comparative perspective', *Ageing and Society* 17: 123–40.

Goodbody Economic Consultants (2001) *Review of the National Anti-Poverty Strategy: Framework Document.* Dublin: Goodbody Economic Consultants.

Gordon, L. (1990) "The new feminist scholarship on the welfare state', pp. 9-35 in Gordon, L. (ed.), *Women, The State and Welfare.* Madison: University of Wisconson Press.

Gordon, P. and A. Newnham (1985) *Passport to Benefits? Racism in Social Security.* London: Child Poverty Action Group.

Government of Ireland (1944) *Report of Commission on Vocational Organisations.* Dublin: Stationery Office.

Government of Ireland (1958) *Economic Development.* Dublin: Stationery Office.

Government of Ireland (1984) *The Psychiatric Services: Planning for the Future.* Dublin: Stationery Office.

Government of Ireland (1989) *Programme for Economic and Social Progress (PESP).* Dublin: Stationery Office.

Government of Ireland (1991) *Child Care Act.* Dublin: Stationery Office.

Government of Ireland (1996a) *First Report of the Ministerial Task Force on Measures to Reduce the Demand for Drugs.* Dublin: Stationery Office.

Government of Ireland (1996b) *Partnership 2000 Agreement.* Dublin: Stationery Office.

Government of Ireland (1997a) *Green Paper on the Community and Voluntary Sector and its Relationship with the State.* Dublin: Stationery Office.

Government of Ireland (1997b) *National Anti-Poverty Strategy: Sharing in Progress.* Dublin: Stationery Office.

Government of Ireland (1998a) *Education Act.* Dublin: Stationery Office.

Government of Ireland (1998b) *The Commission on the Family Final Report to the Minister for Social Community and Family Affairs – Strengthening Families for Life.* Dublin: Stationery Office.

Government of Ireland (1998c) *Social Inclusion: Strategy of the Department of Social, Community and Family Affairs.* Dublin: Stationery Office.

Government of Ireland (2000a) *Programme for Prosperity and Fairness.* Dublin: Stationery Office.

Government of Ireland (2000b) *National Development Plan.* Dublin: Stationery Office.

Government of Ireland (2000c) *White Paper on a Framework for Supporting Voluntary Activity and for Developing the Relationship between the State and the Community and Voluntary Sector.* Dublin: Stationery Office.

Government of Ireland (2001a) *Building on Experience National Drug Strategy 2001–2008.* Dublin: Stationery Office.

Government of Ireland (2001b) *National Action Plan against Poverty and Social Exclusion 2001–2003* (NAPSincl). Dublin: Stationery Office.

Government of Ireland (2002a) *Programme for Prosperity and Fairness Report of the Working Group on the Review of the Parental Leave Act 1998.* Dublin: Stationery Office.

Government of Ireland (2002b) *Traveller Health: A National Strategy.* Dublin: Stationery Office.

Government of Ireland (2002c) *Building an Inclusive Society: Review of the National Anti-Poverty Strategy: Framework Document.* Dublin: Stationery Office.

Government of Ireland (2006) *The All-Party Oireachtas Committee on the Constitution, Tenth Progress Report: The Family.* Dublin: Stationery Office.

Graham, H. (1983) 'Caring: a labour of love', pp. 13–30 in Finch, J. and Groves, D. (eds), *A Labour of Love: Women, Work and Caring.* London: Routledge & Kegan Paul.

Graham, H. (1997) 'Feminist perspectives on caring', pp. 124–33 in Bornat, J. et al. (eds), *Community Care: A Reader.* London: Macmillan.

Gunaratnam, Y. (1990) 'Breaking the silence: Asian carers in Britain', pp. 114–24 in Bornat, J. et al. (eds), *Community Care: A Reader.* London: Macmillan.

Hallstedt, P. and Högström, M. 'Social care: a European perspective', pp. 17–29 in Share, P. and McElwee, N. (eds), *Applied Social Care: An Introduction for Irish Students.* Dublin: Gill & Macmillan.

Handler, J. (2003) 'Social citizenship and workfare in the US and Western Europe: from status to contract', *Journal of European Social Policy* 13 (3) 229–43.

Hann, C. and Dunn, E. (eds) (1996) *Civil Society: Challenging Western Models.* London: Routledge.

Hannan, D. F., McCabe, B. and McCoy, S. (1998) *Trading Qualifications for Jobs: Over-education and the Irish Youth Labour Market.* Dublin: Oak Tree.

Hannan, D. F. and Ó'Riain, S. (1993) *Pathways to Adulthood in Ireland: Causes and Consequences of Success and Failure in Transitions Amongst Irish Youth,* General Research Series no. 161, Dublin: ESRI.

Hantrais, L. (1997) 'Exploring relationships between social policy and changing family forms with the European Union', *European Journal of Population* 13 (2): 339–79.

Harding, S. and R. Balarajan (1996) 'Patterns of mortality in second generation Irish living in England and Wales: longitudinal study', *British Medical Journal* 312: 1389–92.

Harris, P. (2002) 'Welfare rewritten: change and interlay in social economic accounts', *Journal of Social Policy* 31 (3): 377–98.

Harvey, B. (1999) *Emigration and Services for Irish Migrants: Towards a New Strategic Plan.* Dublin: Irish Episcopal Commission for Migrants and Irish Commission for Prisoners Overseas.

Harvey, B. (2002) *Rights and Justice Work in Ireland: A New Baseline.* York: Joseph Rowntree Charitable Trust.

Harvey, B. (2004) *Implementing the White Paper 'Supporting Voluntary Activity'*, The Wheel website, www. wheel. ie.

Hatland, A. (2001) 'Changing family patterns: a challenge to social security', pp. 116–36 in Kautto, M. et al. (eds), *Nordic Welfare States in the European Context.* London: Routledge.

Haughton, J. (2005) 'Growth in output and living standards', pp. 107–32 in O'Hagan, J. and Newman, C. (eds), *The Economy of Ireland: National and Sectoral Policy Issues,* 9th edn. Dublin: Gill & Macmillan.

Hayes, N. (1995) *The Case for a National Policy on Early Education.* Poverty and Policy discussion paper no. 2, Dublin: CPA.

Hayes, N. (2001) 'Early childhood education in Ireland: policy, provision and practice', *Administration* 49 (3): 43–67.

Hayes, N. (2002) *Children's Rights: Whose Right? A Review of Child Policy Development in Ireland,* Policy Paper, Dublin: Policy Institute, TCD.

Hayes, N., Bradley, S. and Newman, C. (2005) *An Accessible Childcare Model.* Dublin: NWCI.

HEA (2005) *A Review of Higher Education Participation in 2003.* Dublin: ESRI.

Heckman, J. and Cunha, F. (2005) *Credit Constraints, Family Constraints and Optimal Policies to Reduce Inequality and Promote Productivity.* Inaugural Lecture, Geary Institute, UCD, 22 Apr.

Heidenheimer, A., Heclo, H. and Adams, C. (1990) *Comparative Public Policy.* New York: St Martin's.

Hickman, M. (1998) 'Reconstructing deconstructing "race": British political discourses about the Irish in Britain', *Ethnic and Racial Studies* 21 (2): 288–307.

Hickman, M. and Walter, B. (1997) *Discrimination and the Irish Community in Britain.* London: Commission for Racial Equality.

Higgins, J. (1989) 'Defining community care: realities and myths', *Social Policy and Administration* 23 (1): 3–16.

Higgs, P. (1998) 'Risk, governmentality and the reconceptualisation of citizenship', pp. 176–97 in Scambler, P. and Higgs P. (eds), *Modernity, Medicine and Health – Medical Sociology Towards 2000.* London: Routledge.

Hill, M. (1996) *Social Policy: A Comparative Approach.* Hemel Hempstead: Prentice Hall/Harvester Wheatsheaf.

Hillyard, P. (1993) *Suspect Community.* London: Pluto.

Hirst, M. (2004) *Health Inequalities and Informal Care.* York: Social Policy Research Unit.

Hirst, P. (1994) *Associative Democracy: new Forms of Economic and Social Governance.* Amherst, MA: University of Massachusetts Press.

Hobsbawm, E. J. (1975) *The Age of Capital, 1848–1875.* London: Abacus.

Hobson, B. (1994) 'Solo-mothers, social policy regimes and the logics of gender', pp. 170–88 in Sainsbury, D. (ed.), *Gendering Welfare States.* London: Sage.

Hobson, B. (ed.) (2002) *Making Men into Fathers: Men, Masculinities and the Social Politics of Fatherhood.* Cambridge: Cambridge University Press.

Hood, S., Mayall B., and Oliver S. (eds) (1999) *Critical Issues in Social Research: Power and Prejudice.* Buckingham: Open University Press.

Housing Unit (2005) *Housing Ireland* 4 (1).

Howard, Kevin (2004) *Constructing the Irish of Britain: Ethnic Recognition and the 2001 UK Census.* Working paper no. 37. Dublin: Institute for British-Irish Studies, UCD.

Huby, M. (1998) *Social Policy and the Environment.* Buckingham Open University Press.

Hudson, B. (ed.) (2000) *The Changing Role of Social Care.* London: Jessica Kingsley.

Hughes, J., Knox, C., Murray, M. and Greer, J. (1998) *Partnership Governance in Northern Ireland: The Path to Peace.* Dublin: Oak Tree.

Hulme, D. and Edwards, M. (1997) *NGOs, States and Donors: Too Close for Comfort?* London: Macmillan.

Hunt, S. (1990) 'Building alliances: professional and political issues in community partici-pation', *Health Promotion International* 5 (3): 179–85.

Hunt. T. (2005) 'The early years of Gaelic football and the role of cricket in County Westmeath' pp. 22–43 in Bairner, A. (ed.), *Sport and the Irish: Histories, Identities, Issues.* Dublin: UCD Press.

Hutton, S. and Hirst, M. (2001) *Caring Relationships Over Time.* York: Social Policy Research Unit.

IBC (2004) *Irish Bishops' Council Conference Proceedings* www.catholic communications.ie

IBEC Survey Unit (2000) *Employment of Non-EU Nationals/Refugees in Ireland.* Dublin, Interact Ireland.

Immigrant Council of Ireland (2003) *Labour Migration into Ireland.* Dublin: Immigrant Council of Ireland.

Immigrant Council of Ireland (2005) '*Summary Analysis and Initial Response to the Government's Proposals for an Immigration and Residence Bill* . Dublin: Immigrant Council of Ireland.

Inglis T. (1987) *Moral Monopoly: The Catholic Church in Modern Irish Society.* Dublin: Gill & Macmillan.

Inglis, T. (1998) *Moral Monopoly: The Rise and Fall of the Catholic Church in Modern Ireland.* 2nd edn. Dublin: UCD Press.

Inter-departmental Committee on the Care of the Aged (1968) *Care of the Aged Report.* Dublin: Stationery Office.

Inter-departmental Working Group to Consider the Recommendations of the Task Force on Policy Regarding Emigrants (2003) *Report.* Dublin: Department of Foreign Affairs.

International Obesity Task Force (2003) *Obesity in Europe,* London: International Association for the Study of Obesity.

IPHI (2001) *Partnership Framework: A Model for Partnership in Health.* Dublin: IPHI.

IPHI (2005a) *Health Impacts of Transport: A Review* Dublin IPHI.

IPHI (2005b) *Inequalities in Perceived Health: A Report of the all-Ireland Social Capital and Health Survey.* Dublin: IPHI.

Irish Refugee Council (2005) *Comments on the Proposed Immigration and Residency Bill (2005)* www. irishrefugeecounci.

Irish Sports Council (2003) *Statement of Strategy 2003–2005.* Dublin: Irish Sports Council.

Irvine, S. and Ponton, A. (1988) *A Green Manifesto: Policies for a Green Future* London Mac Donald and Co.

Jackson, J. (1963) *The Irish in Britain.* London: Routledge & Kegan Paul.

Jenkin, S. and Scott, S. (2000) 'Childhood', pp. 152–67 in Payne, G. (ed.), *Social Divisions* by New York: St Martin's.

Jensen, A. M. (1994) 'The feminization of childhood', pp. 59–76 in Qvortup, J. et al. (eds), *Childhood Matters, Social Theory, Practice and Politics.* Aldershot: Avebury.

Johnson, N. (1999) *Mixed Economies of Welfare: A Comparative Perspective.* London: Prentice Hall.

Joint Committee on Social Care Professionals (2003) *Report.* Dublin: Stationery Office.

Joppke, C. (1999) 'How immigration is changing citizenship: a comparative view', *Ethnic and Racial Studies* 22 (4): 629–52.

Keane, J. (1998) *Civil Society: Old Images, New Visions.* Cambridge: Polity.

Keegan Wells, D., James, K., Stewart, J. L., Moore, I. M., Patterson Kelly, K., Moore, B., Bond, D., Diamond, J., Hall, B., Mahan, R., Roll, L. and Speckhart, B. (2002) 'The care of my child with cancer: a new instrument to measure caregiving demand in parents of children with cancer', *Journal of Pediatric Nursing* 17 (3): 201–10.

Keene, J. (1997) *Drug Misuse Prevention Harm Minimisation and Treatment.* London: Chapman & Hall.

Kellaghan, T. (2002) 'Approaches to problems of educational disadvantage', paper presented to National Forum on Primary Education and Ending Disadvantage, St Patrick's College, Dublin, 1–5 July.

Kelleher, D. and Cahill, G. (2004) 'The Irish in London: identity and health', pp. 78–98 in D. Kelleher, D. and Leavey, G. (eds), *Identity and Health.* London: Routledge.

Kelleher D. and Hillier, S. (1996) 'The health of the Irish in England' pp. in D. Kelleher, D. and Hillier, S. (eds), *Researching Cultural Differences in Health.* London: Routledge. **pp?**

Kelly-Raley, R. and Wildsmith, E. (2004) 'Cohabitation and children's family instability', *Journal of Marriage and Family* 66: 210–19.

Kennedy, F. (2001) *Cottage to Creche: Family Change in Ireland.* Dublin: IPA.

Kennedy, P. (2004) 'Women, autonomy and bodily integrity', pp. 78–94 in Fanning, B. et al. (eds), *Theorising Irish Social Policy.* Dublin: UCD Press.

Kennedy P. and Murphy-Lawless J (2002) *The Maternity Needs of Refugee and Asylum-seeking Women.* Dublin: Applied Social Science Research Programme, UCD.

Kennelly, B, O'Shea, E, and Garvey, E. (2002) 'Social capital, life expectancy and mortality: a cross-national examination', *Social Science and Medicine*, www. Elsevier. com/locate/ soccimed.

Kiely, G. (1995) 'Fathers in families', pp. 147–58 in McCarthy, I. C. (ed.), *Irish Family Studies: Selected Papers.* Dublin: Family Studies Centre, UCD.

Kiely, G. (1998) 'Caregiving within families', pp. 91–100 in Matthijs, K. (ed.), *The Family: Contemporary Perspectives and Challenges.* Louvain: Leuven University Press.

Kiely, G. (1999) 'The family and social policy', pp. 254–68 in Kiely, G. et al. (eds), *Irish Social Policy in Context.* Dublin: UCD Press.

Kiely, G. (2004) 'Individualisation', pp. 62–77 in Fanning, B. et al. (eds), *Theorising Irish Social Policy.* Dublin. UCD Press.

King, D., McCann, M. H. and Adams, J. (2001) *Movers and Shakers: A Study of Community Involvement in Responding to the Drugs Issue.* Dublin: Ballymun Youth Action Project.

Kirby, P. (2002) *The Celtic Tiger in Distress: Growth with Inequality in Ireland.* Basingstoke and New York: Palgrave.

Kirk, P. and Shutte, A. M. (2004) 'Community leadership development', *Community Development Journal* 39 (3): 234–51.

Koenig, M. (2005) 'Editorial', *International Journal on Multicultural Societies* 7: 1–2.

Krieger, H. (2004) 'Family life in Europe - results of recent surveys on quality of life in Europe', paper presented at the Irish Presidency Conference, Families, Change and Social Policy in Europe, Dublin Castle 13–14 May, Dublin: European Foundation for the Improvement of Living and Working Conditions.

Landry, C. and Mulgan, G. (1994) *Themes and Issues: The Future of the Charities and Voluntary Sector*, Working Paper 1. London: Deinos.

Larragy, J. (2002) 'Through the lens of civil society: a perspective on social partnership in Ireland' in Brigid Reynolds, B. and Healy, S. (eds), *Choosing a Fairer Future: An Agenda for Social Partnership after the Celtic Tiger*. Dublin: CORI Justice Commission.

Law Reform Commission (2004) *Consultation Paper on the Rights and Duties of Cohabitees*. Dublin: Stationery Office.

Lawton, D. (1998) *Complex Numbers: Families with More Than One Disabled Child*. York: Social Policy Research Unit.

Leavey, G. (1999) 'Suicide and Irish migrants in Britain: identity and integration', *International Review of Psychiatry*, 11: 168–72.

Lee, A. (2003) 'Community development in Ireland', *Community Development Journal* 3 (1): 48–58.

Lee, J. (1989) *Ireland 1912–1985: Politics and Society*. Cambridge: Cambridge University Press.

Leseman, P. (2002) 'Early childhood education and care for children from low-income minority backgrounds', discussion paper, OECD Oslo Workshop.

Lewis, J. (1992) 'Gender and the development of welfare regimes', *Journal of European Social Policy* 2 (3): 159–73.

Lewis, J. (2001) *The End of Marriage: Individualisation and Intimate Relations*. Cheltenham: Edward Elgar.

Lewis, J. and Glennerster, H. (1996) *Implementing the New Community Care*. Buckingham: Open University Press.

LGFA (2006) *Enhancing Lives and Communities for 100,000 Players*. Dublin: LGFA.

Lillard, L. A. and Waite, L. J. (1995) 'Til death do us part: marital disruption and mortality', *American Journal of Sociology* 100 (5): 1131–56.

Liston, K. (2005) 'Some reflections on women's sport in Ireland', pp. 206–23 in Bairner, A. (ed.), *Sport and the Irish: Histories, Identities, Issues*. Dublin: UCD Press.

Liston, K. and Rush, M. (2006) 'Social capital and health in Irish sports policy', *Administration* 53 (4): 73–88.

Loughrey, S. (1999) 'Sport and education: an examination of the effects of sport on third level aspirations', Unpublished Master's thesis, UCD.

Lovelock, J. (1979) *Gaia: A New Look At Life On Earth*. Oxford: Oxford University Press.

Lynch, K. (1999) 'Equality studies: the academy and the role of research in emancipatory social change', *Economic and Social Review* 30: 41–69.

Lynch, K. and McLaughlin, E. (1995) 'Caring labour and love labour', pp. 250–92 in Clancy, P. et al. (eds), *Irish Society: Sociological Perspectives*. Dublin: IPA.

Lynch, R. (2004) *Exceptional Returns, Economic, Fiscal and Social Benefits of Investment in Early Childhood Development*. Washington: Economic Policy Institute.

Mac an Ghaill, M. (1999) *Contemporary Racisms and Ethnicities*. Buckingham: Open University Press.

McCann, M. H. (1998) 'Drug services in Dublin: selective or comprehensive strategies?' *Journal of Substance Misuse* 3: 150–5.

McCann, M. H. (1999) 'The role of the community in responding to drug related problems', PhD thesis, Dublin City University.

McCarthy P. (1999) *African Refugees: Needs Analysis*. Dublin: African Refugee Network.

McCashin, A. (2004) *Social Security in Ireland*. Dublin: Gill & Macmillan.

McCoy, S. and Smyth, E. (2003) 'Educational expenditure: implications for equality', pp. 90–9 in ESRI, *Budget Perspectives 2004*. Dublin: ESRI.

McDonald, D. and Tallent, N. (2005) 'Obese teenagers may face stomach stapling', *Sunday Times*, 22 May.

McDonald, F. (2000) *The Construction of Dublin.* Dublin: Gandon.

Mac Éinrí, P. (2001) 'Immigration policy in Ireland', pp. 46–87 in Farrell, F. and Watt, P. (eds), *Responding to Racism in Ireland* (Dublin: Veritas).

McGee, H. M., O'Hanlon, A., Barker, M. Stout, R., O'Neill, D., Conory, R., Hickey, A., Shelley. E. and Layte, R. (2005) *One Island – Two Systems: A Comparison of Health Status and Health and Social Service Use by Community-dwelling Older People in the Republic of Ireland and Northern Ireland.* Dublin: Institute of Public Health in Ireland.

McGlone, F. (1992) *Disability and Dependency in Old Age: A Demographic and Social Audit,* Occasional Paper 14. London: Family Policy Studies Centre.

McGlone, F. and Cronin, N. (1994) *A Crisis in Care? The Future of Family and State Care for Older People in the European Union.* London: Family Policy Centre.

McKeown, K., Ferguson, H. and Rooney, D. (1998) 'Fathers: Irish experience in an international context, an abstract of a report to the Commission on the Family', pp. 404–59 in Commission on the Family, *Final Report to the Minister for Social, Community and Family Affairs: Strengthening Families for Life.* Dublin: Stationery Office.

McLaughlin, E. (2001) 'Ireland: from Catholic corporatism to social partnership', pp. 223–60 in Cochrane, A., Clarke, J. and Gewirtz, S. (eds), *Comparing Welfare States.* London: Sage.

Macpherson, W. (1999) *The Stephen Lawrence Inquiry: Report of an Inquiry by Sir William Macpherson of Cluny.* London: HMSO.

McVeigh, R. (1998) *Travellers, Refugees and Racism in Tallaght.* Dublin: European Year Against Racism.

Malcolm, E. (1996) *Elderly Return Migration from Britain to Ireland: A Preliminary Study.* Dublin: National Council for the Elderly.

Malpas, N. and Lampart, P. Y. (1994) *The Europeans and the Family.* Brussels: Eurobarometer.

Mannion A. M. (1991) *Global Environmental Change.* Harlow: Longman.

Manandhar, S., Friel, S., Share, M., Hardy, F. and Walsh, O. (2004) *Food, Nutrition and Poverty Amongst Asylum Seekers in North West Ireland.* Dublin: CPA.

Marks, N. F. (1996) 'Caregiving across the lifespan: national prevalence and predictors', *Family Relations* 45: 27–36.

Middleton N. and O'Keefe P. (2001) *Redefining Sustainable Development.* London: Pluto

Miles, M. S., D'Auria, J. P., Hart, E. M., Sedlack, D. A. and Watral, M. A. (1993) 'Parental role alterations experienced by mothers of children with life-threatening chronic illness', pp. 281–8 in Funk, S. G. et al. (eds), *Key Aspects of Caring for the Chronically Ill.* New York: Springer.

Millar, J. and Rowlington, K. (2001) *Lone Parents, Employment and Social Policy: Cross National Comparisons.* Bristol: Policy.

Miller, S. (2002) 'Respite care for children who have complex healthcare needs', *Paediatric Nursing* 14 (5): 33–7.

Mink, G. (1998) *Welfares End.* Ithaca, NY: Cornell University Press. .

Modood, T., Berthoud, R., Lakey, J. Nazroo, J., Patten, S., Virdee, S. and Beishon, S. (1997) *Ethnic Minorities in Britain: Diversity and Disadvantage.* London: Policy Studies Institute.

Montanari, I. (2000) 'From family wage to marriage subsidy and child benefits; controversy and consensus in the development of family support', *Journal of European Social Policy* 10 (4): 307–33.

Moore, R. (2004) 'Lambegs and bodhrans: religion, identity and health', pp. 123–48 in Kelliher, D. (ed.), *Identity and Health*. London: Palgrave.

Moran, J. (2005) 'Refugees and social policy', pp. 256–76 in Quin, S. et al. (eds), *Contemporary Irish Social Policy*, 2nd edn. Dublin: UCD Press.

Morgan, D. (2002) 'Epilogue', pp. 273–86 in Hobson, B. (ed.), *Making Men into Fathers: Men, Masculinities and the Social Politics of Fatherhood*. Cambridge: Cambridge University Press.

Morris, J (1993) *Independent Lives? Community Care and Disabled People*. Basingstoke: Macmillan.

Morris, J. (1991) *Pride Against Prejudice: Transforming Attitudes to Disability*. London: Women's Press.

Morris, J. (1995) 'Creating a space for absent voices: disabled women's experiences of receiving assistance with daily living activities', *Feminist Review* 51 (1): 68–93.

Morris, J. (1997) 'Care of empowerment? A disability rights perspective', *Social Policy and Administration* 31 (1): 54–60.

Mullaly, G. (2001) 'Ireland – starting late: building institutional capacity on the reform of sub-national governance?', pp. 131–41 in Lafferty, W. (ed.), *Sustainable Communities in Europe*. London: Earthscan.

Munday, B. (1996a) 'Introduction: definitions and comparisons in European social care', pp. 1–20 in Munday, B. and Ely, P. (eds), *Social Care in Europe*. London: Prentice Hall/Harvester Wheatsheaf.

Munday, B. (1996b) 'Conclusion: the future for social care in Europe', pp. 226–30 in Munday, B. and Ely, P. (eds), *Social Care in Europe*. London: Prentice Hall/Harvester Wheatsheaf.

Murphy, G. (2001a) 'The technology-dependent child at home. Part 1: In whose best interest?' *Paediatric Nursing* 13 (7): 14–18.

Murphy, G. (2001b) 'The technology-dependent child at home. Part 2: The need for respite'. *Paediatric Nursing* 13 (8): 24–8.

Murphy, M. (2002) 'Social partnership: is it the only game in town?' *Community Development Journal* 37 (1): 80–90.

Murphy-Lawless, J. and Quin, S. (2004) 'Equity, efficiency and healthcare', pp. 128–46 in Fanning, B et al. (eds), *Theorising Irish Social Policy* Dublin: UCD Press.

Mutwarasibo, F. (2005) 'Participation of third country nationals in the 2004 local elections: new dawn in the emergence of intercultural Ireland', paper presented at Citizens, Non-Citizens and Voting Rights conference Edinburgh, 3–4 June.

National Women's Council of Ireland (2005) *An Accessible Childcare Model*. Dublin: NWCI.

NCC (2004) *The Competitiveness Challenge 2004, Annual Policy Statement of the NCC*. Dublin: NCC/Forfas.

NCCRI (2001) *Racism as a Cause of Poverty: A Submission to the Review of the National Anti-Poverty Strategy*. Dublin: NCCRI.

National Statistics (2005) *Country of Birth*. Available from : //www. statistics. gov. uk/ [Accessed 31 Oct.].

NCA (1985) *Housing for the Elderly in Ireland*. Dublin: NCA.

NCAOP (2004) *Population and Ageing in Ireland 2002–2001*. Dublin: NCAOP.

NCCA (2002) *Towards a Framework for Early Learning*. Dublin: NCCA.

NDA (2002). *Models of Including People with Disabilities in Research*. Dublin: NDA.

NDP/CSF (2003) *Evaluation of the Wual Opportunities Childcare Programme, 2000–2006*. Dublin: Stationery Office.

NDST (2002) *Review of Local Drugs Task Forces Report from the National Drug Strategy Team*. Dublin: National Drug Strategy Team.

Nelson, J. A. (1996) *Feminism, Objectivity and Economics*. London: Routledge.

NESC (1986) *A Strategy for Development 1986–1990: Growth, Employment and Fiscal Balance*. Dublin: NESC.

NESC (1987) *Community Care Service An Overview*, Report no. 84. Dublin: NESC.

NESC (1991) *The Economic and Social Implications of Migration*, Report no. 90, Dublin: NESC.

NESC (1996) *Strategy into the 21st Century: Conclusions and Recommendations*. Dublin: NESC.

NESC (2002) *National Progress Indicators for Sustainable Economic, Social and Environmental Development*. Dublin: NESC.

NESC (2005) *The Developmental Welfare State*. Dublin: NESC.

NESF (2000a) *Alleviating Labour Shortages*, Report no. 19. Dublin: NESF.

NESF (2000b) *The National Anti-Poverty Strategy*, Opinion no. 18. Dublin: NESF.

NESF (2002) *Early School Leavers*. Report no. 24. Dublin: NESF.

NESF (2003a) *Labour Market Issues for Older Workers*, Report no. 26. Dublin: NESF.

NESF (2003b) *The Policy Implications of Social Capital*, Report no 28. Dublin: NESF.

NESF (2005a) *Care for Older People*, Report no. 32. Dublin: NESF.

NESF (2005b) *Early Childhood Care and Education*, Report no. 30. Dublin: NESF.

Newman, J. (2000) 'Beyond the new public management' in Clarke, J. et al., *New Managerialism: New Welfare?* London: Sage.

Neyer, G. (2003) *Family Policies and Low fertility in Western Europe*, MPIDR Working Paper. Rostock: Max Planck Institute for Demographic Research.

Niessen, J. and Schibel Y. (2004) *Handbook on Integration for Policymakers and Practitioners*. Brussels: European Commission.

Nolan, B. (1991) *The Utilisation and Financing of Health Services in Ireland*. Dublin: ESRI.

Nolan, B. (2000) *Child Poverty in Ireland*. Dublin: Oak Tree.

Nolan, B., O'Connell, P. and Whelan, T. (2000) *Bust to Boom: The Irish Experience of Growth and Inequality*. Dublin: IPA.

Northern Ireland Taskforce on Childhood Obesity (2004) *Fit Futures: Focus on Food, Activity and Young People*. Research paper, 1. www.investingforhealthni.gov.uk

NSWQB (2002) *Social Work Posts in Ireland*. Dublin: NSWQB.

Nyberg, A. (2002) 'Gender (de)commodification, economic (in)dependence and autonomous households: the case of Sweden', *Critical Social Policy* 22 (1): 72–95.

O'Carroll, J. P. (2002) 'Culture lag and democratic deficit in Ireland: or, 'Dat's outside de terms of d'agreement' in *Community Development Journal* 37 (1): 10–19.

O'Connell, P., Clancy, D. and McCoy, S. (2006) *Who Went to College in 2004? A National Survey of New Entrants to Higher Education*. Dublin: Higher Education Authority.

O'Connor, J. (2003) 'Welfare State development in the context of European integration and economic convergence: situating Ireland within the European Union context', *Policy and Politics* 31 (3): 387–404.

O'Connor, J., Smyth, E. and Whelan, B. (1988) *Caring for the Elderly, Part I: A Study of Carers at Home and in the Community*. Dublin: National Council for the Aged.

O'Connor, J. S., Orloff, A. S. and Shaver, S. (1999) *States, Markets, Families, Gender, Liberalism and Social Policy in Australia, Canada, Great Britain and the United States*. Cambridge: Cambridge University Press.

O'Connor, P. (1998) *Emerging Voices: Women in Contemporary Society*. Dublin: IPA.

O'Donnell, R. and Thomas, D. (1998) 'Partnership and policy-making', pp. 117–46 in Healy, S. and Reynolds, B. (eds), *Social Policy in Ireland*. Dublin: Oak Tree.

O'Donovan, O. (1997) 'Contesting concepts of care: the case of the home help service in Ireland', pp. 69–84 in Cleary, A. and Treacy, M. P. (eds), *The Sociology of Health and Illness in Ireland*. Dublin: UCD Press.

OECD (1990) *Employment Outlook Study*. Paris: OECD.

OECD (2000) *Starting Strong: Early Childhood Education and Care*. Paris: OECD.

OECD (2001) *Education at a Glance: OECD Indicators*. Paris: OECD.

OECD (2002) *Employment Outlook*. Paris: OECD.

OECD (2003) *Babies and Bosses: Reconciling Work and Family Life Volume 2 Austria, Ireland and Japan*. Paris: OECD.

OECD (2004) *Thematic Review of Early Childhood Education and Care Policy in Ireland*. Dublin: Stationery Office.

OECD (2005) *Education at a Glance 2005*. Paris: OECD.

Office of the Deputy Prime Minister (2003) *Housing and Black and Minority Ethnic Communities: Review of the Evidence Base*. London: HMSO.

O'Hagan, J. and McIndoe, T. (2005) 'Population, employment and unemployment', pp. 76–104 in O'Hagan, J and Newman, C. (eds), *The Economy of Ireland: National and Sectoral Policy Issues*, 9th edn. Dublin: Gill & Macmillan.

O'Hagan, J. W. and Newman C. (2005) *The Economy of Ireland: National and Sectoral Policy Issues*. Dublin: Gill & Macmillan.

O'Hanlon, A., McGee, H., Barker, M., Garavan, R., Hickey, A., Conroy, R. and O'Neill, D. (2005) *Health and Social Services for Older People (HeSSOP II): Changing Profiles from 2000 to 2004*. Dublin: National Council on Ageing and Older People.

Olah, L., Bernhardt, E. M. and Goldscheider, F. K. (2001) 'Co-residential paternal roles in industrial countries: Sweden, Hungary and the United States', pp. 25–60 in Hobson, B. (ed.), *Making Men into Fathers: Men Masculinities and the Social Politics of Fatherhood*. Cambridge: Cambridge University Press.

Oldman, C. and Beresford, B. (1998) *Homes Unfit for Children: Housing, Disabled Children and their Families*. London: Policy Press.

O'Leary, O. and Burke, H. (1998) *Mary Robinson: The Authorised Biography*. London: Hodder & Stoughton.

Oliver, M. (1992) 'Changing the social relations of research production?', *Disability, Handicap and Society* 7: 101–14.

O'Loughlin, A. (2005) 'Social policy and older people', pp. 206–30 in Quin, S. et al. (eds), (eds), *Contemporary Irish Social Policy*, 2nd edn. Dublin: UCD Press.

O'Mahony, J. (2001) *The Performance of Irish Green Schools Programme: Results of the Green Schools Projects* Dublin: An Taisce.

O'Regan, C. (1998) *Report of a Survey of the Vietnamese and Bosnian Communities in Ireland*. Dublin: Refugee Agency

O'Reilly, E. (2004) 'Protecting rights and freedoms', paper presented at the 8th International Conference of the International Ombudsman Institute. Dublin: Office of the Ombudsman http: //www. ombudsman. gov. ie.

O'Reilly, F., Reaper, E. and Redmond, T. (2005) *We're People Too: Views of Drug Users on Health Services*. Dublin: Participation and Practice of Rights Project.

O'Reilly, M. (2005) 'Palliative care for children in the Irish Republic', pp. 71–6 in Ling, J. and O'Síoráin, L. (eds), *Palliative Care in Ireland*. Maidenhead: Open University Press.

Ó'Riain, S. and O'Connell, P. J. (2000) 'The role of the state in growth and welfare' in Nolan, B. et al. (eds) *Bust to Boom? The Irish Experience of Growth and Inequality*. Dublin: IPA.

Orloff, A. S. (1993) 'Gender and the social rights of citizenship: the comparative analysis of gender relations and welfare states', *American Sociological Review* 58: 303–28.

Orloff, A. S. (2002) 'Explaining US welfare reform: power, gender, race and the US policy legacy', *Critical Social Policy* 22 (1): 96–118.

Orton, M. (2004) 'New Labour, citizenship and responsibility: family, community and the obscuring of social relations', pp. 173–92 in Dean, H. (ed.), *The Ethics of Welfare, Human Rights, Dependency and Responsibility*. Bristol: Policy Press.

O'Shea, K. (1985) *The Irish Emigrant Chaplaincy Scheme in Britain 1957–82*. Naas: Leinster Leader.

Owen, D. (1995) *Irish-born People in Great Britain: Settlement Patterns and Socio-Economic Circumstances*. Warwick: University of Warwick Centre for Research in Ethnic Relations.

Owusu-Bempah, J, and Howitt, D. (1997) 'Socio-genealogical connectedness, attachment theory and childcare practice', *Child and Family Social Work* 2: 199–207.

Pahl, R. (2000) *On Friendship*. Cambridge: Polity.

Parekh, B. (2000) *The Future of Multi-Ethnic Britain: Report of the Commission on the Future of Multi-Ethnic Britain*. London: Profile Books.

Parker, G. and Clarke, H. (2002) 'Making ends meet: do carers and disabled people have a common agenda?' *Policy and Politics* 30 (3): 347–59.

Pavee Point (1997) *Part of the Community, Including Travellers in the Community Development Projects*. Dublin: Pavee Point.

Pearse, D. (1993) *Blueprint 3: Measuring Sustainable Development* London: Earthscan.

Peillon, M. (1996) 'A qualitative comparative analysis of welfare legitimacy', *Journal of European Social Policy* 6 (3) 175–90.

Peillon, M. (2001) *Welfare in Ireland: Actors, Resources and Strategies*. London: Praeger.

Penninx, R. (2005) 'Bridges between research and policy? The case of post-war immigration and integration policies in the Netherlands', *International Journal on Multicultural Societies* 7: 33–48.

Pepper, D. (1986) *The Roots of Modern Environmentalism*. London: Routledge.

Pierce, M. (2003) 'Ethnicity and disability' pp. 113–28 in Quin, S. and Redmond, B. (eds), *Disability and Social Policy in Ireland*. Dublin: UCD Press.

Pierce, M. (2003) *Minority Ethic People with Disabilities in Ireland*. Dublin: Equality Authority.

Powell, F. (1992) *The Politics of Irish Social Policy 1600–1990*. New York: Edwin Mellen.

Powell, F. and Geoghegan, M. (2004) *The Politics of Community Development*. Dublin: A. & A. Farmar.

Prugh, T., Constanza, R. and Daly, H. (2000) *The Local Politics of Global Sustainability*. Washington DC: Island Press

Pumares, P. (2002) 'Moroccan families in Madrid', paper presented at the European Observatory on the Social Situation, Demography and Family seminar on Immigration and Family, Helsinki.

Punch, A. (2005) 'Ireland's growing population: an emerging challenge', pp. 1–11 in Reynolds B. and Healy, B. (eds), *Securing Fairness and Wellbeing in a Land of Plenty.* Dublin: CORI Justice Commission.

Putnam, R. D. (2001) *Bowling Alone: The Collapse and Revival of American Community.* New York: Touchstone.

Quadragesimo Anno Encyclical letter of his Holiness Pope Pius XI on reconstructing the social order and perfecting it conformably to the precepts of the gospel in commemoration of the fortieth anniversary of the encyclical 'Rerum Novarum'. (1936, orig. 1931) London: Catholic Truth Society.

Quin, S. (2005) 'Health policy', pp. 30–50 in Quin, S. et al. (eds), *Contemporary Irish Social Policy,* 2nd edn. Dublin: UCD Press.

Quin, S. and Clarke, J. (2004) 'A needs analysis of palliative care services for children in ireland: methodology and some preliminary findings', paper presented at Irish Association of Paediatric Nursing 1st International Conference, Athlone.

Quin, S. and Redmond, B. (2005) 'Disability and social policy', pp. 138–56 in Quin, S. et al. (eds), *Contemporary Irish Social Policy,* 2nd edn. Dublin: UCD Press.

Quirke, B. (2002) 'Traveller proofing health', pp. 6–1 in *Traveller Proofing: Within an Equality Framework.* Dublin: Pavee Point Travellers' Centre.

Quirke, B., Sinclair, H. and Kevany, J. (1994) 'Community participation in primary health care', *Administration* 42 (2): 170–82.

Raftery, M. and O'Sullivan, E. (1999) *Suffer the Little Children: The Inside Story of Ireland's Industrial Schools.* Dublin: New Island.

Reason, P. and Bradbury H. (eds) (2001) *Handbook of Action Research.* London: Sage.

Redmond, B. (2004) *Reflection in Action Developing Reflective Practice in Health and Social Services.* Aldershot: Ashgate.

Redmond, B. and Richardson, V. (2003) '"Just getting on with it": exploring the service needs of mothers who care for babies and young children with severe/profound and life-threatening intellectual disability', *JARID: Journal of Applied Research in Disability* 16 (3): 189–204.

Refugee Information Service (2005) *Submission on the Immigration and Residency Bill* www. ris. ie/progressreport/immigration-residency. doc.

Reich, R. (2002) *The Future of Success.* New York: Vintage.

Renzetti, C. M. and Curran, D. J. (2003) *Women, Men and Society,* 5th edn. London and Boston: Allyn & Bacon.

Rerum Novarum Encyclical Letter of Pope Leo XIII on the Condition of the Working Classes. (1983, orig. 1981) Catholic Truth Society, London.

Richardson, V. (1995) 'Reconciliation of family life and working life', pp. 127–46 in McCarthy, I. C. (ed.), *Irish Family Studies: Selected Papers.* Dublin: Family Studies Centre, UCD.

Richardson, V. (2001a) *Young Mothers: A Study of Young Single Mothers in Two Communities,* Dublin: Social Science Research Centre, UCD.

Richardson, V. (2001b) 'Legal and constitutional rights of children in Ireland', pp. 21–44 in Cleary, A. et al. (eds), *Understanding Children,* vol. 1: *State, Education and Economy.* Cork: Oak Tree.

Richardson, V. (2003) 'Evaluation of policies in relation to the division of unpaid and paid work between men and women in Ireland', paper for Working in Ireland Symposium, TCD.

Richardson, V. and Rush, M. (2006) 'Family and work in Ireland', pp. 199–216 in Rossi, G. (ed.), *Reconciling Family and Work: New Challenges for Social Policies in Europe* (Milan: Franco Angeli).

Rifkin, S. B. (1978) 'Politics of barefoot medicine', *The Lancet*, 7 Jan.: 34.

Rifkin, S. B. (1996) 'Paradigms lost: toward a new understanding of community participation in health programmes', *Acta Tropica* 61 (2): 79–92.

Rifkin, S. B., Lewando-Hundt, G. and Draper, A. K. (2000) *Participatory Approaches in Health Promotion and Health Planning A Literature Review*. London: Health Development Agency.

Robins, J. A. (1960/2003) 'The Irish hospital: an outline of its origins and development', pp. 143–67 in Fanning, B. and MacNamara, T. (eds), *Ireland Develops: Administration and Social Policy 1953–2003*. Dublin: IPA.

Roche, M. (2000) *Comparative Social Inclusion Policies and Citizenship in Europe: Towards a New European Social Model*. Brussels: European Commission. Targeted Socio-Economic Research (TSER) SOE2–CT97–3059)

Rostgaard, T. and Lehto, J. (2001) 'Health and social care systems, how different is the Nordic model?', pp. 137–67 in Kautto, M. et al. (eds), *Nordic Welfare States in the European Context*. London: Routledge.

Rourke, S. (2003) *Research Project on The Community Development Support Needs of 'New Communities' Within the Inner City of Dublin*. Dublin: Tosach.

Rouse, P. (2005) 'Sport in Ireland in 1881', pp. 7–21 in Bairner, A. (ed.), *Sport and the Irish: Histories, Identities, Issues*. Dublin: UCD Press.

Ruddle, H., Prizeman, G. and Jaffro, G. (2000) *Evaluation of Local Drugs Task Force Projects: Experiences and Perceptions of Planning and Implementation*. Dublin: Stationery Office.

Rummery, K. (2002) *Disability, Citizenship and Community Care: A Case for Welfare Rights?* Aldershot: Ashgate.

Rush, M. (1999) 'Social partnership in Ireland: emergence and process', pp. 155–77 in Kiely, G. et al. (eds), *Irish Social Policy in Context*. Dublin: UCD Press.

Rush, M. (2003) *Children, Diversity and Childcare*. Waterford: Waterford City Childcare Committee.

Rush, M. (2004a) *Including Children: Childcare Audit 2003: Diversity, Disability and Additional Needs*. Waterford: Waterford County Childcare Committee.

Rush, M. (2004b) 'Fathers, identity and well-being', pp. 95–111 in Fanning, B. et al. (eds), *Theorising Irish Social Policy*. Dublin: UCD Press.

Rush, M. (2005a) 'Fathers and family policy', *Studies* 94 (374): 171–9.

Rush, M. (2005b) 'Family policy, reproductive work and comparative social policy', paper presented to the *Counting, Measuring, Valuing: Four Decades of Social Science Research at UCD Social Science Research Centre* conference, 7 Apr. Dublin: RIA.

Ryan, S., O'hUallacháin, S. and Hogan, J. (1998) *Early Start Pre-School Programme: Final Evaluation Report*. Dublin: Education Research Centre.

Sabel, C. (1996) *Ireland: Local Partnerships and Social Innovation*. Paris: OECD.

Sainsbury, D. (1996) *Gender Equality and Welfare States*. Cambridge: Cambridge University Press.

Sainsbury, D. (ed.) (1999) *Gender and Welfare State Regimes*. Oxford: Oxford University Press.

Sassen, S. (1999) *Guests and Aliens*. New York: New Press.

Schon, D. A. (1973) *Beyond the Stable State: Public and Private Learning in a Changing Society*. Harmondsworth: Penguin.

Schweinhart, L. (2005) *The High/Scope Perry Preschool Study Through Age 40: Summary, Conclusions and Frequently Asked Questions.* Ypsilant: High/Scope Press.

Sen, A. (1984) *Resources, Values and Development.* Cambridge MA: Harvard University Press.

Senge, P. (1990) *Fifth Discipline: The Art and Practice of the Learning Organisation.* New York: Doubleday.

Shakespeare, T. (2000) 'The social relations of care', pp. 52–65 in Lewis, G. et al. (eds), *Rethinking Social Policy.* London: Sage.

Shapiro, M., Cartwright, C. and Macdonald, S. (1994) 'Community development in primary health care', *Community Development Journal* 29 (3): 222–31.

Share, P. and McElwee, N. (2005) 'What is social care?' pp. 3–18 in Share, P. and McElwee, N. (eds), *Applied Social Care: An Introduction for Irish Students.* Dublin: Gill & Macmillan.

Share, P. and McElwee, N. (2005) *Applied Social Care: An Introduction for Irish Students,* Dublin: Gill & Macmillan.

Silke, D. (2005) 'Housing policy', pp. 51–79 in Quin, S. et al. (eds), *Contemporary Irish Social Policy,* 2nd edn. Dublin: UCD Press.

Smith, S. and Mutwarasibo, F. (2000) *Africans in Ireland: Developing Communities.* Dublin: African Cultural Project.

Smyth, E. and Hannan, D. F. (2000) 'Education and inequality', pp. 109–26 in Nolan, B. et al. *Bust to Boom? The Irish Experience of Growth and Inequality.* Dublin: IPA.

Solesbury, W. (2001) *Evidence Based Policy: Whence It Came and Where it's Going.* London: ESRC Centre for Evidence Based Policy and Practice.

Solomos, J and Back, L. (1996) *Racism and Society.* London: Macmillan.

Sommerstad, L. (1997) 'Welfare state attitudes to the male bread winning system: the United States and Sweden in comparative perspective', pp. 153–74 in Janssens, A. (ed.), *The Rise and Decline of the Male Breadwinner Family.* Cambridge: Cambridge University Press.

Spicker, P. (1995) *Social Policy Themes and Approaches* Essex: Prentice Education.

Stainton, T. (1998) 'Rights and rhetoric of practice: contradictions for practitioners' pp. 135–44 in Symonds, A. and Kelly, A. (eds), *The Social Construction of Community Care.* London: Macmillan.

Stienberg, S. (2000) 'America again at the cross roads', pp. 461–72 in Solomos, J. and Back, L. (eds), *Theories of Race and Racism.* London: Routledge.

Stocpol, T. (2001) *Social Policy in the United States: Future Possibilities in Historical Perspective.* Princeton, NJ: Princeton University Press.

Stoesz, D. (2002) 'The American welfare state at twilight', *Journal of Social Policy* 31 (3): 487–503.

Sweeney, J. (2001) 'Prosperity and well-being', *Studies* 90 (357): 7–16.

Task Force on Childcare Services (1980) *Final Report to the Minister for Health.* Dublin: Stationery Office.

Task Force on Policy Regarding Emigrants (2002) *Ireland and the Irish Abroad.* Dublin: Department of Foreign Affairs.

Task Force on the Travelling Community (1995) *Report.* Dublin: Stationery Office.

Taylor, M. (2003) *Public Policy in the Community.* Basingstoke: Palgrave Macmillan.

Taylor-Gooby, P. (2001) 'Sustaining state welfare in hard times: who will foot the bill?' *Journal of European Social Policy* 11 (2): 133–47.

Tilki, M. (1996) *The Health of the Irish in Britain.* London: Federation of Irish Societies.

Tilki, M. (1998) *Elderly Irish People in Britain: A Profile.* London: Federation of Irish Societies.

Timonen, V. and McMenamin, I. (2002) 'Future of care services in Ireland: old answers to new challenges?', *Social Policy and Administration* 36 (1): 20–35.

Tormey, W. P. (1992/2003) 'Two-speed public and private medical practice in the Republic of Ireland, pp. 191–200 in Fanning, B. and MacNamara, T. (eds), *Ireland Develops: Administration and Social Policy 1953–2003.* Dublin: IPA.

Tronto, J. (1993) *Moral Boundaries: A Political Argument for an Ethic of Care.* London: Routledge.

Truman, C., Mertens, D., and Humphries B. (eds) (2000) *Research and Inequality.* London: UCL Press.

Twigg, J. (2000) 'The changing role of users and carers' pp. 103–19 in Hudson, B. (ed.) *The Changing Role of Social Care.* London: Jessica Kingsley.

UN (1976) *International Covenant on Economic, Social and Cultural Rights.* Geneva: UN.

UN (1989) *United Nations Convention on the Rights of the Child* Adopted by the UN General Assembly, 20 Nov.

UN (2002) *Strengthening of the United Nations: An Agenda for Further Change.* New York: UN (A/57/387).

UN (2004) *Report of the Secretary-General in response to the report of the Panel of Eminent Persons on United Nations-Civil Society Relations.* New York: UN (A/59/354).

UN Economic and Social Council (1999) *The Right to Education,* General Comment no. 13 – Twenty-first Session, 1999 Geneva; UN, http: //www. unhchr. ch/tbs/doc. nsf.

UNESCO (2001) *Bridging Research and Policy: Annual Report.* Paris: UNESCO, MOST Programme.

UNICEF (2005) *Child Poverty in Rich Countries,* Innocenti Report, Card No. 6, Florence: UNICEF.

UNHCHR (2002) *Draft Guidelines on a Human Rights Approach to Poverty Reduction Strategies.* UN, Geneva. http: //193. 194. 138. 190/development/povertyfinal. html#guid8.

Varley, T. and Curtin, C. (2002) 'Communitarian populism and the politics of rearguard resistance in rural Ireland', *Community Development Journal* 37 (1): 20–31.

Victor, C. (2005) *The Social Context of Ageing: A Textbook of Gerontology.* London: Routledge.

Village Ireland (2005) *Building Sustainable Communities.*http: //www. village. ie [Accessed 14 Oct.].

Vincent, J. (2003) *Old Age.* London: Routledge.

Waite, L. (2004) 'Changing demographic patterns in the United States: highlights of program research', *RAND, Labour and Population Demography.* htlm.

Walsh, J., Craig, S. and McCafferty, D. (1998) *Local Partnerships for Social Inclusion?* Dublin: Oak Tree.

Walsh, T. (2003) *An Audit of Research on Early Childhood Care and Education in Ireland, 1990–2003.* Dublin: Centre for Early Childhood Development and Education.

Walter, B. (2004) 'Invisible Irishness: Second generation identities in Britain', *Association of Migration Institutes Journal* 2: 185–93.

Walter, B., Gray, B. Almeida Dowling, L.and Morgan, S. (2002) *A Study of the Existing Sources of Information and Analysis of Irish Emigrants and Irish Communities Abroad.* Dublin: Department of Foreign Affairs.

WCED (1987) *Our Common Future* (Braundtland Commission). Oxford: Oxford University Press.

Weeks, J., Donovan, C. and Heaphy, B. (1996) *Families of Choice: Patterns of Non-Heterosexual Relationships. A Literature Review.* London: School of Education, Politics and Social Science, South Bank University.

Whelan, B. (2001) 'Introduction', in *Green and Bear It? Implementing Market-Based policies for Ireland's Environment*, Proceedings of a conference,10 May. Dublin: ESRI no. 166: 1–4.

White Paper (1996) *Challenges and Opportunities Abroad: White Paper on Foreign Policy.* Dublin: Stationery Office.

WHO (1978) *Declaration of Alma Ata International Conference on Primary Health Care, Alma-Ata, USSR, 6–12 September.* Geneva: WHO.

WHO (1986) *Ottawa Charter For Health Promotion* Geneva, *First International Conference on Health Promotion Ottawa, 21 November 1986.* Geneva: WHO.

WHO (1991) *Technical Report Series 809.* Geneva: WHO.

Whyte, G. (2002) *Social Inclusion and the Legal System: Public Interest Law in Ireland.* Dublin: IPA.

Whyte, J. H. (1980) *Church and State in Modern Ireland, 1923–70.* Dublin: Gill & Macmillan.

Willemsen, T. M., Jacobs, M. J. G. and Frinking, G. A. B. (1998) *Do Policies Influence the Gender Division of Work? Empirical Evidence from Two Different Approaches* Tilburg: Tilburg University Press.

Willemsen, T. M. and Frinking, G. A. B. (eds) (1995) *Work and Family in Europe: The Role of Policies.* Tilburg: Tilburg University Press.

Williams, F. (2001) 'In and beyond new labour: towards a new political ethics of care', *Critical Social Policy* 21 (4): 467–93.

Williams, I. and M. Mac an Ghaill (1998) *Health, Accommodation and Social Care Needs of Older Irish Men in Birmingham.* Birmingham: Irish Community Forum.

Williams, S. J. (2003) 'Beyond meaning, discourse and the empirical world: critical realist reflections on health', *Social Theory and Health* 1: 42–71.

Wilson, E. (1977) *Women and the Welfare State.* London: Tavistock.

Winston, N. (2000) *Between Two Places: A Case Study of Irish-born People Living in England.* Dublin: Irish National Committee of the European Cultural Foundation.

Winston, N. (2002) *The Return of Older Irish Migrants: An Assessment of Needs and Issues.* Dublin: IECE and Department of Social, Community and Family Affairs.

Winston, N. (2005) 'Explaining the deficit: implementing sustainable housing in Ireland', paper presented to the ENHR conference in Reykjavik June.

Working Group on Services for the Elderly (1988) *The Years Ahead: A Policy for the Elderly.* Dublin: Stationery Office.

Wrench, J (1997) *Preventing Racism at the Workplace.* Dublin: European Foundation for the Improvement of Living and Working Conditions.

Yeates, N. (1997) 'Gender, informal care and social welfare: the case of the carer's allowance', *Administration* 45 (2): 21–43.

Young, I. M. (2000) *Inclusion and Democracy.* Oxford: Oxford University Press.

Index